MODELING AIRCRAFT

Edited by Aaron Skinner

Kalmbach Media

On the cover: Paul Boyer's B-52H project, top, shows how to correct even the most up-to-date kits, while Chuck Sawyer shares how to make the most accurate F-15C possible.

Back cover: Chuck Davis shares tips for building HK Model's 1/32 Lancaster (top), and Vladimir Kafka builds America's first operational jet fighter, the P-80.

Kalmbach Media
21027 Crossroads Circle
Waukesha, Wisconsin 53186
www.KalmbachHobbyStore.com

© 2019 Kalmbach Media
All rights reserved. This book may not be reproduced in part or in whole by any means whether electronic or otherwise without written permission of the publisher except for brief excerpts for review.

All photos were taken by the respective authors, except pages 5, 32, 46, 66, and 102, © 2019 Kalmbach Media; and page 4, U.S. Marine Corps/Lance Cpl. Jackson Ricker, U.S. Navy Photo/Mass Communication Specialist 2nd Class Scott Barnes, U.S. Air National Guard/Master Sgt. Vincent De Groot, and National Museum of the U.S. Air Force

Published in 2019
23 22 21 20 19   1 2 3 4 5

Manufactured in China

ISBN: 978-1-62700-698-9
EISBN: 978-1-62700-699-6

Editor: Eric White
Book Design: Lisa Bergman
Additional Photography: Bill Zuback

Library of Congress Control Number: 2019945764

CONTENTS

Introduction — *Aaron Skinner* 4

1. Mastering the basics — *Aaron Skinner* 5
Build your skills with Airfix's 1/48 scale Defiant
Sidebars: Working with photo-etched metal and resin parts, Airbrushing basics

2. HobbyBoss's Pfiel made better — *Anders Isaksson* 16
Elevate an easy assembly kit with aftermarket parts and scratchbuilding

3. The all Canadian affair — *Massimo Santarossa* 23
Building the BPK CRJ-200

4. Building a classic Phantom — *Darren Roberts* 26
Basic techniques get Monogram's F-4 up and away

5. Building a better BUFF — *Paul D. Boyer* 32
Assembly tips and detail improvements for ModelCollect's 1/72 scale B-52H

6. Painting poached eggs on a Folgore — *Vladimir Kafka* 40
Hasagawa's 1/72 scale Macchi C.202 Folgore made a fine canvas for this project

7. Modeling done large — *Chuck Davis* 46
Building HK Models' 1/32 scale Avro Lancaster

8. 'Unpainting' a Hornet — *Darren Roberts* 56
A few fixes and odd colors make a unique F/A-18

9. Building *Queenie* — *Paul D. Boyer* 66
Kitbashing the first presidential jet in 1/72 scale

10. Finishing America's first operational jet — *Vladimir Kafka* 78
Refining Sword's 1/72 scale Lockheed P-80A

11. Folding the wings on a Cold War sub hunter — *Andy Cooper* 84
Get Classic Airframes' 1/48 scale Gannet fit for a hangar

12. A gaucho dressed as a pirate — *Ricardo Dacoba* 92
Building Hasagawa's 1/48 scale Sea King for Argentine service

13. Mastering biplanes — *Chuck Davis* 102
Special techniques bring early planes to life

14. Building Hasegawa's 1/8 scale Fokker Dr.1 — *Bob Steinbrunn* 112
A *very* large-scale static display model

15. Going aggressive with an Eagle — *Chuck Sawyer* 126
Improving Tamiya's 1/32 scale F-15

INTRODUCTION

Since the dawn of time, human beings have sought to slip the surly bonds of earth. Even today when flying is a regular occurrence, the sound of a passing plane has many looking skyward to marvel at the engineering wonder on display. This fascination explains why aircraft have been at the center of scale modeling since the earliest plastic kits. And why we've gathered some of the hobby's leading figures to introduce the subject with 15 projects. So strap yourself in with the seatback up and your workbench down and ready to go. It's time for your modeling to take off!

—*Aaron Skinner*

U.S. Marine Corps Lance Cpl. Dustin Delgado prepares to launch an F/A-18C Hornet at Andersen Air Force Base, Guam, in 2019. *U.S. Marine Corps/Lance Cpl. Jackson Ricker*

A German Westland Sikorsy WS-61 Sea King search and rescue helicopter departs the command and control ship USS Mount Whitney during exercise Baltic Operations 2019. *U.S. Navy Photo/Mass Communication Specialist 2nd Class Scott Barnes*

A Vietnam War era F-4 Phantom flaunts a show-quality paint restoration after being painted at Sioux City, Iowa. *U.S. Air National Guard/Master Sgt. Vincent De Groot*

A Lockheed F-80C Shooting Star from the U.S. Air Force 80th Fighter-bomber Squadron, 8th Fighter-Bomber Group awaits a mission in Korea. *National Museum of the U.S. Air Force*

Mastering the basics

Build your skills with Airfix's 1/48 scale Defiant

BY AARON SKINNER

Aaron Skinner, senior editor of FineScale Modeler magazine, shows you how to get results like this from your first kit.

Building aircraft, like any other scale model, takes a combination of techniques. None of these skills are necessarily difficult by themselves but mastering each will make each model you finish better than the last.

Picking your first subject is important. Here are a few things to look for. First, make sure it is all plastic. Many modern kits contain photo-etched or white metal and cast resin parts. You'll learn to use those in later projects, but for now, let's get the hang of building plastic kits. Second, pick a subject that is all or mostly one color. We're going to paint with spray cans to start and a monochromatic finish minimizes masking. Think late-World War II U.S. Navy or Marine Corps aircraft in overall sea blue. Another good option is a British Cold-War fighter as many were painted in high-speed silver.

I picked the night fighter version of Airfix's 1/48 scale Boulton Paul Defiant because it met all of the requirements. It's all-plastic and overall black: perfect!

You'll also need some basic tools to get started. Pick up a pair of sprue or side cutters, a pack of sanding sticks in various grits, liquid cement, a hobby knife with replacement No. 11 blades, fine-tipped tweezers, and a couple of good-quality paintbrushes.

Now, let's get started!

1 To remove parts from the trees, place the flat side of the cutter against the needed piece and gently squeeze the jaws closed through the attachment point. Only remove the parts as you need them, one, to avoid losing them and, two, to keep track of similar items.

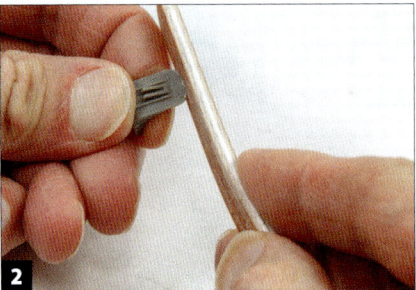

2 Take care of the remnants of the attachment point with a sanding stick. Unless it is especially large, I usually start with a medium grit sanding stick and all it takes is a few gentle strokes to smooth the surface. Using the next finest grit will take care of scratches.

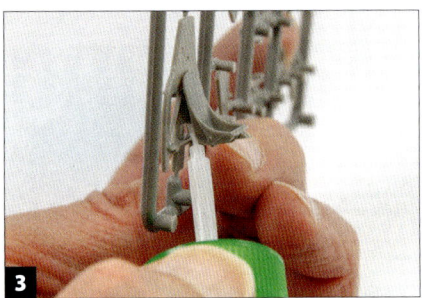

3 The part trees make a great handle to hold small parts for painting, so I prefer to build certain subassemblies on the tree. On the Defiant, that included some of the cockpit components like the seat on the back wall. Hold the part in place a flow a little liquid cement into the joins with a fine brush. Go easy: It doesn't take much.

4 Hold small parts in place with tweezers as you apply cement. This will help you control the part and help prevent you from touching with the glue. The cement works by dissolving the plastic along the joint, then welding the surfaces together as it cures. That also means you can leave a perfect fingerprint in plastic if you come in contact with glue.

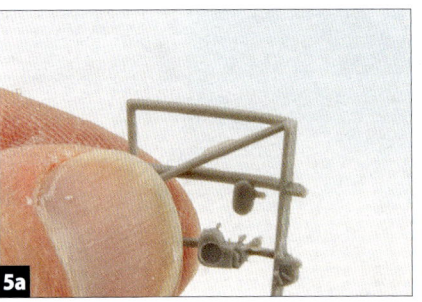

5a **5b** Occasionally, a little plastic can flow between the mold halves during manufacturing, producing a thin film that is known as flash (left). It's easily removed with a sharp No. 11 blade. Be careful and go slowly to avoid cutting too deeply into the part or slipping and cutting yourself. Blood rarely improves your models.

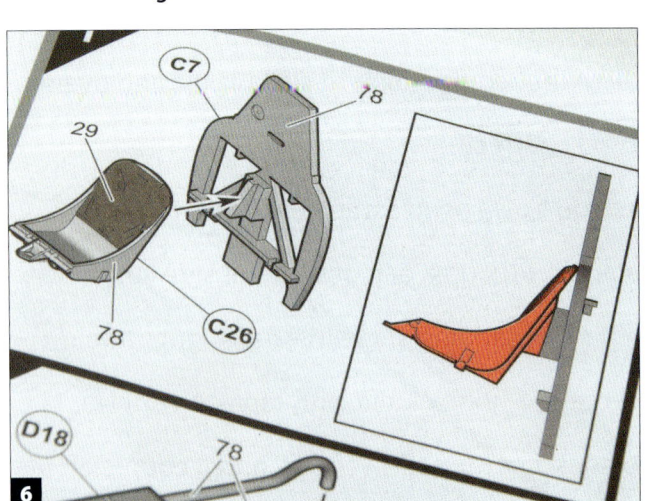

6 Many instructions provide color information for painting details as you go. Airfix uses numbers without any boxes around them that refer to the Humbrol range of colors. In this case, 78 indicates British interior gray-green; 29 is dark earth for the seat's leather back cushion.

7 I wanted to use Tamiya acrylic paint for this project, so I mixed a little dark gray (XF-24) with cockpit green (XF-71) for a base coat. A little Tamiya thinner in the mix helped the paint flow.

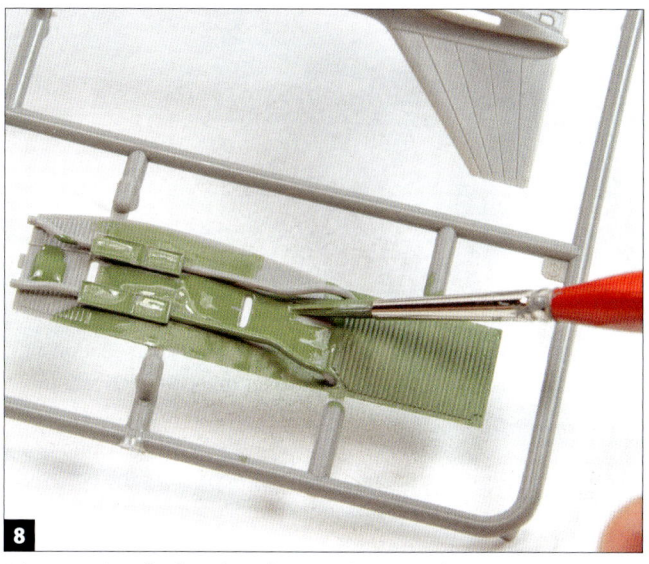

8 After wetting the bristles of a No. 2 brush with Tamiya acrylic thinner to prevent paint drying in the brush, I dipped it in the paint and began painting the interior parts. Apply the paint in a few long strokes.

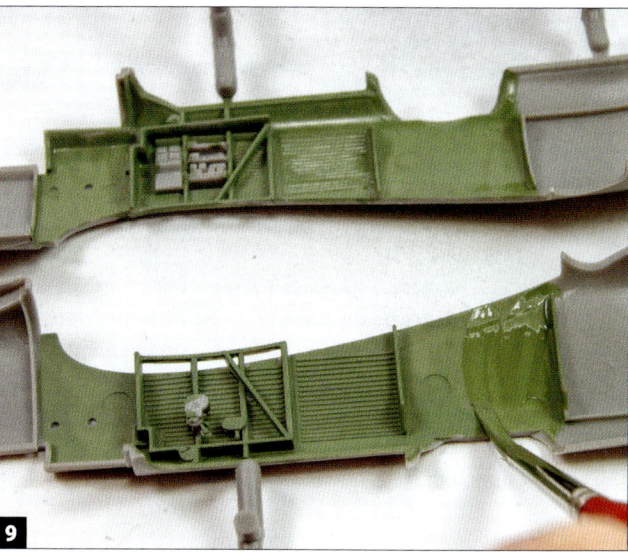

9 The slightly thin paint may not completely cover the first time, but wait until the first coat is dry before applying a second.

10 Black is used for many of the parts, including the turret interior and instrument panel, which I painted with the No. 2 brush …

11 … and small details such as the controls and boxes along the walls. I painted these with a No. 0 brush for more control on the small surfaces.

12 To punch up detail, I mixed a wash of burnt umber artist oil—you only need a little color and odorless turpentine. The important thing is to thoroughly mix the paint and thinner with the goal of something akin to colored thinner.

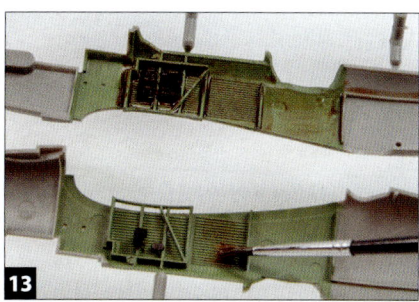

13 Using a No. 2 brush, I flowed the wash into the cockpit detail; the thin color naturally wants to settle into recesses. As it dries, the brown wash outlines raised details and deepens shadows.

14 Then, I pick or mix lighter shades of the basic green and black—in this case cockpit green with a drop of white added for the interior surfaces, and dark gray for the black. After picking a little up on a stiff, flat brush, I drag the bristles repeatedly across scrap paper until almost nothing was coming off on the sheet.

15 Dragging the brush across the parts leaves just enough paint on raised edges and ridges to highlight the detail. Combined with the washes, the effect is cockpit detail that pops when seen through the cockpit openings.

16 Airfix provides a decal to detail the dials on the painted instrument panel. I carefully cut around it with fine scissors.

17 After dipping the panel decal in warm water for a few seconds, I placed it on a paper towel to let the water activate the adhesive on the back of marking. Don't leave the decal in the water too long or the marking may float off or the adhesive may become too diluted to be effective.

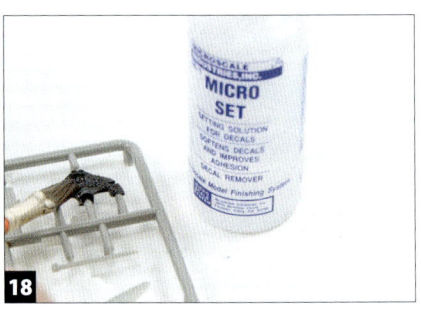

18 While the decal is soaking, I brushed the panel with a setting solution, in this case, Microscale Micro Set. It helps break the surface tension of water so the decal will settle over and around molded detail. You always want decals to look either painted on if they are markings or part of the panel in this case.

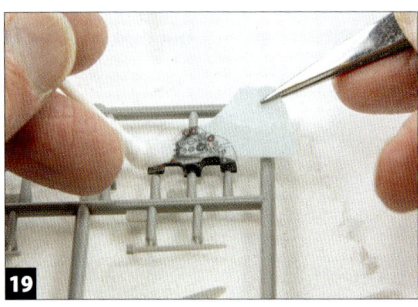

19 Once the decal moves freely on the backing paper, place it in position on the model or part, hold it in place with a cotton swab, and gently slide the paper out from under the film. Don't succumb to the temptation to use your finger to slide or hold the decal as it will likely stick to your skin better than the model.

20 Once you are sure the decal's location is spot-on, use a wet brush or cotton swab to gently press the film into the detail.

21 Finally, apply a decal solution, such as Microscale Micro Sol. This mild solvent will soften the decal film and help it conform to detail. The decal may wrinkle as the solvent does its work, but don't touch it. It should flatten as dries.

22 Paint interferes with plastic cement and can prevent firm joints from forming, so remove it from joining surfaces. In this case, I dragged the edge of a No. 11 blade held perpendicular to the surface across the gluing surfaces on the wall and the corresponding areas on the floor.

23 After pushing the cockpit's rear wall into the slot on the floor, I flowed liquid cement into the joint. Doing it from underneath minimizes the damage the glue might do to surrounding paint. Placing the cockpit parts in one of the fuselage halves will align the floor and bulkheads as the glue dries.

24 To join the fuselage halves, I held them together and flowed liquid cement into the joint an inch or two at a time. Rubber bands or small clamps will keep the parts together overnight so the seams are tight.

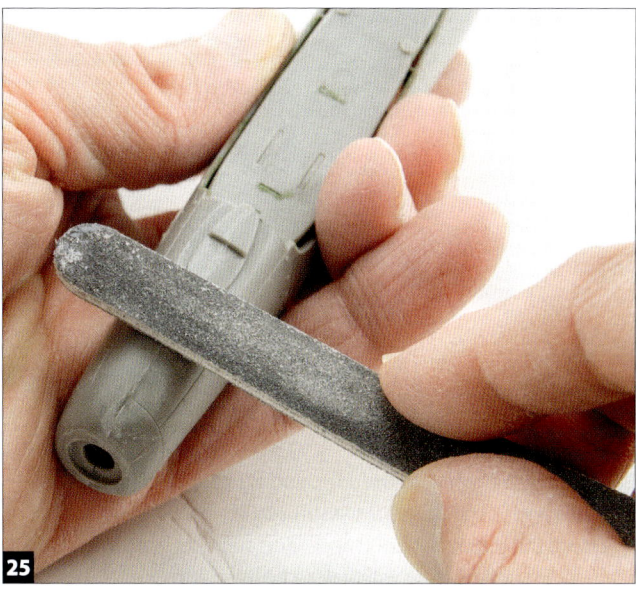

25 Checking the seams, I found a couple areas where the halves were mismatched, causing a step. I smoothed them with progressively finer sanding sticks.

26 To ensure a solid joint for the wings, I applied Testors liquid cement from a container equipped with a metal tube. This thicker glue will flow through the joints as pressure is administered.

27 Wooden clothes pins make useful clamps to apply gentle pressure to the wings as the glue sets. You can flip the parts of the clothes pins over to get a different shape, above.

28 Ideally, a thin bead of glue will be squeezed out of the joint as the parts are pushed together. You want this as it fills the gap as it hardens; removing it is easy with sanding sticks, but be sure to rock them over the leading edge to preserve the airfoil shape.

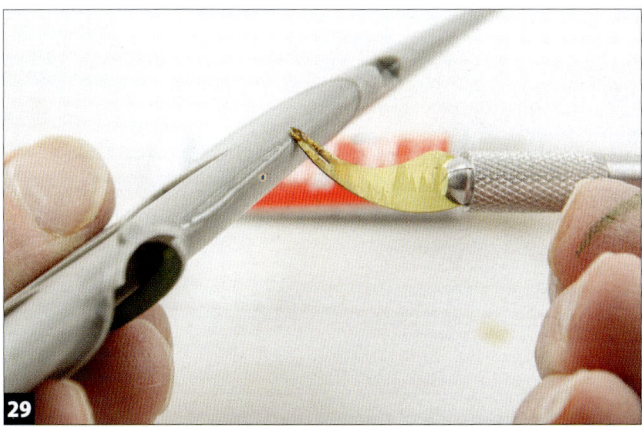

29 In a couple of places, the seam was still visible. Filling these gaps sets good models apart from average builds and the easiest filler is superglue. First, apply a little to the problem seams.

30 Then flow a little accelerator (sometimes called kicker) over the superglue, taking care not to touch the brush directly to the glue. It will set instantly and you don't want the brush sticking to the model.

31 Sand the glue flush with the surrounding surface within a few minutes and you should have a smooth surface with no hint of the joint. If it remains, apply more glue and accelerator, and sand it again. Extra time here will make a better model.

32 Sanding seams often partially eliminates panel lines. I restore them by placing tape along the line to serve as a guide, then drag a fine razor saw gently along the edge. A few passes will remove just enough plastic to produce a consistent line across the seam.

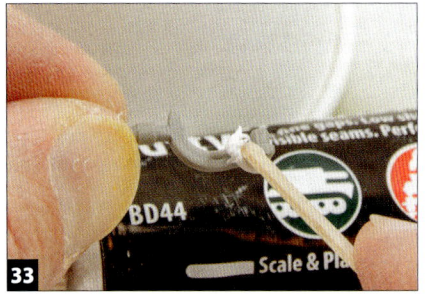

33 Sink marks mar the landing gear legs. These depressions occur when the plastic cools and contracts after being removed from the molds during manufacture. I filled them with Deluxe Materials Perfect Plastic Putty, sanding it flush after the putty hardened.

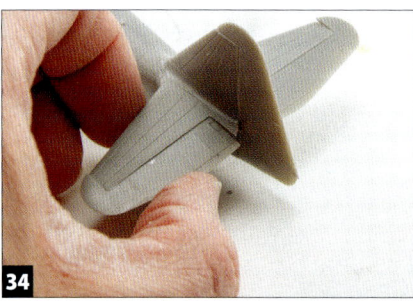

34 After attaching the wings, I glued the horizontal stabilizers with their separate elevators onto the rear fuselage. Check and double-check your alignment here to ensure they match.

35 In preparation for painting, I masked the cockpit openings with pieces of masking tape carefully placed along the edges of the openings and pressed into the holes.

36 There aren't a lot of shortcuts when it comes to masking clear parts. I usually start by taking small pointed triangles of Tamiya tape and placing them into the corners of panes with a hobby knife. Then, I gradually fill the pane with small sections of tape until it is entirely masked.

37 Then I mask the inside of the part with large sections of tape burnished into place. You want to ensure no overspray reaches the inside of the clear parts. Tamiya masking tape is available at hobby shops and is thinner than masking tape you might find at the hardware store. That helps it conform better around details.

38 Before using a spray can, vigorously shake it for a minute or two. Then you can spray the model, starting the flow of paint off the model …

39 … and go over the model in smooth, even passes ending each one off the model. Starting or stopping the flow of paint on the model can produce splatters.

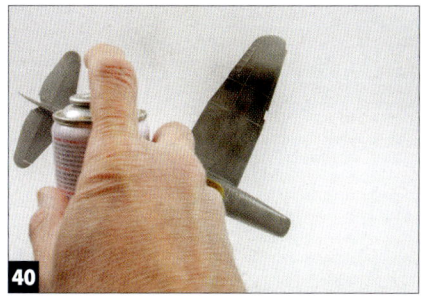

40 Ideally, you should be able to spray the model in three passes waiting a few minutes between each. The first won't entirely cover the model but provides bite for subsequent layers to hang on to. The second one should cover, and the third will even everything out and should produce a smooth surface.

41 I attached the masked clear parts to cardboard that will serve as a handle during painting. Go slowly when spraying canopies to avoid flooding the parts and having paint bleed under the tape.

42 Unfortunately, no matter how many times I try to spray in a clean environment, dust particles and stray hairs end up in the wet paint.

43 These blemishes are usually easy to remove with the gentle application of 1000-grit sandpaper. But that work can affect the finish. If you sand through the paint and reveal bare plastic, simply respray the affected areas.

44 Otherwise, use progressively finer sanding pads—they often come in sets that include these grits: 3200, 3600, 4000, 6000, 8000, and 12000. Start with the coarsest and by the time you reach the last, the surface should be glass smooth.

45 That provides the perfect surface for decals, which adhere better on gloss paint. To remove water from under large markings like the Royal Air Force roundels, I rolled a cotton swab from the center out. Don't drag it across or the marking may move. If you need to move a decal, work water under the edge with a brush until it floats.

46 Normally washes are darker than the surrounding color, so black presents a problem. I mixed light gray artist oil with Turpenoid and flowed it into panel lines. Touch the tip of a fine brush loaded with wash to a line and it should be drawn into it by capillary action.

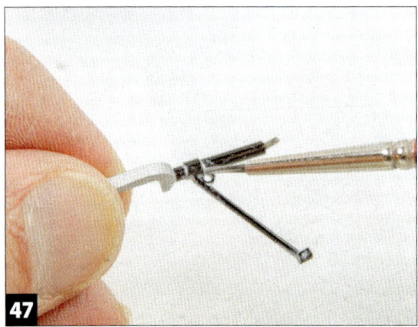

47 The wash also works to highlight the detail on parts like the landing gear legs and wells.

48 Don't panic if you color outside of the lines. Take a cotton pad damp with Turpenoid and draw it gently back across the surface. It should remove the excess wash from the surface and leave it in the recessed detail.

49 Go carefully to be sure the thinner doesn't lift the paint. Tamiya spray cans are acrylic lacquers, so the Turpenoid shouldn't affect the finish. It's a good idea to test this issue before using it on a full model. Avoid using the same paint for a wash you used for the finish; never use an enamel wash on enamel paint, but enamel over acrylics is usually fine.

50 Finally, for a more realistic finish and to tie the decals and paint together, I sprayed the Defiant with Tamiya clear flat using the same three-step process I used for the black.

51 I hand-painted details like the wheels—Tamiya flat aluminum (XF-16) worked perfectly—and tires. For the latter, I used Tamiya rubber black (XF-85), but a dark gray would have worked; straight black is always too stark for tires.

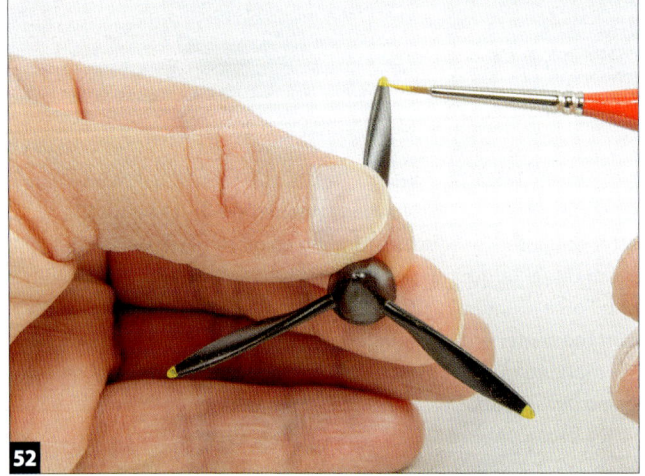

52 The tips of many propellers were contrasting colors; in the case of the Defiant, yellow. After assembling the propeller and spinner and spraying them gloss black with the rest of the airframe parts, I hand-painted the tips. I started with the inner edge of each to keep them even and used two coats for color density.

53 After scraping paint from the mounting pins and holes for the landing gear, I glued the legs and struts in place. Now's the time to check the alignment on them to ensure they match photos of the real thing and that they are aligned with one another.

54 The hole to the tailwheel was partially closed while I was filling the seam around it during fuselage construction. To mount the strut, I bored the hole with a fine bit in a pin vise, a great tool to keep on hand

55 To remove the tape from the clear parts, I placed the tip of a No. 11 blade under the edge of the mask and gently lifted it straight up. Tweezers gripped the lifted edge to pull the section away. Never force the knife under the tape or you risk scratching the clear plastic.

56 Normal plastic cement and superglue can permanently scar clear plastic. Instead, use clear part cement to attach clear parts. Some will likely squeeze out of the joint, but you can remove it with a little water on a brush.

57 A little clear flat on a brush will dull any shine from the glue after it dries. You can also touch up bare plastic exposed during cleanup of pre-painted parts after they have been removed from the parts trees.

58 For light lenses and the oleo on the landing gear legs, I used a Molotow chrome pen. The shiny fluid flows easily onto the surfaces and dries quickly.

59 Weathering adds realism to a model. I kept it to a minimum on the Defiant, but used a silver Prismacolor pencil to draw chips in the paint around engine access panels, the edge of the propeller blades, and wing leading edges.

60 In addition, powdered gray and light brown artist pastels were brushed on for staining from the exhausts. I swept them back along the fuselage in the direction of airflow. Be careful handling the model going forward as the pastels are easily removed with fingers. The exhausts were hand-painted with Tamiya dark iron (XF-84) before installation.

WORKING WITH PHOTO-ETCHED METAL

Photo-etched metal (PE) is thin steel or brass onto which shapes are transferred through a photographic process and then etched. The parts are thin, can be easily bent, and do a great job of representing metal. The material used to be primarily an aftermarket item, but it is now widely included in kits of every genre, so it's important to be comfortable using it. Whether aftermarket or kit-supplied, brass or steel, the techniques for handling and attaching PE are the same.

Like plastic, PE needs to be removed from its fret before use. A fine chisel pushed straight down through the attachments while the fret is held against a hard surface such as plate glass will do the work without bending the part.

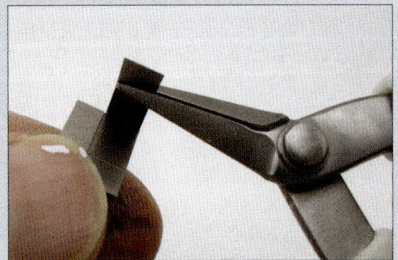

Most aircraft PE is small so smooth-jawed pliers are all you'll need to make required bends. They hold the part and give you a straight edge to bend the metal against without marring the surface.

To attach PE, place the part on the model, then flow thin superglue into the join with a fine applicator and let it set.

WORKING WITH RESIN

Resin has become an increasingly important ingredient of modeling over the last 15 to 20 years and many kits include resin parts and some kits are entirely resin. Resin can hold a sharp edge better than styrene plastic, so these parts provide a level of detail not usually possible with kit parts. But resin parts need to be handled slightly differently than plastic ones, although they are generally easy to handle.

Preparation is a big part of working with resin. Before doing anything else, soak the parts overnight in a cleaner like Westley's Bleche-Wite to remove any mold-release agent left from the casting process. Although it won't harm the resin, Westley's is corrosive so wear gloves and eye protection.

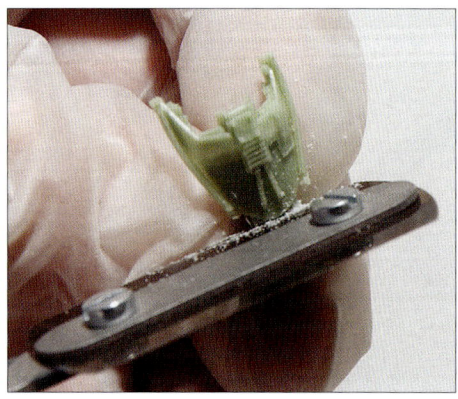

Resin parts usually have excess resin—pour plugs—attached to them where the liquid resin was poured into the mold. Most can be removed with a knife or saw. Clean up the attachment points with sanding and fill any pinholes or other blemishes with superglue; use the same adhesive or 5-minute-epoxy to attach parts. Resin dust can be irritating so wear a respirator and eye protection during cleanup.

AIRBRUSHING BASICS

What is an airbrush? In simple terms, an airbrush uses air under pressure to atomize paint in a controllable pattern. It's like a can of spray paint, but much more precise, and it's the perfect tool for applying paint to scale models.

Designs differ, but airbrushes can be divided into two basic categories: single-action and double-action. The types differ in the way paint is applied, ease of use, and cleaning.

In a single-action brush, the trigger controls only air flow, and it's usually either on or off. Paint flow is preset by adjusting either the nozzle or the needle. This makes them easy to use, especially for beginners, because there's only one thing to consider while spraying—and a lot less chance of applying too much paint. On the other hand, single-action brushes tend to be less versatile because adjusting the paint flow is generally done while the brush is not in use.

On a double-action airbrush, the trigger controls air flow and paint volume. Generally, the air pressure is controlled by depressing the trigger. Pulling back on the trigger moves the needle within the nozzle, which allows more paint through and results in a wider pattern. Skilled painters can manipulate double-action brushes to easily create interesting effects. But the versatility of double-action brushes makes them harder to use as there are more variables to master.

Airbrushes mix paint and air externally or internally. External brushes are usually less expensive than internal brushes, but they tend to produce a wider, harder-to-control spray pattern. I find internal-mix brushes easier to use and control, but I know many talented builders who achieve terrific results with external-mix brushes.

The position of paint supply also differentiates airbrushes. The reservoir can be a bottle that attaches to the brush, usually underneath or in an open-top color cup. Bottles hold more paint and are by definition closed, a handy way to prevent unfortunate spills or splashes. Most color cups mount on top of the brush. They hold less paint, but because gravity helps move paint into the body of the brush as opposed to air pressure in a bottle-fed brush, you don't have to use as

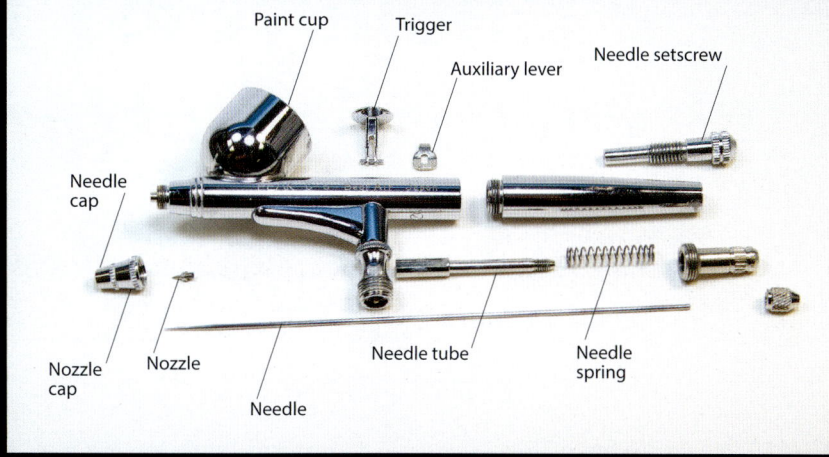

This image shows the breakdown of a double-action internal-mix airbrush. Single-action and external-mix brushes operate slightly differently but share terminology.

high a pressure to spray. That means you can achieve subtle effects more easily.

Most airbrush starter sets come with a can of propellant, which is a good starting point for powering the brush. The disadvantages are the expense of constantly having to replace the cans and the difficulty of controlling the pressure.

Most modelers end up using a compressor once they are comfortable with airbrushing, and like the airbrush, they can be an important investment in your hobby. Many manufacturers sell different styles. Try a diaphragm or piston-powered unit that can maintain a steady pressure of at least 22 psi. A unit with a storage tank is even better. That said, even small, tabletop compressors will move paint through a brush. Some compressors come with built-in regulators. If you get one that doesn't, consider purchasing one because it'll give you control over one of the variables of airbrushing—pressure.

You may also need a moisture trap. As air is compressed, any moisture present condenses. If water from the air line hits the fresh paint on the model, the color may be ruined. The trap will stop water from reaching the brush.

Another thing to consider is noise. Compressors are, as a rule, loud. If you live alone, miles from your nearest neighbor, you can use the biggest, loudest machine you can find. If you share a house with others or live in an apartment, your friends and neighbors will thank you for choosing a quiet alternative.

A third option for powering your brush is compressed air or gas. You can use an industrial gas cylinder filled with air, nitrogen, or carbon dioxide. These are available from specialized outlets—restaurant or bar supply stores for CO_2 and welding shops for nitrogen—and come in several sizes. You won't need a moisture trap if you use nitrogen or CO_2 but you'll need a regulator. Portable air tanks and gas cylinders have a big advantage—they are silent.

Airborne paint is easily inhaled, which is unhealthy. Airbrush where there is good ventilation—outdoors or in a garage with the door open—rather than in an enclosed space. (Some paint fumes are even flammable, so it's really a bad idea to let them build up in a room or basement containing a gas-fired heater or stove.)

The best option is a spray booth. Not only will the fan pull paint fumes and particles out of the room, but it will contain stray paint.

Airbrushing takes practice to master, but it's fun and will improve your models.

2 HobbyBoss' Pfiel made better

Elevate an easy assembly kit with aftermarket parts and scratchbuilding

BY ANDERS ISAKSSON

This Dornier Do 335 replicates an aircraft captured by the Allies near the end of World War II. Resin parts from Freightdog Models and decals from EagleCals helped bring the project together.

I have always found the Dornier Do 335's odd design fascinating, so when HobbyBoss released a 1/72 scale kit I couldn't pass it up. I can say from the beginning that this is a sound kit with fine surface detail in the form of consistent, recessed panel lines. However, a few of the details are lacking or completely wrong. The most egregious errors are the misplaced propeller shaft in the nose and incorrectly shaped props that turn the wrong directions. Fortunately, a small firm called Freightdog Models, from the United Kingdom, offers a simple resin set that corrects both of these shortcomings, as well as providing a few other detailed replacement pieces to use on the kit.

In addition, I added EagleCals decals which include American national insignia for a Do 335 captured by the Allies near the end of WWII. The sheet's instructions included photos that helped during finishing.

1
The Do 335 is part of HobbyBoss' Easy Assembly range, so the part count is low but the detail is rather good and all of the major features are included. Most of the fuselage comes in one part, while the entire wing is a single piece molded as part of the rest of the fuselage. These are large pieces and quite impressive!

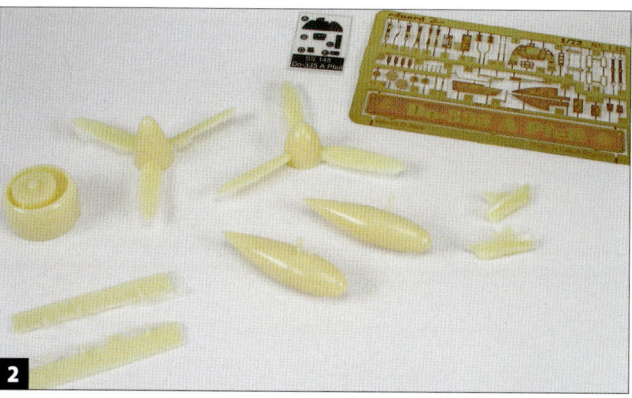

2
To improve the kit, I used a small resin correction set from Freightdog Models that includes a replacement nose with the correct propeller shaft position and a pair of new propellers. In addition, a old Eduard photo-etch (PE) set designed for Dragon's Do 335 enhanced detail in the cockpit and landing gear. Not pictured here was a set of Master Detail turned brass barrels and pitot tube.

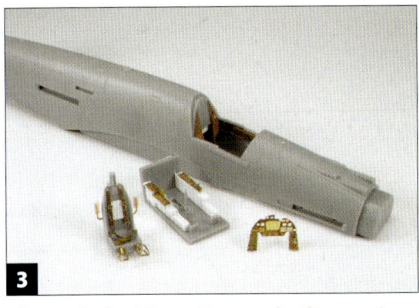

3 The cockpit side walls were built up using scrap styrene and appropriate PE parts for the side consoles and instrument panel. I overhauled the seat with a pair of scratchbuilt armrests and a few PE bits. Then, the cockpit was painted with MRP RLM 66 schwarzgrau (No. 56).

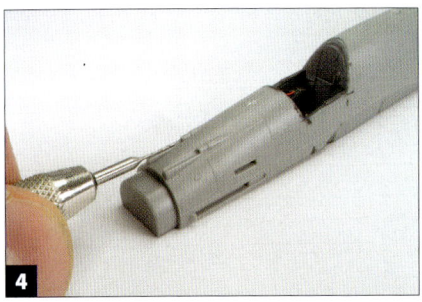

4 The dual gun barrels on top of the nose are molded on. Rather than embarking on the complex operation of replacing them with similar turned-brass barrels, I opted to simply drill out the muzzles; good enough for my purposes.

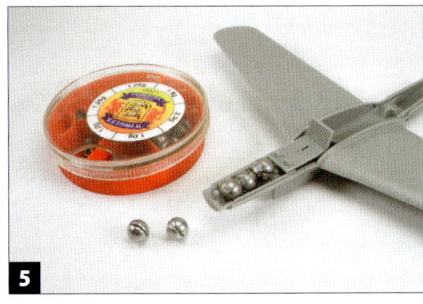

5 The instructions don't mention the need for weight to keep the nose wheel grounded, but I felt it was better to be safe than sorry. I added what seemed like a good amount of lead fishing sinkers, but it ended up being just enough!

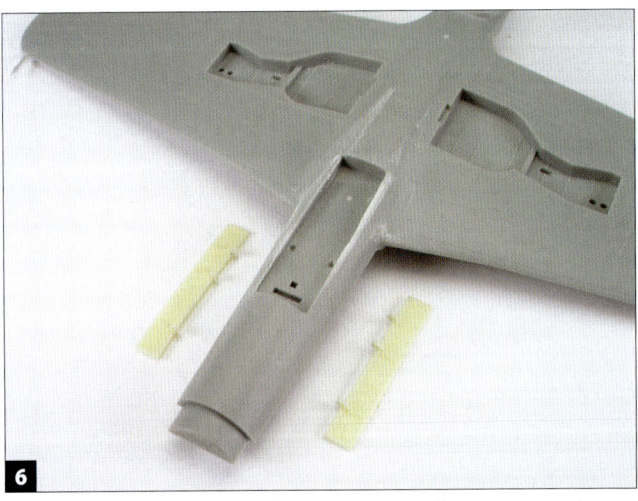

6 The major drawback of the kit's Easy Assembly nature was the nose gear doors, which are set in the open position and molded with the lower fuselage. This toy-like feature was corrected by the Freightdog set that provides replacement doors complete with accurate inner surface detail.

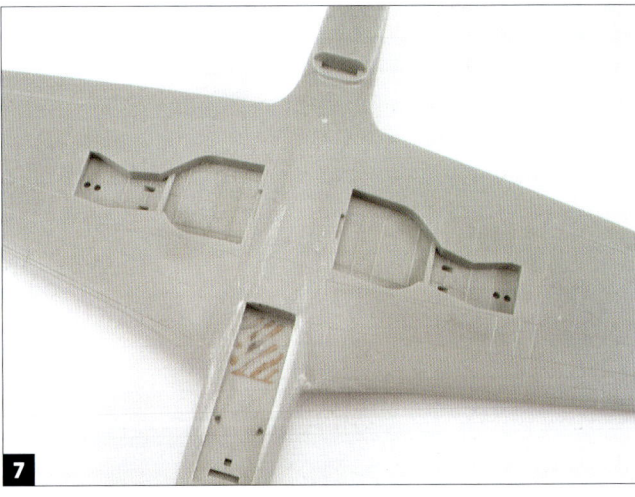

7 I rarely spend time detailing areas that will be difficult to see under normal circumstances. But, after taking a look at the landing gear bays, I decided they could do with a little improvement. This was especially true of the too-shallow nose-wheel well, so I marked the area to be modified and went to work.

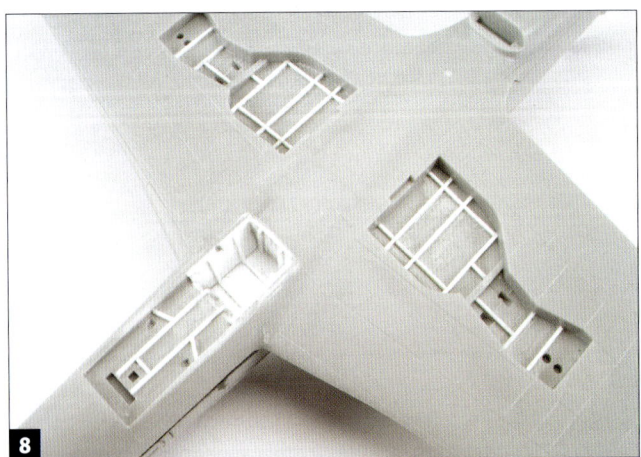

8 Referring to a photo of the Aires resin 1/48 scale gear bays and a fair amount of my imagination, I ended up with something that's not totally accurate but better than the kit wheel wells. In addition to deepening the nose well, I added frames and detail using styrene strip.

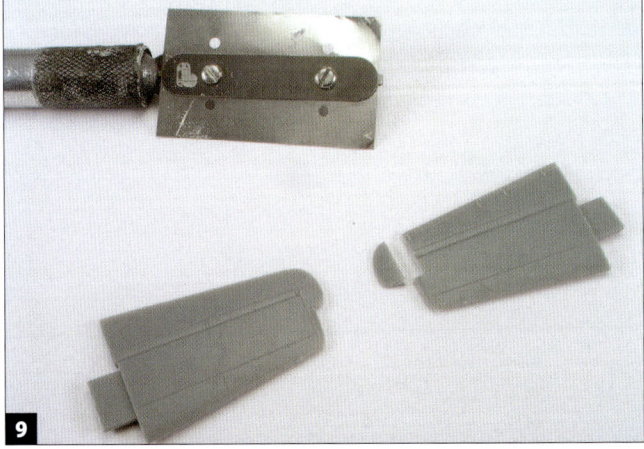

9 When possible, I like to droop elevators as this modification makes the model look more dynamic and realistic. The design of the Do 335's stabilizer made the operation more complex as each elevator section had to be cut apart and rejoined in the new position. A fine razor saw made clean cuts.

10 Once attached, the stabilizers show the added realism provided by the repositioned elevators.

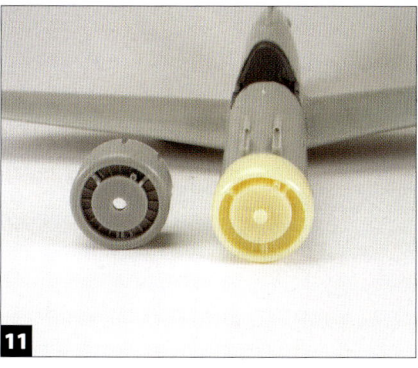

11 Nose job: A quick comparison of the kit part with the Freightdog replacement.

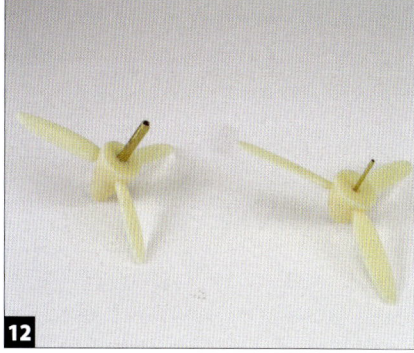

12 After cleaning up Freightdog's resin props, I gave each a brass-tube shaft to make installation easy.

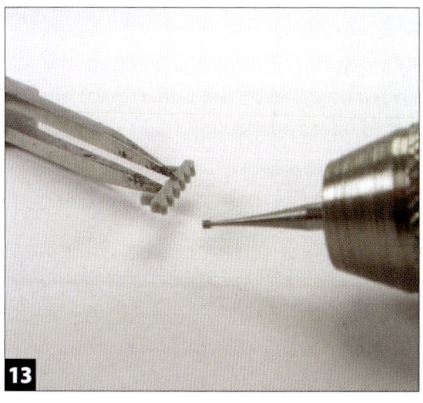

13 I carefully opened each stub of the kit exhausts using the smallest grinding bit I could find. A steady hand coupled with low speed is the key to success here.

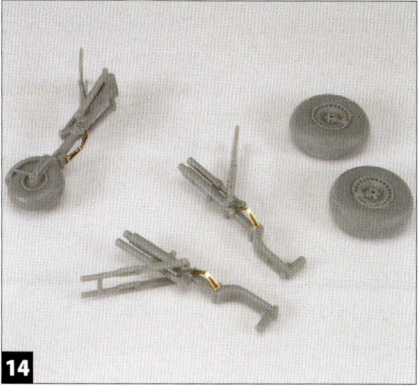

14 Unfortunately, the nose wheel is molded with the gear leg. I deemed the problem not-too-serious and decided to let it pass as the improvement would require substantial work. Instead, I focused on adding detail, such as the PE oleo scissor links.

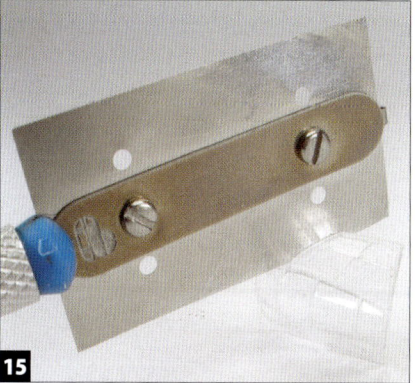

15 After detailing the cockpit, I wanted to open the canopy to better display the interior. A fine-toothed saw quickly separated the sections.

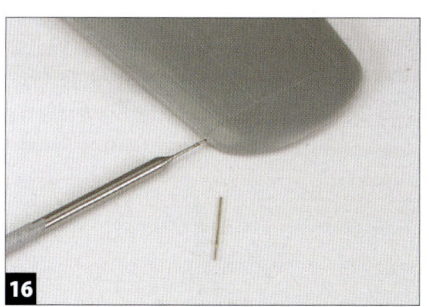

16 In preparation for installing the turned-brass pitot tube, I drilled a mounting hole in the wing's leading edge with a small-diameter bit.

17 A set of pre-cut canopy masks from Pmask made painting much easier. Considering the intricate framework of the Do 335, it was an easy decision to use this time-saver.

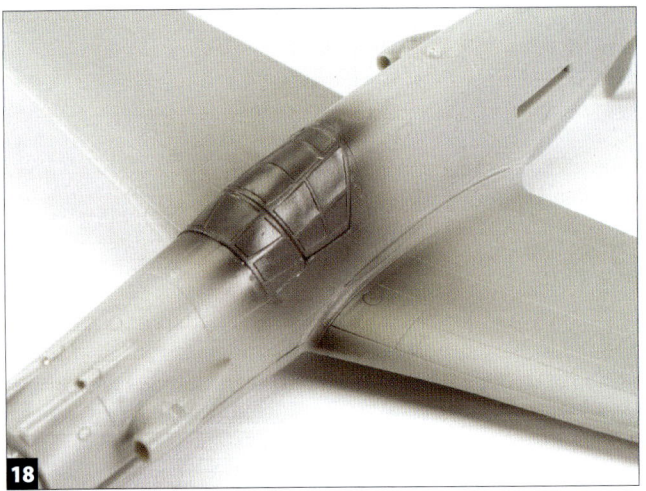

18 Before applying primer, I sprayed the canopy with the cockpit color—RLM 66—so the inside faces of the frames matches the interior.

19 To prepare for the camouflage colors, I base-coated the entire model with gray Tamiya Fine Surface Primer straight from the spray can. Any imperfections revealed by the primer were eliminated with small amounts of filler and sanding sticks.

20 I painted the wheel wells with MRP RLM 02 grau (50), then masked with pieces of sponge cut to shape.

21 To get the Luftwaffe splinter camouflage right, I used pre-cut masks from AML. While the angular shapes and sharp demarcation lines are rather easy to mask with tape, sets like this save time.

22 Here's the upper camouflage pattern on the model. I airbrushed it with MRP RLM 81 braunviolett (70) and RLM 82 hellgrun (71).

23 After masking the upper surfaces, the underside was painted with MRP RLM 65 hellblau (58).

24 Rather than decals, I used an old set of Eduard masks for the German national insignia on the fuselage and upper wings. These simple white crosses will be painted over later to replicate the captured Do 335 I was building.

25 The painted insignia were complemented with decals from the EagleCal sheet to complete the markings.

26 Then, all of the Luftwaffe insignia were covered with a thin layer of flat black as per the real thing.

27 I started weathering by airbrushing streaks of dirt along the wings using thin flat black paint. Masking adjacent panels isolated the streaks to specific areas like the flaps.

28 I continued weathering with dark artist-oil washes flowed along selected panel and hinge lines to simulate collected dirt as well as to deepen shadows and define detail.

29 Chips and scuffs in the paint were added using a various colored pencils, focusing around panels and high-wear areas.

30 Referring to photos, I built up heavier deposits and streaks of dirt and oil under the nose. To make these effects, I used thin black and brown artist oils applied with a paintbrush and then streaked downward.

31
To mimic fading and general discoloration on horizontal surfaces, I used dot filters—spots of several colors of artist oils applied to the surface, then blended and feathered with a broad paintbrush damp with turpentine.

32
To give the propellers a battered and worn appearance, I applied light gray paint with a chunk of sponge producing a suitably uneven and more interesting look versus the otherwise monochromatic propellers.

33
As a final step to improve the detail, I scratchbuilt a pair of hydraulic actuators for each inner main landing gear door. These were easily fabricated using sections of brass tubing with styrene rod inside.

With the final parts attached, my Do 335 was finished. I appreciate the approach HobbyBoss has taken with Easy Assembly kits producing a decent model with few parts and fine surface detailing, while still getting the basic shapes and panel lines about right. This leaves it up to the modeler to add any detail if desired, and one can choose exactly how much extra time and effort to put into the build.

The all Canadian affair

Building the BPK CRJ-200

BY MASSIMO SANTAROSSA

Big Planes Kits, or BPK, made a big splash in 2012 with the release of a 1/72 scale 737-200, and it probably ranks as the best kit of the baby Boeing in that scale. As a result, many airliner modelers wanted to see what the Ukrainian company would do next. We didn't have to wait long as a short time later BPK's 1/144 scale Bomdardier CRJ 100 hit hobby store shelves. It was a welcome addition as it represented the first fully injection-molded plastic kit of this plane.

Let's get this out of the way straight away: This is a limited-run kit, not a shake 'n bake variety of plastic. As such it possess a number of features that we normally associate with this type of kit, namely no locating pins, a certain amount of flash and mold seams, and some small parts that lack some detail and need cleaning up to really come into their own. That said, the kit has some serious pluses, including a set of resin intakes and exhausts for the engines, a photo-etched (PE) metal fret that provides a number of small details, recessed panel lines, and thin trailing edges. My boxing came with a set of well-printed decals covering three liveries. From the beginning, this project had the hallmarks of an enjoyable build.

Airliners, such as this Big Planes Kits Bombardier CRJ-200, have their own unique skill sets. Massimo Santarossa shares some tips for getting that glossy white finish.

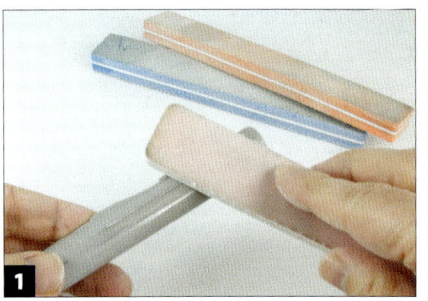

1 With airliners, you can get right into building; there's no interiors or subassemblies to paint ahead of glue. BPK does provide a clear windscreen and basic flight deck parts, but I intended to use decal windows so I omitted the interior parts. In short order, I had the fuselage together and the clear cabin windows attached. Although a snug fit, the drop in strip needs extra work for a seamless fit. I filled gaps with Mr. Surfacer and sanded the areas smooth.

2 This is still a limited run kit don't forget, and some sanding and thinning of mating edges was needed for the parts to meet correctly. Some of the edges of limited-run kit parts can be a little soft, so I sanded mating surfaces flat and square using sandpaper on a hard surface.

3 Assembly of the wings proved to be straightforward, although the wheel well parts needed clean-up for perfect fit. I had the main fuselage, cockpit, and wings together into what was quickly looking like a proper airplane pretty quickly. Overall fit was good, but clamps maintained alignment while the glue set. Note the weight in the cockpit to keep the plane from rocking back on its tail.

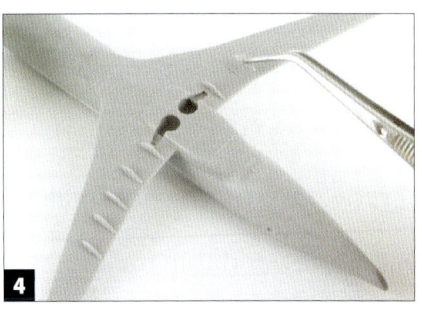

4 The locators on some of the smaller parts, such as the flap actuators, were a bit oversized and not perfectly formed. Instead of spending a lot of time and energy trying to clean them up, I removed the mating tabs and simply glued the parts to the wings' surfaces. They are not weight bearing, so the strength of the joints wasn't going to be an issue. The same was true for the winglets, which butt up to the wingtips.

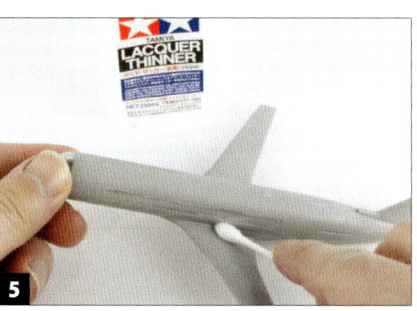

5 The kit includes an optional resin tail fin, but, for the life of me I could not figure out why. It is identical to the plastic part and the instructions make no mention of it. I used the plastic part, reasoning that it would bond with the plastic for a sturdier model. A smear of Mr. Surfacer filled gaps. Tamiya lacquer thinner is excellent for smoothing Mr. Surfacer; even days later. This technique will dissolve putty, virtually eliminating the need for sanding.

6 My chosen paint scheme was simple—overall white—so I applied two coats of Testors Model Master flat white. Between each coat, be it flat or gloss, I sanded the finish with a 3600-grit polishing cloth to guarantee a glossy, smooth finish. The final layer is Model Master classic white. After sanding, I buffed the CRJ to a high shine with Novus Plastic Polish.

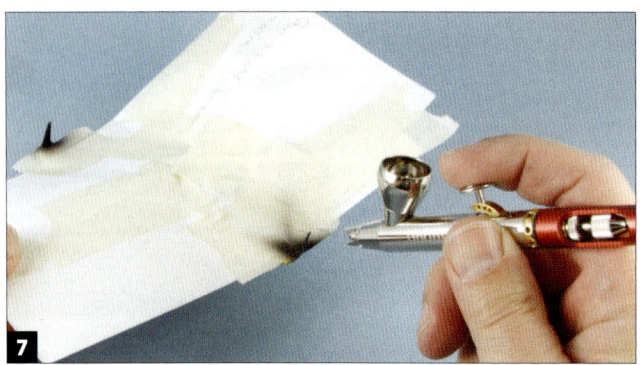

7 You can't mask too much when spraying black paint over white. I sprayed the winglets with gloss black to match the livery.

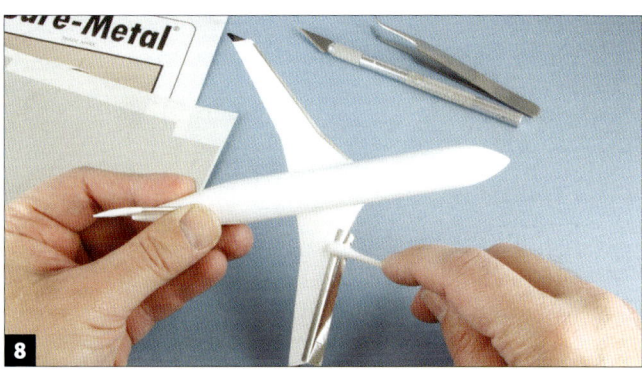

8 Nothing looks like metal like metal. For the shiny leading edges, I used Bare-Metal Foil chrome; it's quicker than masking and painting and it looks very realistic. To apply the self-adhesive foil, I burnished an oversized piece into place with a cotton swab.

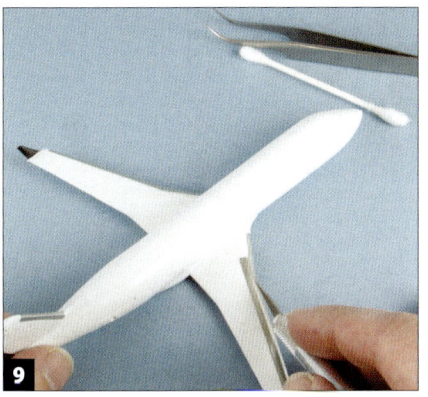

9 Then, using the recessed panel lines as a guide, I trimmed away the excess with a sharp, new blade. The foil is thin so you don't need to use a lot of pressure cut it, just enough to keep the knife on course.

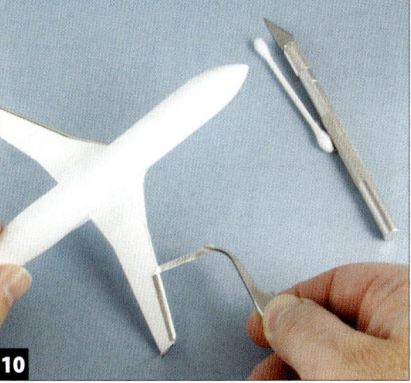

10 Using tweezers to pull off the excess foil revealed a neat, shiny leading edge that really makes the model come to life.

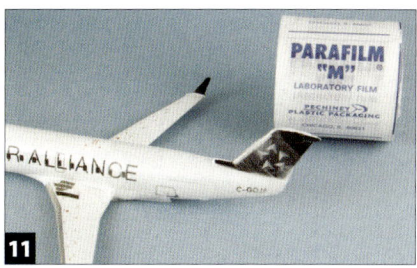

11 The kit's decal were fine, but I wanted a subject closer to home, namely Air Canada Jazz in Star Alliance livery from Canadian manufacturer V1 Decals. They performed flawlessly and included the major livery components, but also some details to boost the model's appearance. Unfortunately, the tail decal was touch small so I touched it us with gloss black. Parafilm "M" is ideal for masking over decals.

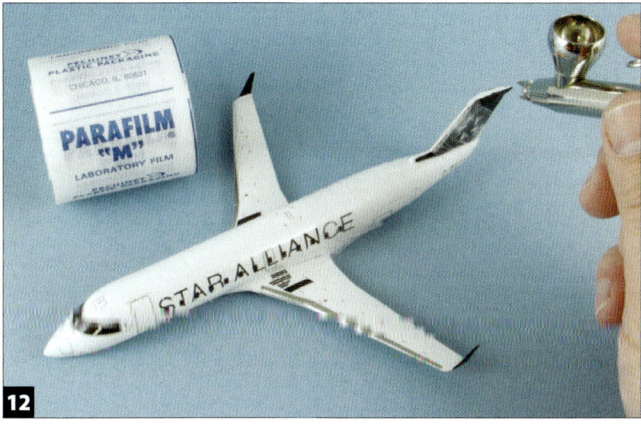

12 After spraying gloss black, I removed the Parafilm and airbrushed the entire tail with Pledge Floor Gloss to seal the decals and blend the paint touch ups.

13 The CRJ is not a big plane and in 1/144 scale it is smaller yet, so mounting the landing gear is slow, delicate work. It took a little time and patience to get everything attached and aligned, but when I was done the plane sat squarely on its tires.

14 To bring out the fine detail of the resin engines, I flowed Model Master black stain into the fans. Despite its diminutive size, this little addition makes the whole engine pop with eye catching life. The engine pylons needed a bit of adjusting with a file to mount correctly, which added a grand total of 10 minutes to the build.

15 Finally, I attached the PE antennas and other small exterior details using Microscale Kristal Klear as an adhesive. I enjoyed this build and the limited-run nature of the model should not stop anyone with a bit of modeling experience from tackling the kit. With the likes of V1 Decals and others, the sky's the limit when it comes to what one can produce.

4 Building a classic Phantom

Basic techniques get Monogram's F-4 up and away

BY DARREN ROBERTS

A new hobby shop recently opened up by me, which is a pretty big deal these days. You don't see many new shops starting up. So, wanting to support the cause, I made my way over and began meandering through the aisles. There was a pretty good selection of both new and old kits. I really wasn't looking for anything in particular, but then a kit from my childhood caught my eye. It was Monogram's 1/48 scale F-4C. This particular boxing contained markings for the 136th Fighter Interceptor Squadron based out of Niagara Falls. Having grown up in upstate New York, I'd seen quite a number of F-4s from that unit at airshows. That made it a no-brainer. I plunked down my money (technically I inserted my credit card with security chip) and headed home with my new-found project.

There are newer, more detailed F-4 kits on the market, but that doesn't mean the Monogram kit should be cast aside. It's actually quite nice, and with some TLC, can be turned into a finished model every bit as good as one of the newer wonder kits. Plus, there's something about building a Monogram kit that strikes a chord. Working on one of these old kits is like wrapping yourself up in a warm, soft blanket on a cold, rainy day. There's just something comforting about it.

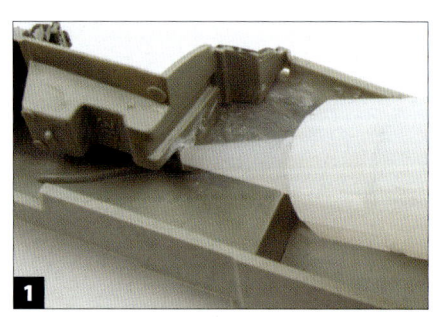

When the cockpit was ready for installation, I discovered that securing it to the fuselage was going to be tricky. There wasn't a lot of surface area to attach the cockpit tub, so I reinforced the bond with superglue.

Darren Roberts grew up in upstate New York and remembered seeing these F-4s from Niagara Falls at airshows. This was just one of the nostalgic effects of building this venerable Monogram kit.

2 With the cockpit tub secured, I dry-fitted the fuselage halves to get the best fit—this would be a recurring theme throughout the build. While nicely detailed, Monogram kits were not known for their fit. Once the fuselage halves were together, I cleaned up the seam. To minimize damage to the raised surface detail, I ran masking tape along the seam's sides before adding putty.

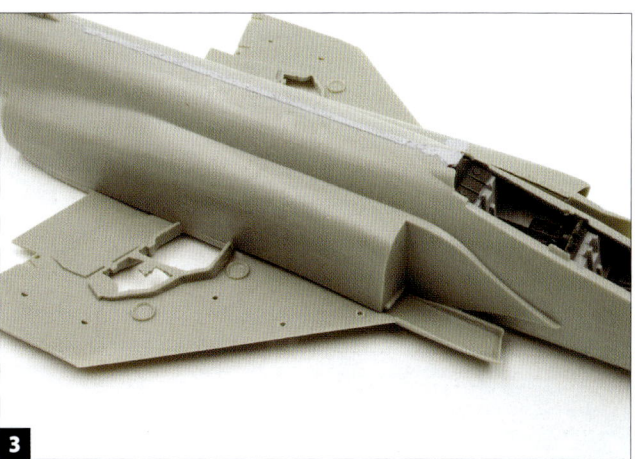

3 At this point, I deviated from the instructions, which would have you assemble the wings and then attach that completed assembly to the fuselage. I've found that by changing up the sequence, you can get a much better fit. I attached the bottom of the wings first.

I focused my attention on the front underside of the fuselage, making sure to align it with the upper fuselage as much as possible for the best possible fit.

Next came the intakes, probably the most problematic area of the entire kit. I decided early on that intake plugs were the way to go as there was very little depth to the intakes — they are simply blanked off. I cut the splitter plate from the interior intake piece.

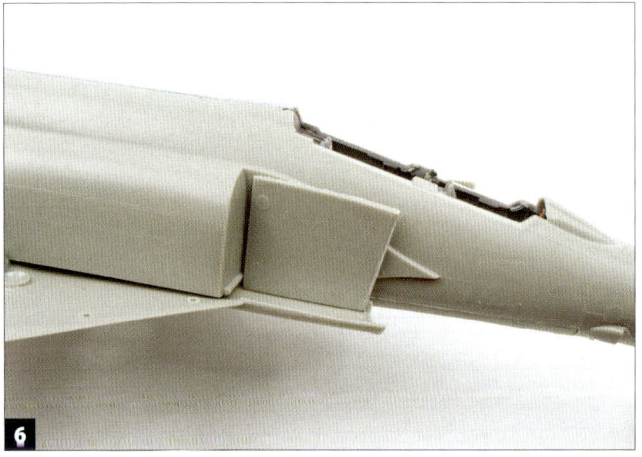

Then, I attached the inboard intake piece to the fuselage.

I took quite a bit of dry-fitting to adjust the fit of the exterior intake piece.

I thinned the top of the piece with a sanding stick …

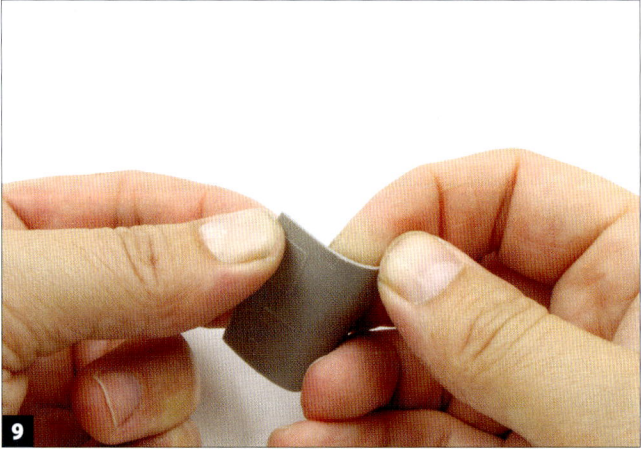

… and resorted to brute force to bend the curvature of the piece to match the fuselage.

10 Quick-setting liquid cement was used to prevent the intake piece from shifting out of place.

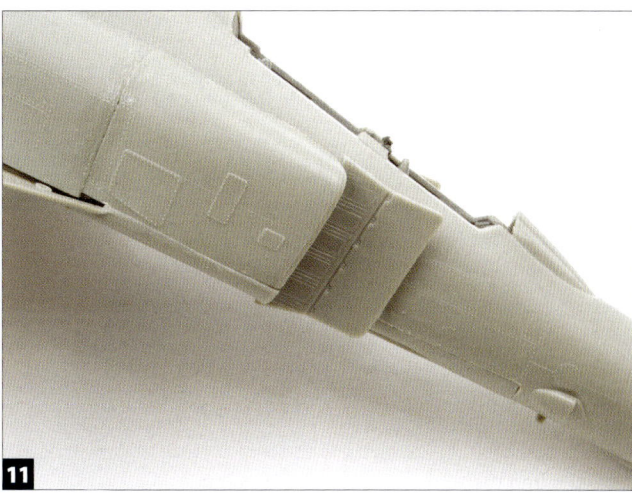

11 Finally the splitter plate was added.

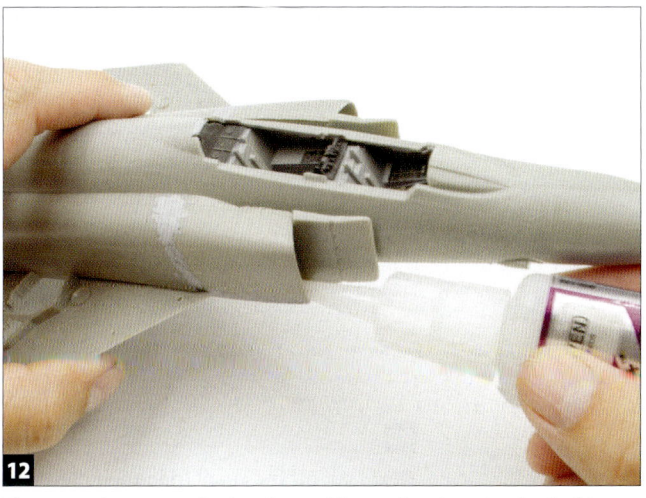

12 The seam between the intake and lower fuselage looked a bit weak, so I reinforced it with super glue on the inside of the intake. This was another reason I decided to use intake plugs.

13 In cleaning up the seam between the fuselage halves, some of the raised detail was lost. However, there's a quick little trick that can restore the detail. With strips of masking tape as a guide, I used a hobby knife to make grooves where the panel line should have been. Doing this pushes up a ridge of plastic that, when painted, mimics the look of the raised detail surrounding it.

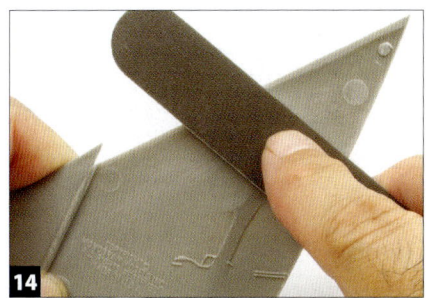

14 With the fuselage complete, I added the tops of the wings. To ensure a good fit, I sanded all of the mating surfaces as well as removing the locating tabs. This allowed me to have a bit of wiggle room to get the best fit possible.

15 The flaperons didn't quite fit snuggly into the recess, so I cut off the locating tabs, …

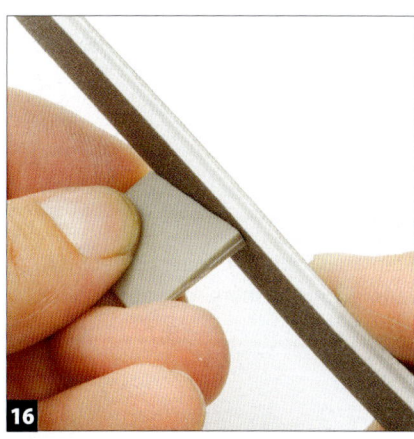

16 … sanded the mating surface at an angle, …

17 … and glued them to completed wings.

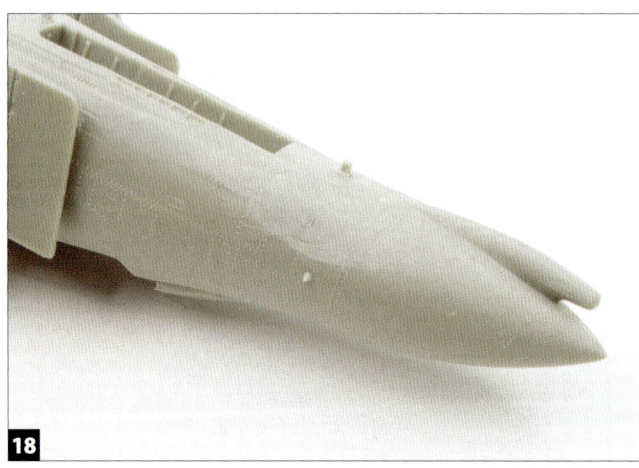

18 While the Monogram Phantom has nice detail, there are small things that can be improved. The first upgrade was to replace the air-conditioning scoops alongside the nose with resin parts from Steel Beach.

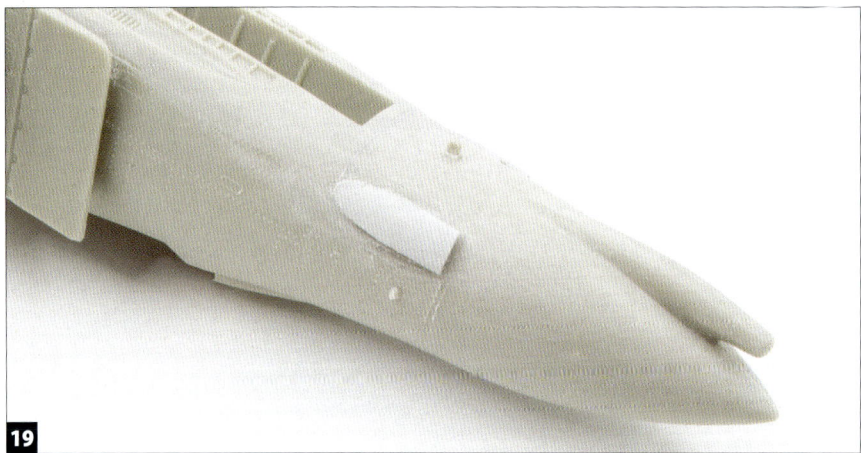

19 After sanding off the molded scoops, I glued on the resin replacements.

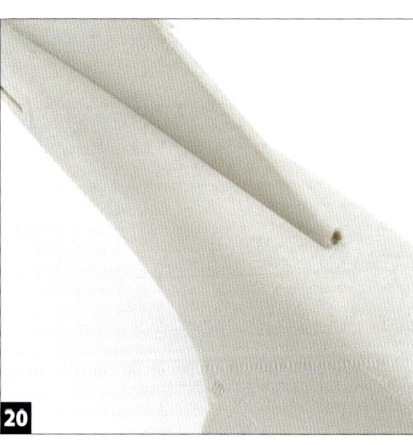

20 Next I cut off the small triangular piece at the base of the tail and hollowed out the area behind it.

21 I replaced it with a thinner piece of styrene, giving it a more scale appearance.

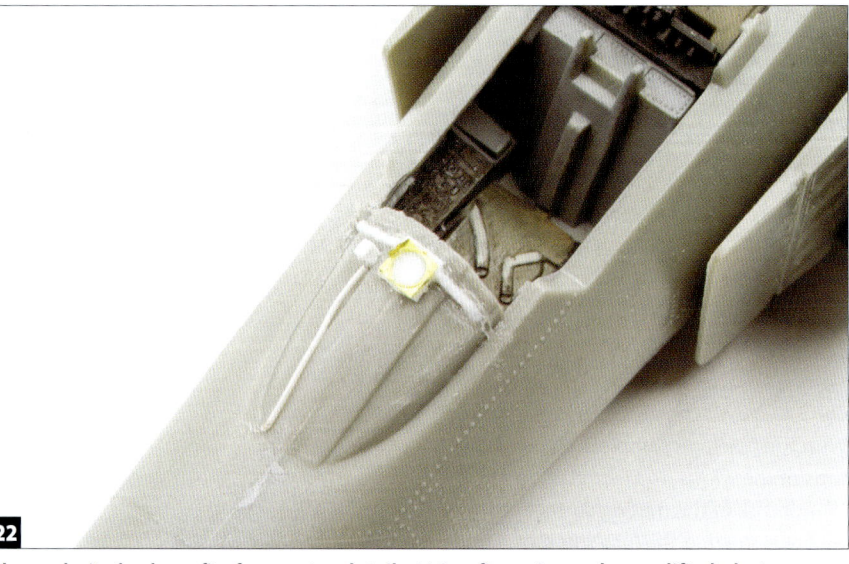

22 The cockpit also benefits from extra details. Using fine wire and a modified photo-etched HUD for the gunsight, I spruced up the front glare shield.

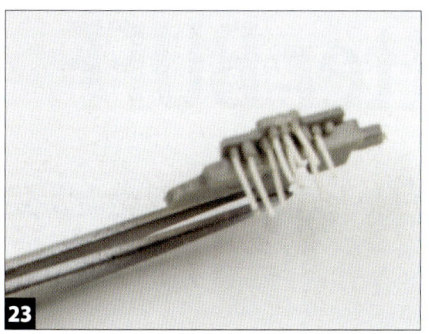

23 I also wired the rear instrument panel, which is exposed.

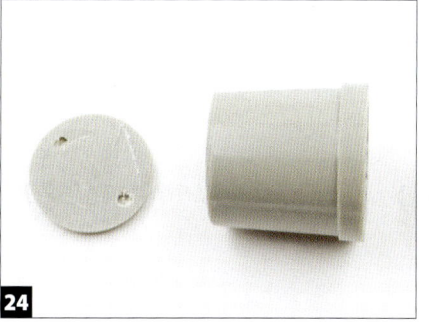

24 The kit jet nozzles lack detail, even omitting flame holders at the end of the burner cans. Styrene half-round rod and channel, along with a bit of resin and some items from the spares box, added some much-needed detail. First, I cut off the end of the burner can and separated the nozzle with a razor saw.

25 From my spares box, I used an open exhaust nozzle from a 1/72 scale F-14 Tomcat to create the inner ring on the inside of the kit nozzle.

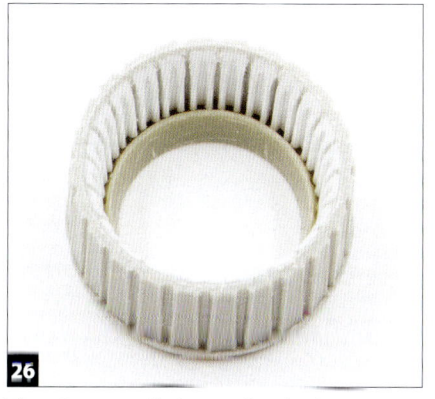

26 Then I cut small pieces of 1/16-inch styrene channel and glued them inside of the nozzle and sanded them to shape.

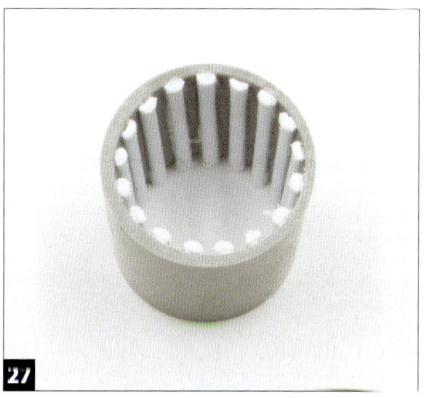

27 I glued sections of half-round rod inside of the burner can and painted it with four coats of Mr. Surfacer 1000 to represent the corrugated look.

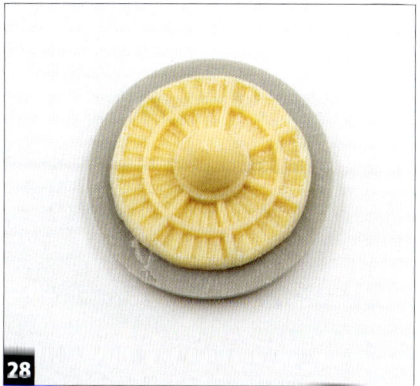

28 I glued a resin flame holder from Steel Beach onto the piece of burner can and put everything back together.

29 I painted the overall ADC gray scheme using a mix of Hataka, Mr. Color, Alclad, and Testors Model Master acrylics, and the model was ready for the decals. Unfortunately, while removing masks, I inadvertently took out the ram-air and pitot tubes on the leading edge of the tail. I should have known better, as I've done that same exact thing building this kit in the past. I replaced them with turned-metal aftermarket probes.

30 The decals for the 136th FIS were, surprisingly enough, straight from the kit. They actually performed quite well, despite their age, and conformed nicely after an application of Microscale Micro Sol. This was a nostalgia-filled project, both for the Monogram kit and my childhood memories. Now, let's see what other classic gems are hiding in my stash. Maybe it's time to dust those off and give them a go.

5 Building a better BUFF

Assembly tips and detail improvements for ModelCollect's 1/72 scale B-52H

BY PAUL D. BOYER

Even brand-new kits can use some correction. Paul Boyer shares some techniques to improve the accuracy of this Big, Ugly, Fat ... umm ... Fellow.

The ambitious flight plan put forth by ModelCollect to produce new, up-to-date kits of U.S. Air Force strategic bombers rolls on with several versions of the venerable Boeing B-52 Stratofortress. But there has been some turbulence along the way, with the manufacturer offering corrected parts for its initial B-52G kit.

So when the kit of the B-52H model was issued, I expected a smooth ride. Well, not so much. Before we take off, be sure your seatbelts are securely fastened.

A reasonably acceptable model can be made out of the box—if you don't look too closely and if you don't know the B-52 well. I'm not a BUFF expert, but some dimension errors and shape problems were obvious. Some puzzling detail mistakes and omissions, and questionable design decisions by the manufacturer are going to frustrate beginners looking to build the ultimate B-52 model.

So what follows is a tour of the improvements I made to my BUFF. I'll also show you some diversions to avoid some air pockets during assembly. I modified some kit parts, scratch-built some antennas, but had to divert to aftermarket markings. Still, my model isn't perfect. I'll have to head for an alternate aftermarket destination to fix other problems someday.

1 In the cockpit, the kit provides moderate detail for six crew stations, but any assembly and paint work you do aft of the pilot and co-pilot seats is wasted—you can't see any of it on the finished model. I didn't have alternatives, so I installed the kit's ACES II seats even though they are not correct for the B-52. Also, the seats on their rails won't fit under the low ceiling of the lower crew stations.

2 I decided to build and paint the fuselage in forward, center, and aft sections, then assemble them and add the wings later. With the forward fuselage closed, I worked on the "glass." The windscreen fits perfectly, but the small overhead windows needed to be sanded on all sides and repeatedly test-fit.

3 I burnished Bare-Metal Foil to mask canopies and windows. Then with a sharp blade, I scored around each pane and remove the foil from the framing. I rubbed off what little adhesive is left with my fingers.

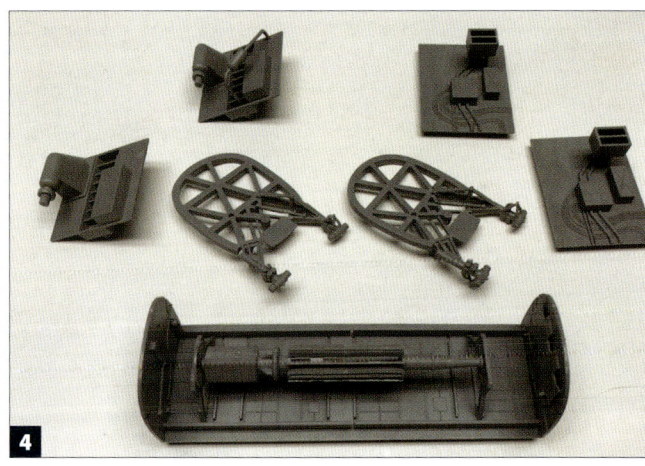

4 I built all the bomb-bay and landing-gear subassemblies and prepped them for painting.

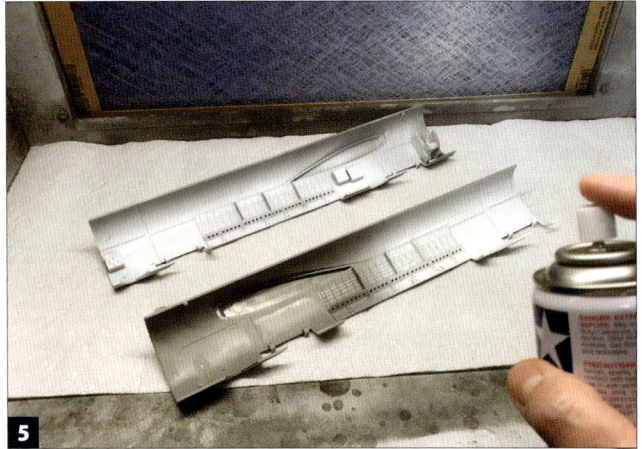

5 I sprayed the interior surfaces of the center fuselage section with Tamiya Fine White Primer, then did the same on the bomb-bay and landing-gear subassemblies.

6 After adding the subassemblies to one side of the center section, I masked the interior surfaces with tape and sprayed the outer surfaces of both halves with Tamiya spray-can gunship gray (AS-27).

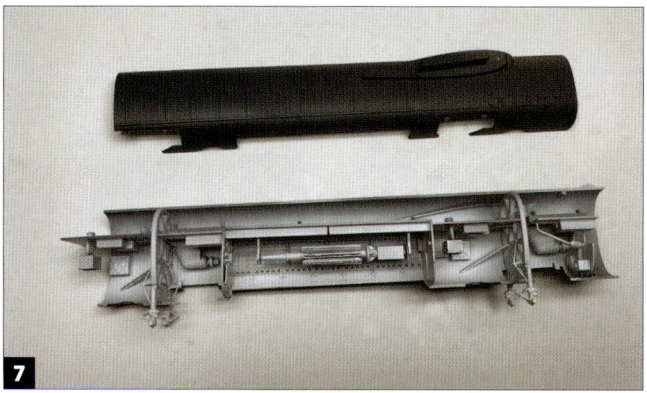

7 Here are the painted halves of the center section.

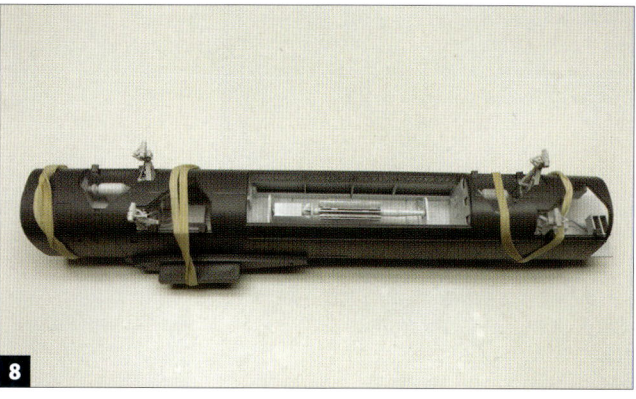

8 Next I glued the halves together and wrapped rubber bands around the assembly to ensure the glued surfaces were making good contact. I touched up the seams with a brush later on.

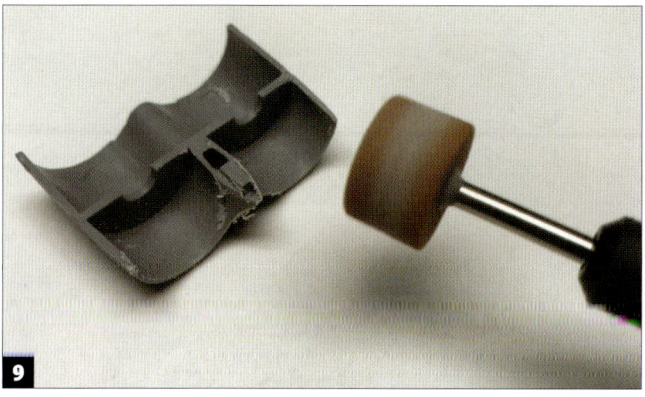

9 The shape of the engine intakes is not correct with the divider being too thick and squared off. I found a grinding bit that was exactly the right size and used it in a motor tool to flare out the intake ramps and correct the shape.

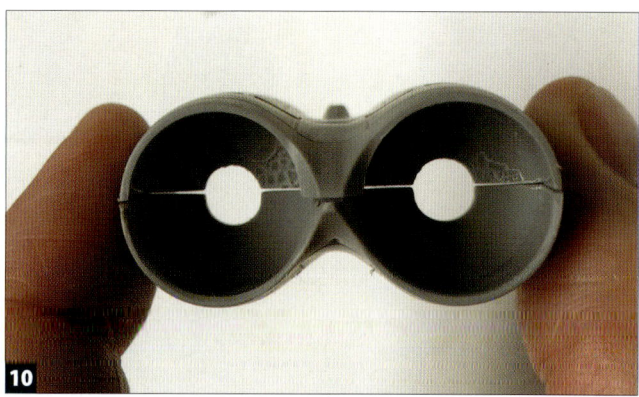

10 Here's a before-and-after-shot of the intakes. The top half is kit stock, the bottom half has been flared open. I had to correct each nacelle half separately as the engine fans in an assembled nacelle would not provide room for the grinding bit.

11 After assembling the nacelles, I cleaned up the seams inside the intakes with a homemade tool of sandpaper attached around a cutoff drop tank half with double-sided tape. This tool reached the seams without damaging the fan or intake cone of the engine.

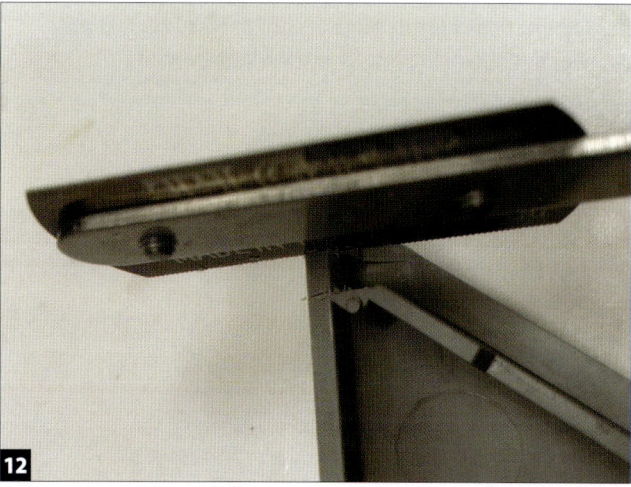

12 There is a rectangular intake near the root of each wing's leading edge, but the kit parts don't show it. I cut away a small section of plastic from the root of both lower wing halves to represent the intakes

13 Here's the opened intake in the left wing.

14 You have to open holes in the wing for the tip tanks and external weapon pylons. Impressions for these holes are molded on the inside face of the bottom wing halves. I use a blade to first center the hole from the inside, then broaden the holes from the outside.

15 The suspension arms molded to the dropped flaps are very thin and break off easily. I reinforced them with a drop of gap-filling superglue applied where they meet the flap.

16 I painted each engine nacelle separately with the spray can of gunship gray, then attached them to the wing. There's only one small hole and pin at the leading edge of the pylon, but no other mounting pins or holes to guide assembly. I had to eyeball the attachment. I found that aiming the aft tip of each pylon at the third rib from the outside edge of each flap bay aligned the pylon as liquid cement flowed into the surface joints.

17 With the engine pylons attached and the joints cleaned up, I sprayed each wing assembly gunship gray before attaching the wings to the fuselage.

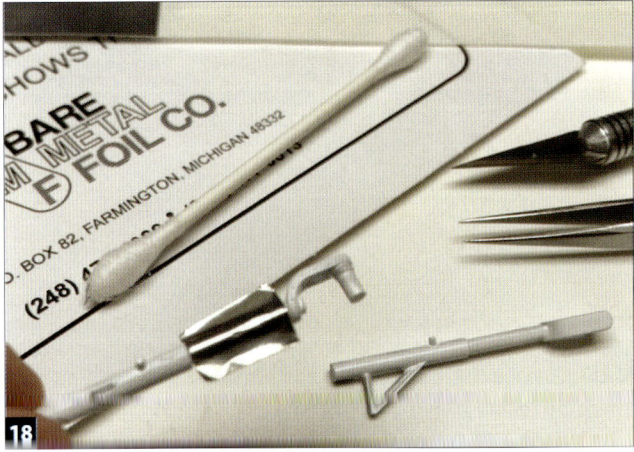

18 I applied a piece of Bare-Metal Foil to simulate the oleo strut of each outrigger.

19 The fit of the outriggers to the wing is poor. I had to cut down the "pin" and shave off the tip of the triangular aft support to get each strut to fit into the opening in the wing.

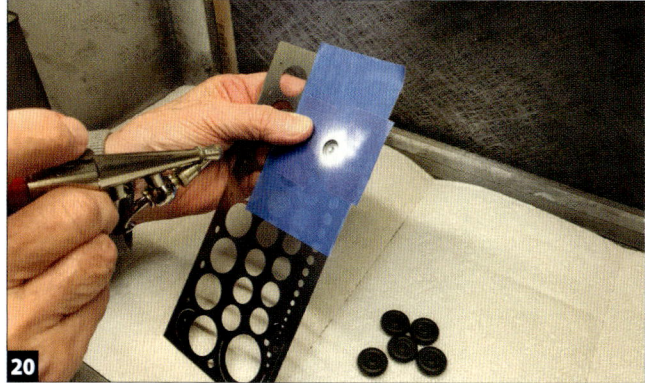

20 I painted each main wheel with a dark-gray rubber color, then used a circle template as a mask to airbrush the wheels with white.

21 There's no indication of the landing lights mounted in the edges of the forward main gear doors, so I simulated them with drops of chrome paint from a Molotow marker.

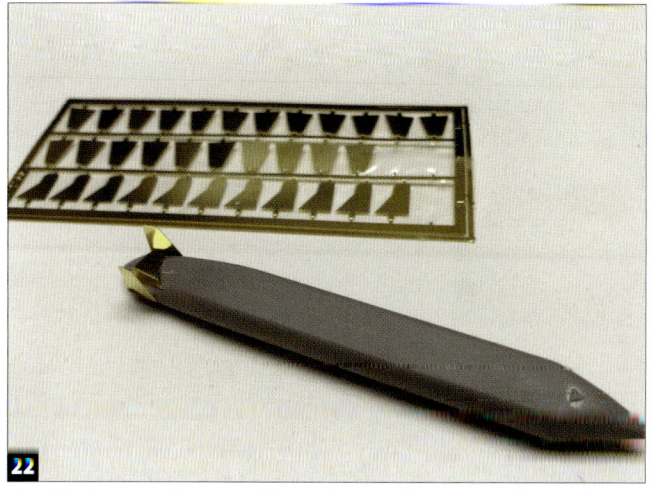

22 The Modelcollect kit provides a dozen AGM-129A Advanced Cruise Missiles, but the photo-etched (PE) metal fins included are for the earlier AGM-86B missiles. Because the fins were to be mounted in the folded position, the mismatch wasn't obvious.

23 Before joining the three main fuselage sections and cleaning up the seams, I added some of the obvious antennas omitted from the kit. Eyeballing the dimensions, I used a simple office hole punch to fashion a disc from .010-inch sheet styrene for the GPS antenna, and a section of ½-inch PVC pipe, shaped with sanding sticks, for the transverse magnetic antenna for the AN/ARR-85 Miniature Receiver Terminal on the upper fuselage.

24 I drilled holes in the rear fuselage to provide mounts for anticollision beacons and antennas.

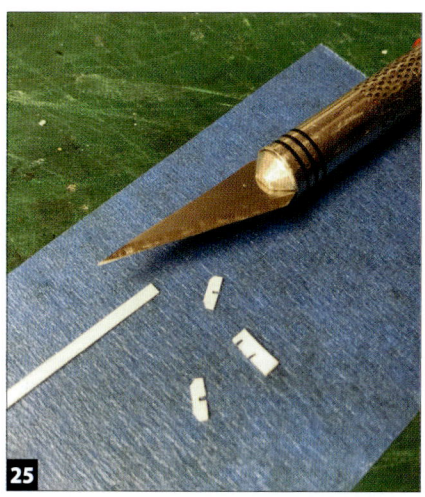

25 I fashioned the upper and lower ALQ-122/ALT-16S ECM "tree" antennas from .010-inch styrene strip. The notches make assembly easier with fewer parts.

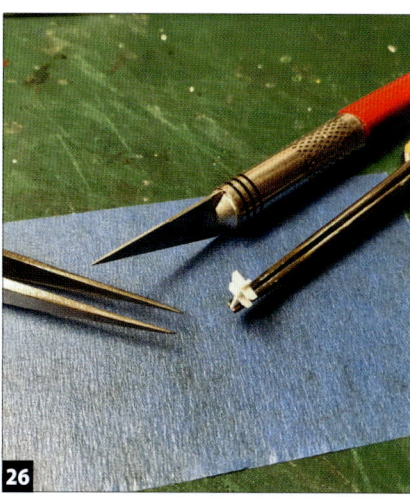

26 Here's a finished tree antenna. Again, the dimensions were eyeballed. Too small? Too big? I have no idea.

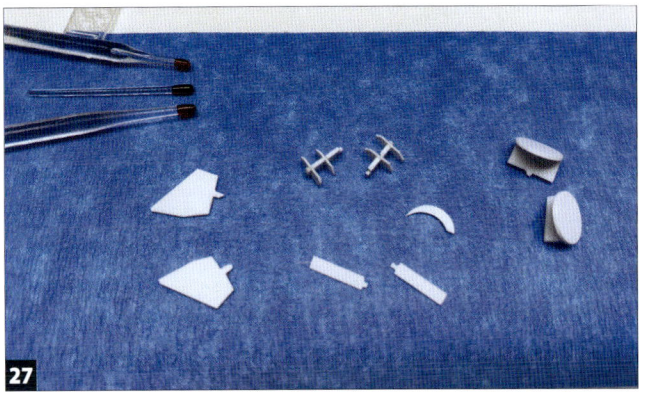

27 Here is the group of small antennas to be added to the fuselage. The three anticollision beacons were made from stretched clear sprue that were painted with clear red acrylic. The "elephant ear" fins are not antennas, but recognition devices in accordance with the START treaty. The "Frisbees" are AN/ARC-210(V) satellite communication antennas made from sheet styrene.

28 So here are the antennas on the finished model. I painted the GPS antenna a cream color.

29 There's a pair of anticollision beacons flanking the sat/com Frisbee and ECM "tree" antennas on top of the rear section of the fuselage.

30 A single anticollision beacon, Frisbee, tree, and ID fins on the bottom of the rear section.

31 Also missing from the kit were four pitot/air sensor masts near the nose. I made them from .010-inch styrene rod and strip.

32 The kit provides these four ECM antennas, but they are hard to find on the sprues and not mentioned in the kit instructions. I'm not sure I have them in the correct positions, but at least they are there!

33 There are two prominent air scoops missing from the right side of the kit's forward fuselage. I couldn't see a way of carving them out, so I simulated their shapes and shadows with strips of black decal. Looks good, eh?

34 One of the big disappointments of the kit were the decals. Although well printed by Cartograf, there were some errors. Insignia and wing walks were provided in light gray, but photos show that wing walks are either black or not applied at all. I left them off. The kit's two representations of the SAC Time nose art are not as good as that provided on Caracal's B-52H sheet (No. CD 72058).

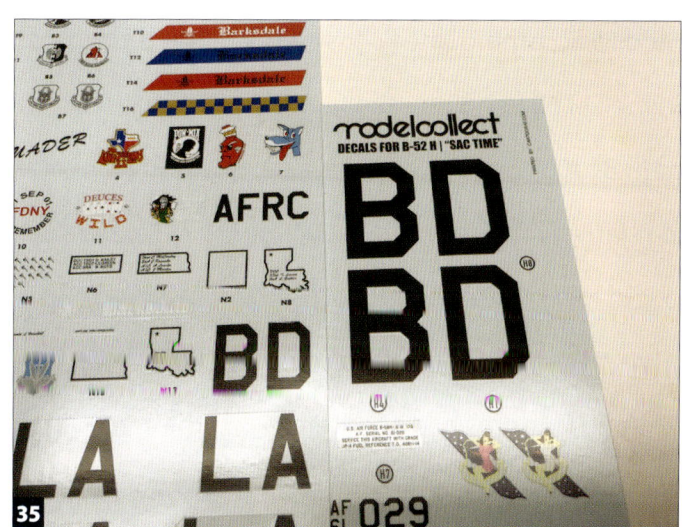

35 Modelcollect's representation of the BD tail codes were overscaled—75 scale inches instead of the proper 42! I ended up using none of the kit decals and went with the Caracal sheet for everything.

So that's it. I couldn't fix every error in the kit and will have to live with the remaining inaccuracies until the aftermarket steps up. In addition to the fixes I made, I want to replace the poor representations of the upper wing spoilers—the "fingers" of the spoilers are too short and misplaced, and the underwing tanks are way too big. I attached my tanks with minimal cement so I can pop them off and replace them easily. Someday soon, I hope.

6 Painting poached eggs on a Folgore

Hasagawa's 1/72 scale Aer.Macchi C.202 Folgore made a fine canvas for this project

BY VLADIMIR KAFKA

The C.202 Folgore was the C.200 Saetta design adapted to accommodate license-built German inline DB 601 engines, the famous powerplant used in Bf 109 and Ki-61 aircraft.

There are two relatively modern kits to choose from, Hasegawa and Italeri. After building three Italeris, I decided to try its Japanese predecessor.

Some of these early Folgores had an interesting camouflage, sometimes called "poached eggs," a dark green base with sand yellow blots, the blots mostly oversprayed with red brown. I always look for an airbrush challenge and this surely looked like one.

I experimented with isopropyl alcohol with Gunze H and Tamiya paints for fine freehand work, which sped up drying time at the cost of thinner paint. I use two airbrushes for quicker retouching without having to change paint.

An interesting paint scheme allowed Vladimir Kafka to stretch his airbrushing skills and learn new techniques. He started with a simple kit so he'd have the energy to see the painting project through to the end.

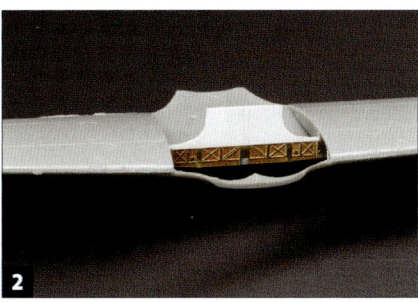

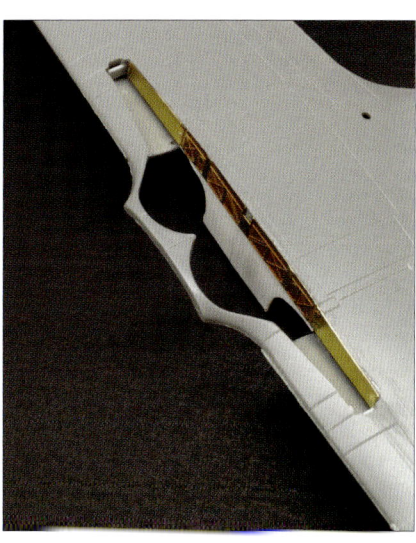

1. The wheel wells are blanked out with a flat, shallow bottom. That won't do, so I began removing material with a motor tool to make room for more detail.

2. I made a new rear bulkhead from sheet styrene and detailed it with a piece of Eduard photo-etched metal (PE) from set SS138. Note the small plastic insert in the middle of the bulkhead. I had to extend it a bit after measuring wrong. In general, I like to move quickly with approximate dimensions and trim and adjust when needed, instead of precisely measuring everything.

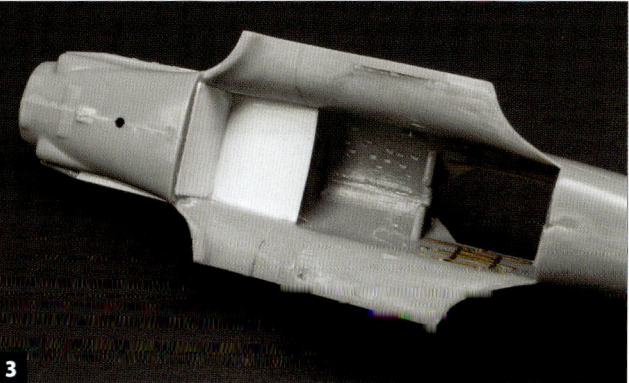

3. I added a front bulkhead and top. I don't know if and where these bulkheads were on the real airplane, but I had to define the wheel well somehow. I glued the fuselage halves together, my preferred solution whenever it's possible to insert the cockpit later from below. You can see bits of the Eduard PE on the sides of the cockpit.

4. Since I was modeling the early version, I added a proper early supercharger intake, part of a resin set I market from Airone Hobby.

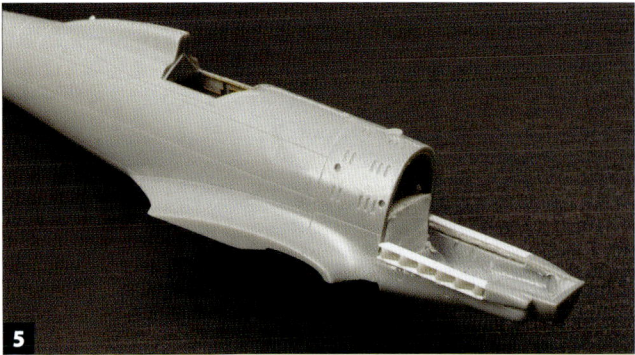
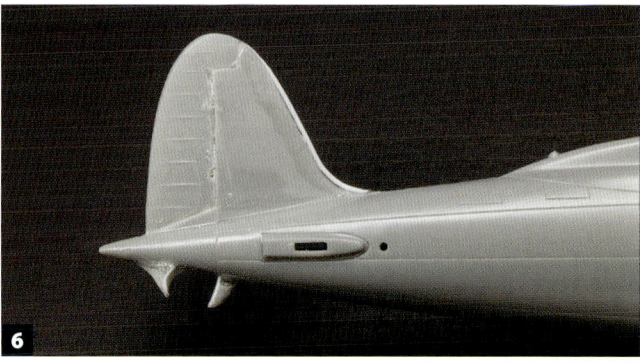

5 I replaced simplified kit exhausts with SBS resin aftermarket parts SBS-72038, intended for Tamiya's Bf 109E. They fit in place without any trouble. As on the Bf 109, the exhausts are in an oblong fairing. Instead of cutting and filing out an accurate, narrow slit in the fairing, I cut away its upper half, inserted the new exhausts from above, then rebuilt the fairing with plastic strip.

6 I added some bulk to the vertical stabilizer leading edge, which seemed to be a bit too narrow (this was indirectly proven later by how hard it was to fit all the decals there). Both the front and rear tailwheel mudguards were scratchbuilt using styrene strip and thick superglue sanded to shape.

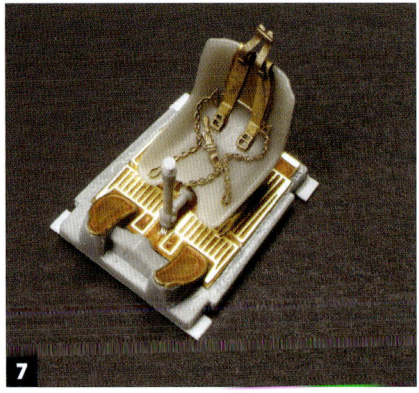
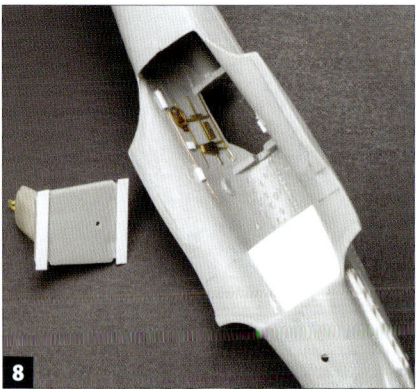

7 I used a correct seat and belts of that peculiar Italian style, with chains, from Airone Hobby, and Eduard PE floor and pedals. The control stick has a scratchbuilt knob-shaped handle instead of original, generic joystick-shaped one.

8 I couldn't manage to fit the cockpit floor at the correct height, so I cut away the original location pegs and after some dry fitting, glued it in the proper location using supports made of strip styrene. I used Eduard PE for the sidewalls, and a Yahu instrument panel—my automatic choice whenever available.

9 In a hindsight I think Italian cockpit green should have been a bit lighter. I used a Squadron acetate canopy (SQ9154). I didn't want it open as that ruins the aircraft's elegant silhouette.

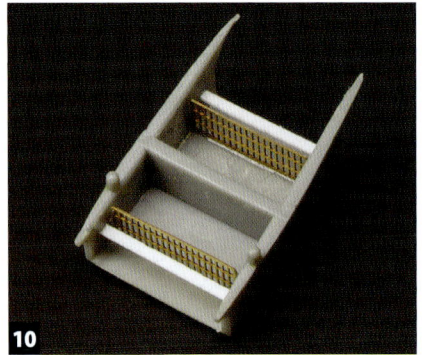
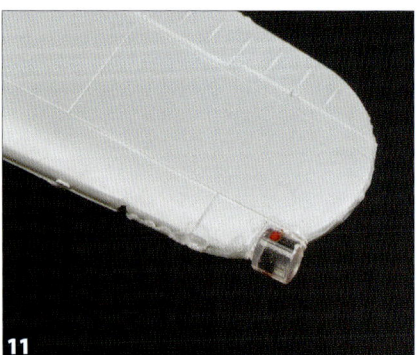
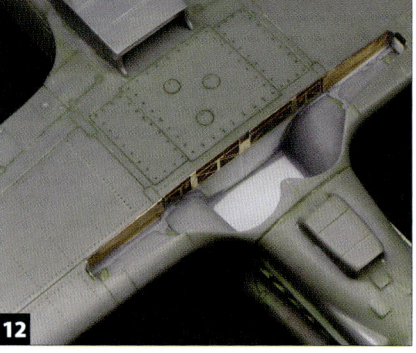

10 The radiator received Eduard PE mesh. The thin slats are Evergreen strip styrene.

11 I made the position lights from clear sprue. I sanded the mating surfaces at a right angle, drilled a small hole inside and filled it with red or green paint. Then I attached them with superglue and sanded them to the correct shape. Finally, I polished it with Tamiya compounds.

12 After gluing the fuselage and wings together, I returned to the wheel wells, which were now ready to accept the "snakes" into the pit. Also note the circular hatches and fasteners I added to the bottom panels. You can see I didn't quite manage to pierce all the screws in correct locations on my first attempt.

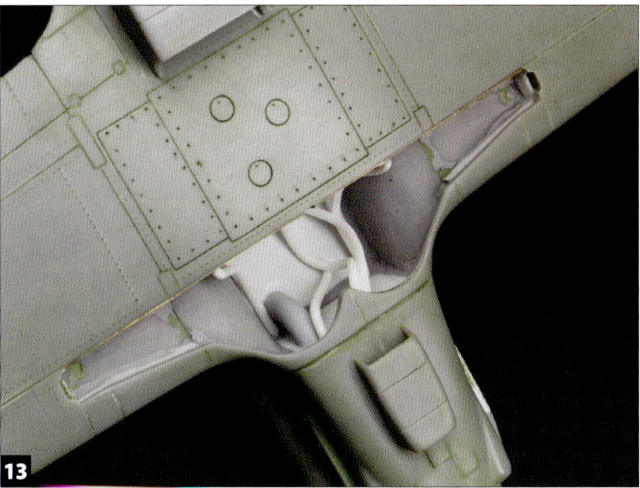

For the larger stuff, made from bent styrene rod, I tried to more or less stick to available photos and drawings.

But all the small stuff, made from brass wires, is just my artistic license. As per a well worn modeler's phrase, "just to make it look busy."

The complete cockpit has a scratchbuilt armored headrest. Again, note added fasteners on the panels in front of the cockpit. After the usual preparation—spraying primer, final sanding and polishing and thorough cleaning of the plastic dust, it was painting time.

And finally plastic rods forming the inner framing, and small triangular fillets from Eduard PE. Walkaround photos of museum machines show the wires and hoses in various colors. However, these would be nearly impossible to paint cleanly on a model, so I settled with metal colored girders and all remaining stuff in uniform interior green.

The first of many attempts at finding the correct color, shape and density of the mottling. In black and white photos of the real machines with "poached eggs," it is quite hard to see any pattern, because the whole scheme is very dark. Tamiya and Gunze paints thinned with isopropyl alcohol created a patchy looking finish, but all the spots disappeared after a varnish.
I decided to switch the dark green (Tamiya XF-13, mixed beyond recognition though) to a darker shade (Tamiya XF-27, slightly lightened by white and yellow). Then I tried experimenting with a bit more dense, and wilder-shaped mottling. Apparently, size and style differed not only from plane to plane, but also on different parts of the same machine, sometimes being quite far from neatly defined, concentric, two-tone blotches. After so many trials and errors, I got so frustrated I stripped the paint and resprayed the whole model with uniform XF-27 dark green—the so-called metropolitan camouflage.

18 Shortly after that I went to a vacation and when I came back after two weeks of no modelling, my courage renewed, I sprayed the blotches back on, swearing to myself to keep whatever result I arrive at on the first attempt—which I did. Contrary to some of the early attempts with more eccentric, irregular shapes, I intentionally went for a relatively neat, regular scheme of round-ish blots, I guess more "organized" looking than it actually was in reality.

19 I struggled a bit with a camo demarcation line on the rear fuselage. There is no photo of an aircraft in service showing where the line was. Museum machines and various drawings show different results, their authors probably also just guessing. The situation is much clearer with later Breda-built machines, which had a higher demarcation line, visible from the sides.

20 The decals are by Sky Models. There are some minor inaccuracies, the white crosses on rudder are far too big and have to be trimmed both in height and width. I also omitted some of the decals: a large stencil plate below the cockpit, which looked out of scale (too prominent and contrasty), and a serial number on the rear of the fuselage. The decal sheet offered dense "123456789" lines, and cutting the minuscule individual numbers out of them would be far beyond my skills and patience.

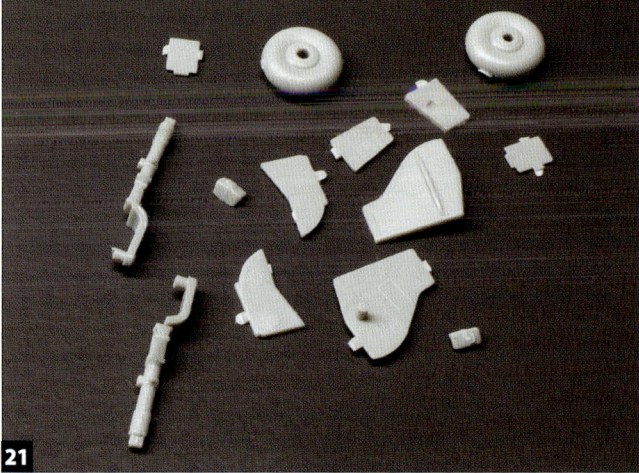

21 The undercarriage bits and pieces. Note the unfortunate engineering solution of the "U" shaped fork, with one half missing.

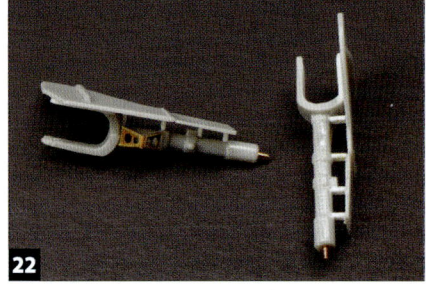

22 Fixing it wasn't that hard. I glued in a rough piece of plastic, which I filed into the correct shape with a sanding stick, using the existing fork arm as a guide. Then I drilled holes for an axle into both arms so I could thread the axle through and attach the wheels after painting.

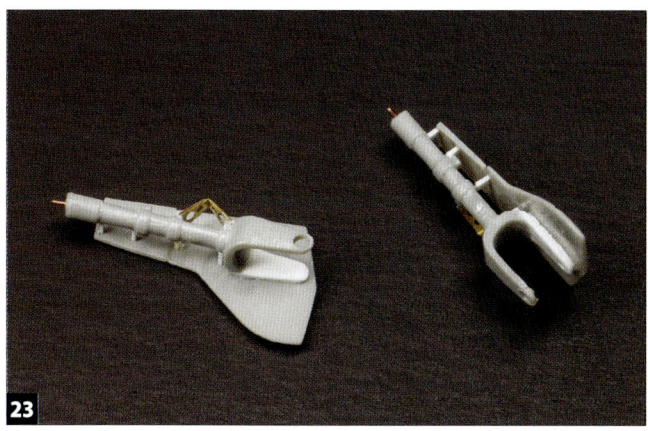

23 I thinned down all the undercarriage covers and attached them to the main legs via simplified fittings made of plastic strips. I also replaced the oleo scissors with Eduard PE.

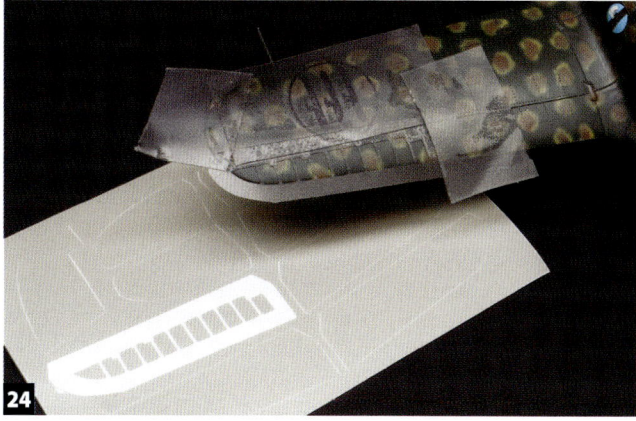

24 As usual, I used Airone Hobby masks to recreate the fabric effect on all control surfaces. I sanded the existing raised plastic ribs, starting on a flat surface. I used Oramask vinyl to protect the wings while painting. As long as the surface is sprayed with matt or semi-matt varnish to reduce adhesion, you don't have to worry about masking over decals. The Oramask vinyl is very soft and low-tack.

The shading was created using a highly diluted mix of black and red-brown, airbrushed with quick passes along the mask outlines. On upper surfaces it is very subtle, while on lower surfaces the effect is more eye-catching, but not overpowering.

25

Finally, after gluing all the small parts carefully and adding an antenna wire (Uschi van der Rosten thread), I called the model done. Despite some setbacks during painting, I enjoyed the build. Starting with a simple, quality mainstream kit meant I had enough energy left for detailing, difficult camouflage, and other self-imposed complications. With two more Folgores in my stash, I am definitely not done with this subject yet.

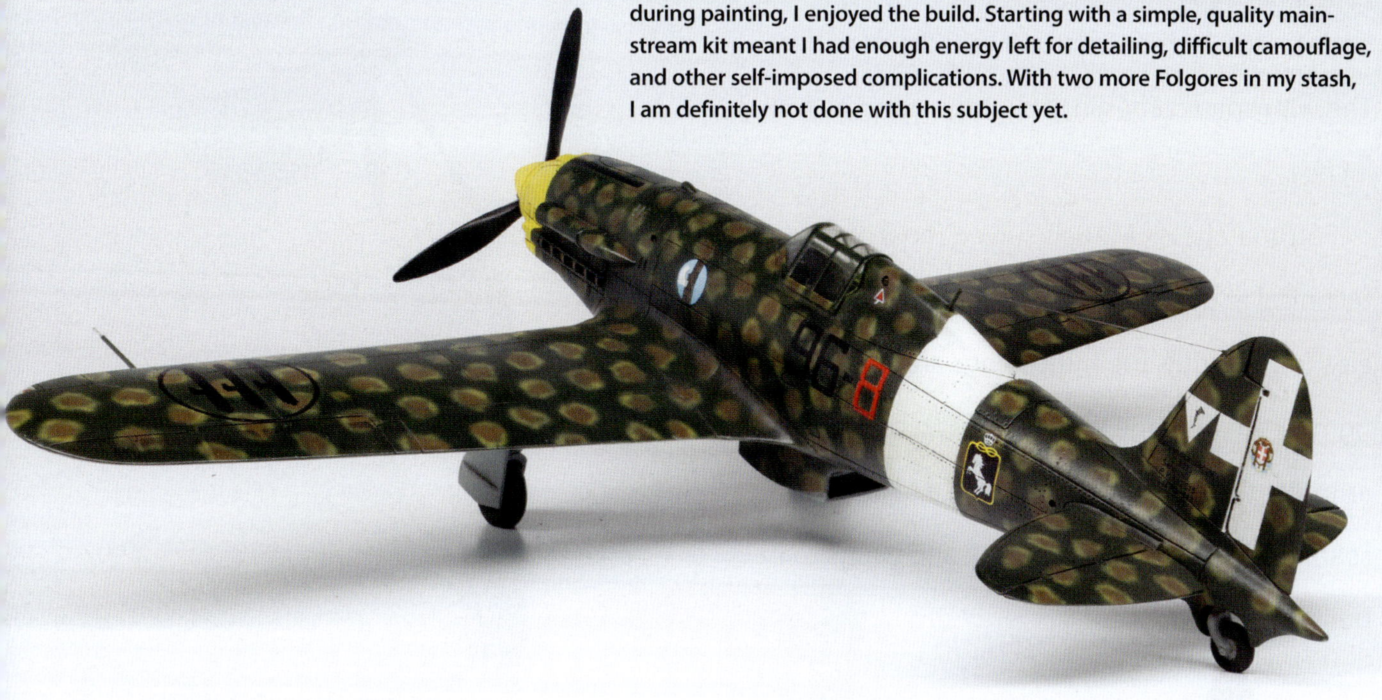

7 Modeling done large

Building HK Models' 1/32 scale Avro Lancaster

BY CHUCK DAVIS

The Avro Lancaster falls into that category of aircraft that truly don't need an introduction, especially if you hail from the United Kingdom. Even in the U.S., the Lanc's fame as Royal Air Force Bomber Command stalwart precedes it. Roughly equivalent in role and fame to the USAAF's B-17 Flying Fortress, the Avro Lancaster was bigger and could carry a larger bomb load, both in weight and physical dimensions.

Given the Lanc's size, translating the real thing into 1/32 scale poses some unique challenges, both for the kit manufacturer and the modeler. The wingspan comes in at slightly more than 38 inches.

Fortunately, HK Models solved most of the technical issues in a manner that helps the modeler. Importantly, the huge wings are solidly held tight to the fuselage with a robust tab-and-slot arrangement. Test-fitting showed a near perfect seam line, allowing the fuselage and wings to be built separately.

That's a huge help to the modeler and meant my desk light stayed in one piece and I did not have to construct an addition for my airbrush booth to paint the behemoth—although it was close.

HK Model's mastery of molding and engineering is apparent in the lack of ejector-pin marks

inside the fuselage halves and the one-piece wings molded open at the back, like a folded piece of paper. The fuselage is made from long rear halves and separate nose halves. HK has designed them with interlocking tabs and the joint is just ahead of the massive wing root, so alignment is easy and the connection strong. The stabilizer-to-fuselage and the rudder-to-stabilizer joints are tight enough that they can be painted, decaled, and installed at the end of the build. Overall, the kit design and molding help tackle issues that might have put modelers off finishing a kit this large.

Once the major sections are assembled, painted, decaled, and weathered, final assembly takes just minutes. You are reminded how large this kit really is as it gets heavier and heavier the more you add to it. Follow along for the big build — but be warned, you'll need to bank one way or the other flying through doorways with this one!

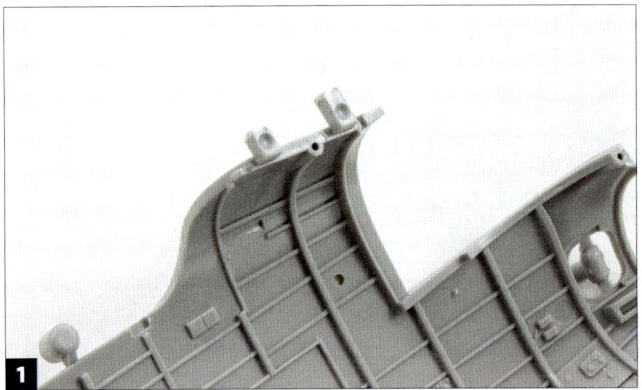

1 Big kits use a lot of plastic. HK's Lancaster has some large injection-molding gates that allow plastic to flow into the mold. As a result, careful trimming is needed to ensure good fits.

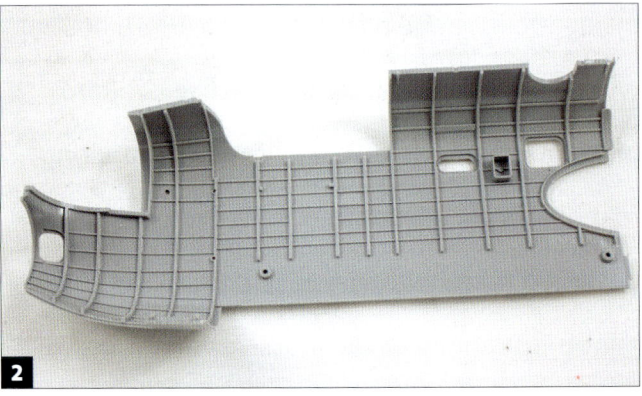

2 Considering the kit's size and complexity, and the amount of plastic needed, HK did a splendid job minimizing ejector-pin marks—circular marks created when pins are used to push the parts out of the mold. The major components of the kit, including the interior walls, were almost free of these marks.

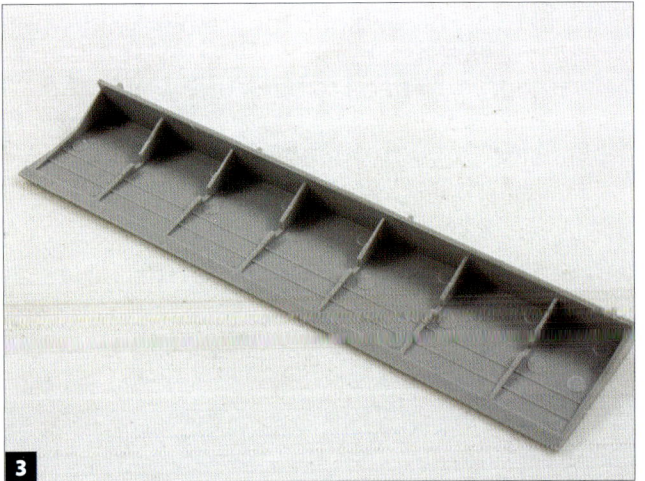

3 However, some of the "smaller" parts are quite large and need work to eliminate ejector-pin, or knockout, marks. For example, the flap interiors have a number of raised marks that are quite visible even on the finished model.

4 A micro chisel makes short work of the offending disks.

5 Carefully check all parts for visible ejector-pin marks. Keep in mind angles of view, especially in a large-scale kit where you can actually see things through windows and other openings. Here, a couple of interior bulkheads need work on their reverse sides.

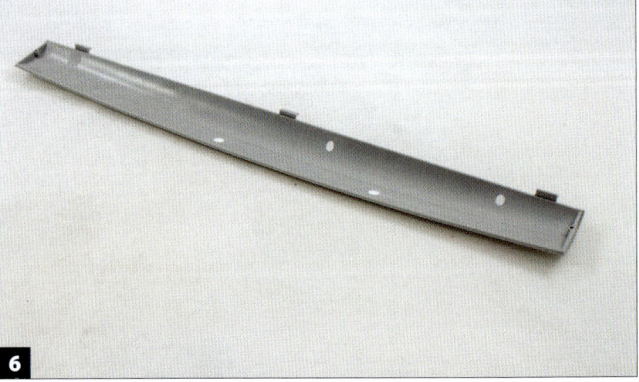

6 The interior of the long, slender bombbay doors suffered from indented ejector-pin marks. Deluxe Models Perfect Plastic Putty is, well, perfect for filling these shallow depressions in tight, hard-to-sand spaces.

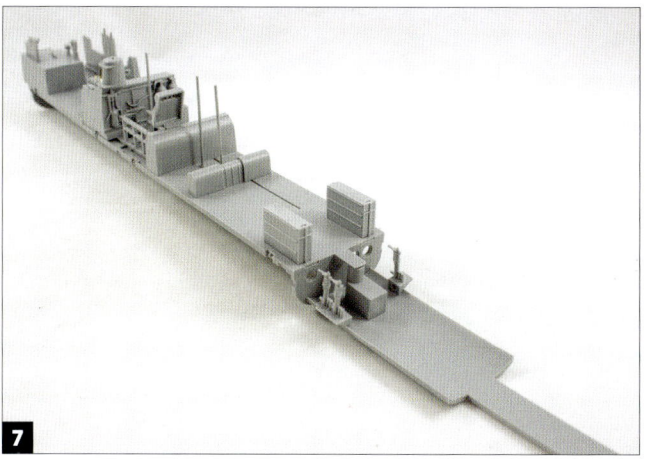

7 HK has included the major items of detail for the long interior. I assembled all but the radio equipment to make painting easier.

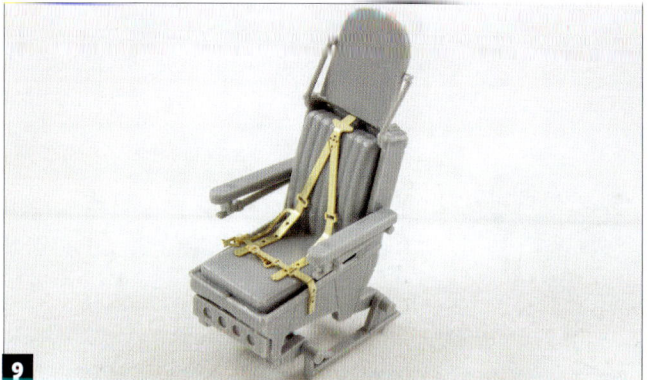

9 The pilot seat is well detailed and accurate, including PE seat belts. I realized after this shot was taken that the armored head rest was installed at the wrong angle; it isn't clear from the instructions or the layout of the parts, but it should be mounted at the rear of the seat, not the front.

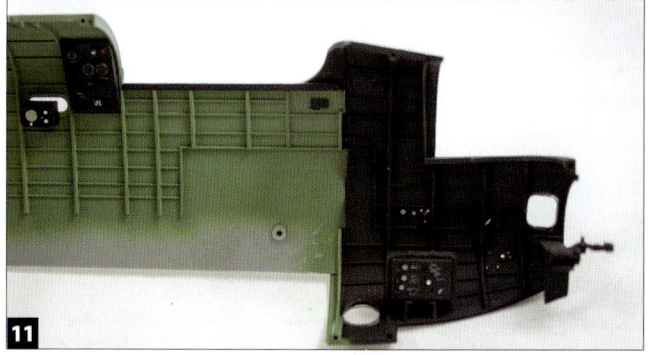

11 References differ—and likely the real thing did as well—as to the breakdown of interior colors in the Lancaster. Generally, the interior from the cockpit aft was painted interior green while the "visible" areas of the nose was painted black. HK includes plenty of accurately molded detail, and the fit of all components is very good. Since no decals are included for the interior, I added a few scribbles with a white pencil to simulate stencils on some of the black boxes. I had to add a sheet plastic rear face to the black box mounted near the window in this picture—remember to look at all parts from every possible viewing angle on a large-scale kit to pick up on these details.

8 Once a patchy coat of interior green is in place, details can be picked out and a wash of Flory Models dark dirt applied. The engineer's panel must be hand-painted as no decals are included in the kit. Luckily, pictures are readily available online. Note the photo-etched (PE) seat belts included in the kit.

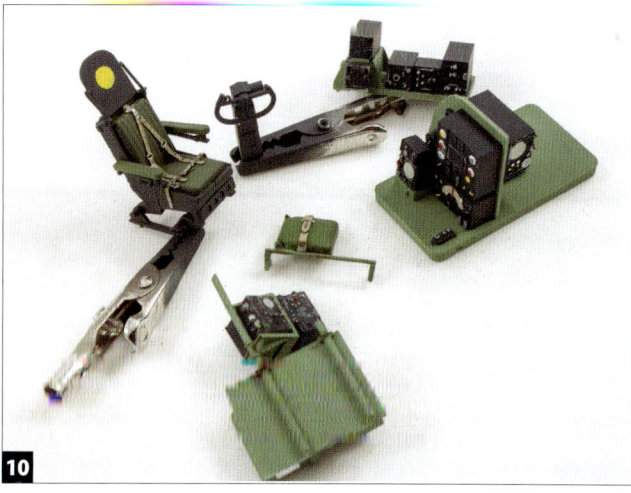

10 Here are the interior subassemblies after painting. Again, online references were used to determine colors for the various pieces of radio and navigation gear. The instructions point to adding a yellow dot on the headrest—indicating a piece of armor plate to the ground crew—but it seems to indicate the dot is on the front. After researching online, I realized this is incorrect. I moved the yellow dot to the rear side when I glued the headrest at the proper angle.

12 Some more scribbles—and a very non-camouflaged safety railing—are included on the opposite side.

13. The vast interior of the Lancaster before adding in all the parts—and look, Ma—no ejector-pin marks! Beautiful!

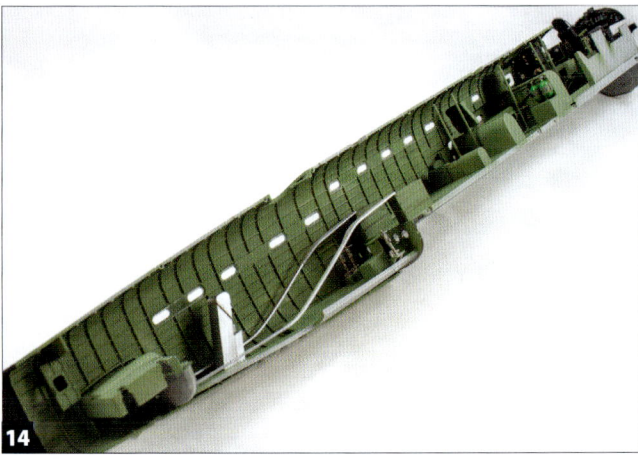
14. Plenty of detail is included for the interior—including ammunition tracks for the rear turret.

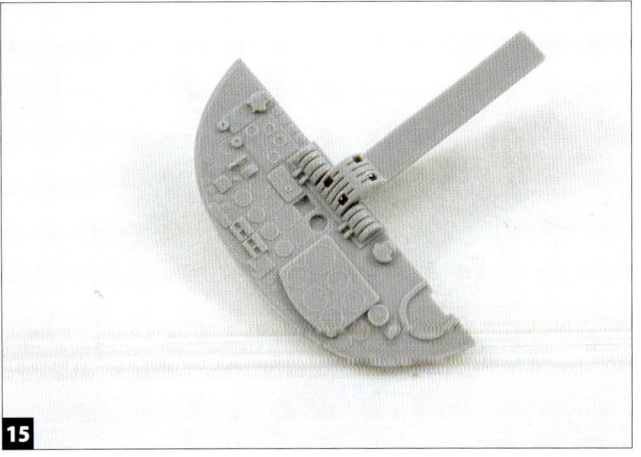
15. While the instrument panel is molded with accurate relief, I was very disappointed to discover that the kit does not include any instrument dial decals, forcing the builder to make do.

16. There are numerous aftermarket options to accomplish this task; I used 1/32 scale RAF WWII instruments decals from Airscale (AS32 RAF).

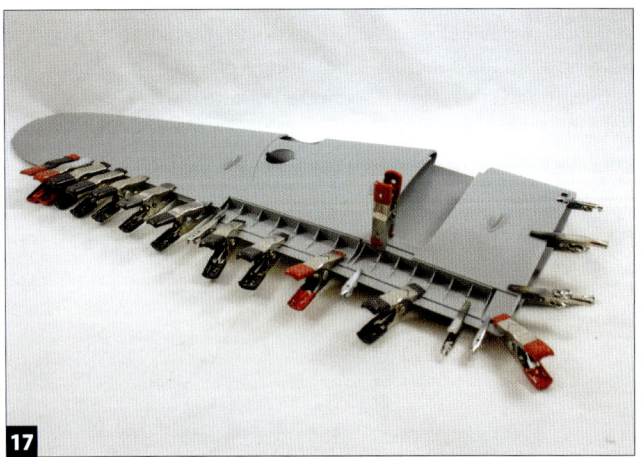
17. Large aircraft need lots of helping hands for assembly. In this case, numerous clamps were used to ensure all the wing connections were as tight as possible to aid structural strength for this behemoth.

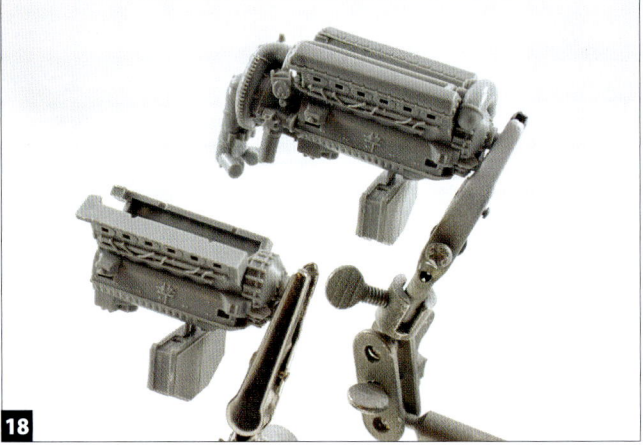
18. HK includes parts for four fully detailed Merlin engines. I decided to open up one for viewing. However, the radiator and exhaust for each Merlin are mounted to the engine. Careful study of the instructions reveals the fewest parts necessary to allow mounting these details. The engine in the upper right is fully detailed while the lower left engine merely places the mounting points in the proper places.

19 Painted and detailed with the hoses included in the kit, the engine looks ready to run. The engine mount is a bit fiddly to assemble but mimics the real version well. This Merlin was set aside for mounting once all other steps are complete.

20 Here are the two "support engines" installed. You can see how the engines are just hanging in the breeze holding the radiator and exhaust attachments in their proper place in space.

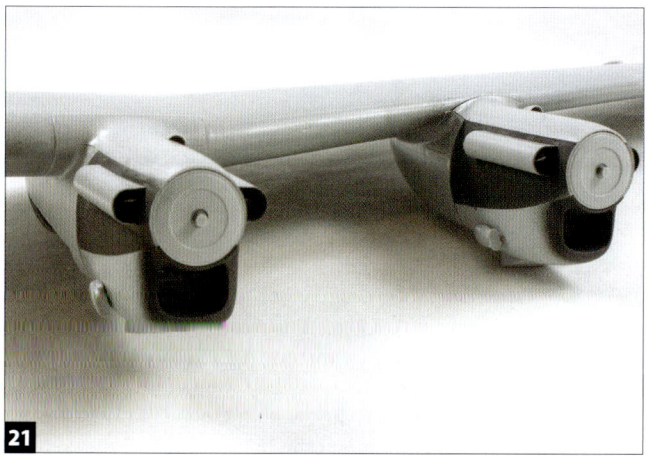

21 I decided to pre-paint several areas prior to assembly to not back myself into a tight corner when masking later. The inside of all the exhaust shrouds were painted black before they were attached to the cowlings.

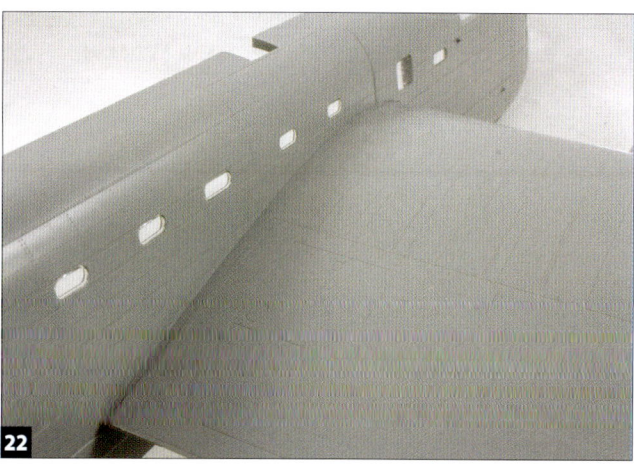

22 Despite the size and complexity of this kit, the wing joints are absolutely superb and allow the wings to be built and finished separately and attached later. This is a terrific advantage when dealing with a wingspan equal to most doorways.

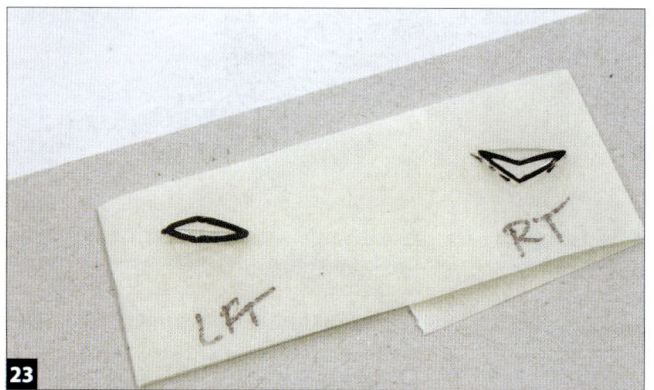

23 Here's an old but useful trick: Paint the edges of all glass black to cut down on reflections when it's in place on the model. With a kit this large and complex, I often label parts while I'm shuffling them around my basement work space.

24 Again with the clamps! On a kit this big, parts can flex during assembly. I wanted to make sure the flap mounts were firmly tied down, so I added long-nose clamps that had just enough reach.

25 All three turrets have complete internal structures. However, they all needed ejector-pin cleanup. The rear turret frame on the left has been scraped flat while the one on the right still has the ejector-pin marks visible.

26 This is the fully assembled mid-upper turret, fully detailed with controls, seat, and PE seat belts. I left the guns and barrels off to be painted separately.

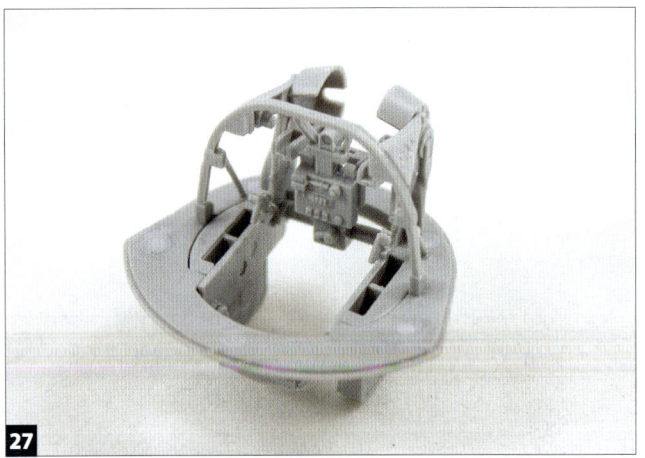

27 The nose turret has nearly identical parts to the mid-upper, so pay attention during clean up. Notice the Tamiya putty filling in the ejector-pin marks on the turret base.

28 Here's the nose turret assembly fully painted and ready to go under glass. Don't forget to paint the brass ammunition where its exposed briefly on its way to the weapons.

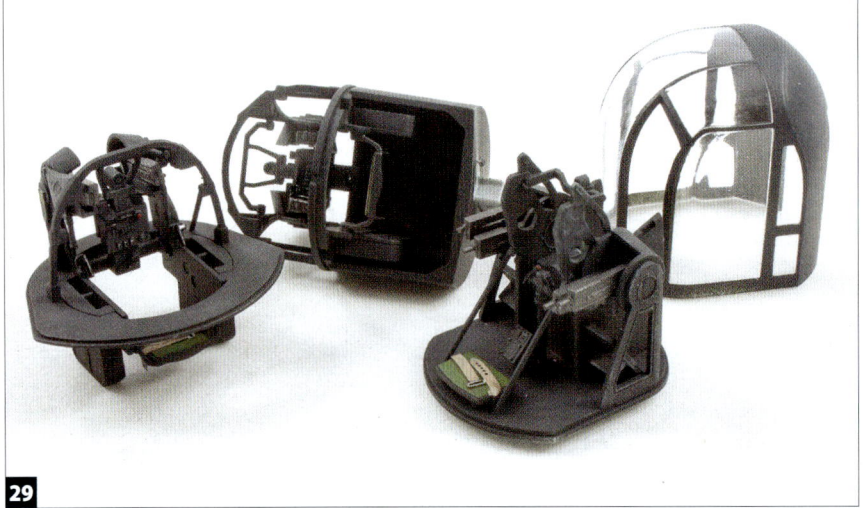

29 The turrets include numerous details—but they're black on the inside. To help bring out the detail, I used multiple shades of black and dark gray, along with tiny bits of color. A bit of "fogging" with the airbrush using dark gray helped pick out details as well.

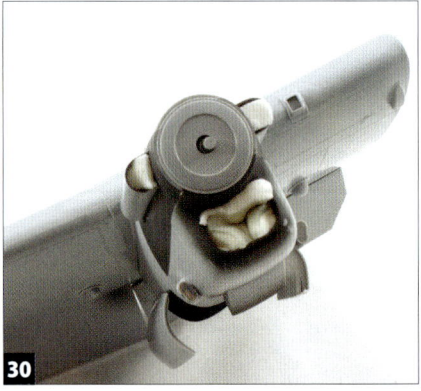

30 No, my Lanc hasn't had surgery for a deviated septum—I've placed chunks of makeup sponge in the exhausts and radiator intakes to keep overspray out. Pre-painting these areas meant I didn't need precise masking.

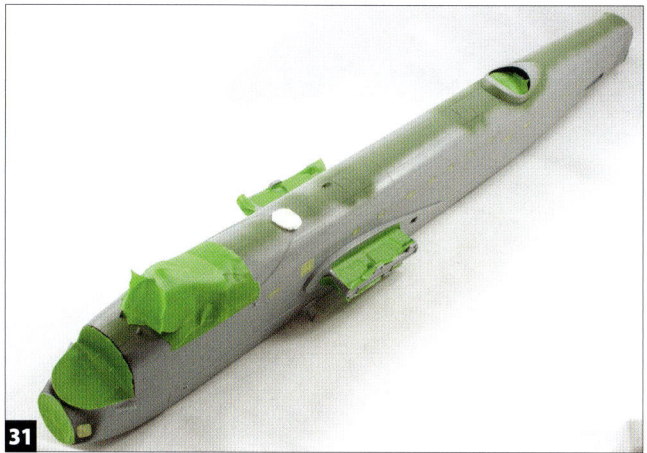

31 The fuselage all buttoned up and masked. Eduard's mask set has provided for the numerous windows in the fuselage; be aware that many Lancs had some or all these windows painted over, so check your references—like I should have. I've used a piece of makeup sponge for the astrodome opening aft of the cockpit, while tape has been placed and trimmed for all the other openings. Note that includes the wing root mounting points as well.

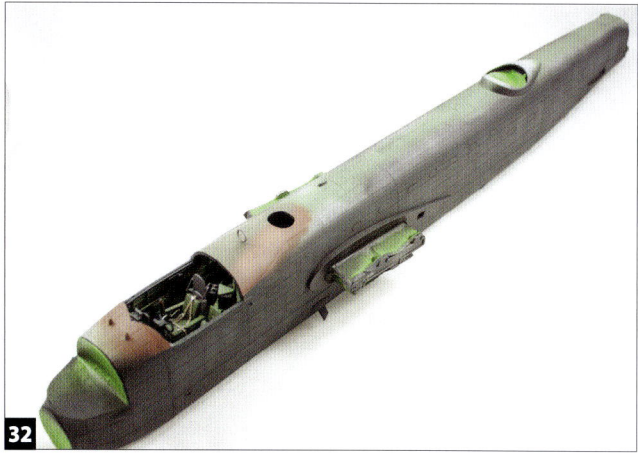

32 I painted the extensive black areas using a spray can of Tamiya flat black as a base coat. This was then faded and fogged with a dark gray to add variation. I then pre-painted the camouflage around the cockpit so I could mask the area using the canopy.

33 Note the Eduard mask set in use on the canopy—these sets are huge timesavers for complicated framing like the Lanc. The "bubble" areas are masked with Wilder Red Masking Fluid.

34 Because the areas to cover were so large on this kit, I decided to use spray cans for the top surface camouflage in addition to the underside black. After spraying Tamiya dark earth (AS-22), I added fading and shading with an airbrush using lighter mixes of dark earth. I then used paper to mask off the "brown" areas of the camouflage. This requires care to make sure all angles are covered—spray cans are merciless when it comes to coverage.

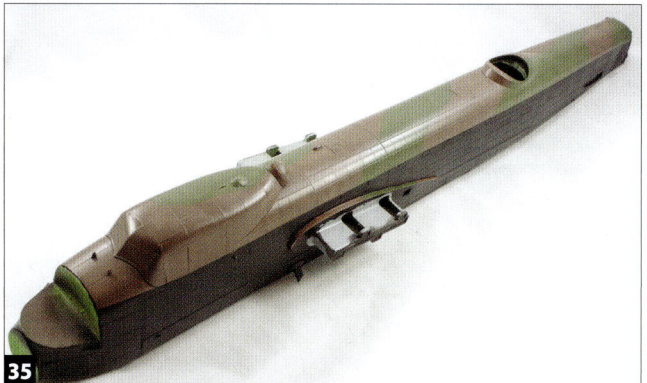

35 The "green" was applied using Tamiya dark green (AS-9), followed by the normal highlighting. The camouflage masks were removed and thankfully there were minimal areas requiring touch-up.

36 The wings were painted in the same manner as the fuselage—the underside was hit with a spray can then faded and shaded. There's a lot of black on this model!

37 Once again, paper masks were used for the camouflage pattern. It's easy to reverse the color you're masking, so check the plan one last time before spraying. And check all spraying angles too—overspray is a killer!

38 The final result—much better than if had I tried applying the camouflage freehand.

39 The Lancaster has unique exhaust stains due to the outer wing dihedral and airflow patterns—the outboard exhaust of the outer engines stain the bottom of the wing, while all the other exhausts muck up the upper wing surface. The great wing root fit arranged by HK allows easy access to the exhausts after painting to get the staining right without bumping into the rest of the model.

40 The landing gear is robust and detailed. I kept the parts segregated by left and right side to ensure they didn't get mixed while cleanup and painting was underway. The wheels are "keyed" for alignment—make sure you have them attached with the flat angled the correct way!

41 After decals and exhaust stains were added, the landing gear was installed. The fit is tight—I didn't even need to glue the front legs in place. HK instructs you to add the door closing links when assembling the gear, but I waited until the gear was installed to fit them between the legs and the gear doors.

8 'Unpainting' a Hornet

A few fixes and odd colors make a unique F/A-18

BY DARREN ROBERTS

It's hard to believe that the F/A-18 Hornet was a product of the 1970s; its first flight occurred Nov. 18, 1978. Designed as a replacement for the A-7 Corsair II and remaining F-4 Phantoms, it was also intended to supplement the F-14 Tomcat. Originally there were two different designations, the F-18 and the A-18, but with advances in technology, it was realized that one airframe could perform both the fighter and attack missions. This led to the birth of the new F/A designation which, strangely enough, was only applied to the Hornet series of aircraft. The F/A-18 has served with both the U.S. Navy and Marine Corps, as well a number of foreign countries. During Desert Storm, it proved its dual-capability worth when a flight of Hornets from VFA-81, on

A couple of grainy photos in some old books showed a Full Scale Development (FSD) airframe that Darren Roberts couldn't let pass by. Realizing the original Monogram release in his stash was an FSD model sealed the deal.

their way to bomb an airfield in Iraq, were vectored toward a bogie, which turned out to be a pair of Iraqi MiG-21s. The Hornets promptly shot the MiGs down and continued on their way to bomb their assigned target. But even with this dual-threat capability, age is inevitably catching up with the F-18, and they have been replaced with either the Super Hornet or the new F-35, with only the Marines and Blue Angels still flying them for the time being.

I've built quite a few Hornets, so I felt the urge to try something different. I found inspiration looking through some old books I had on the Hornet where I found a couple of grainy pictures of one of the Full Scale Development (FSD) air frames making a test flight minus any paint. The various materials used to make the Hornet were on full display, as well as some areas that were painted in yellow zinc chromate to protect from corrosion. This was too interesting to pass up! The problem was that the FSD Hornet differed slightly from the production models. I was trying to figure out how to backdate one of the kits I had in my stash when I realized I had an original Monogram release that was actually an FSD model. I pulled it off the shelf and browsed what was in the box. It was almost perfect for what I needed.

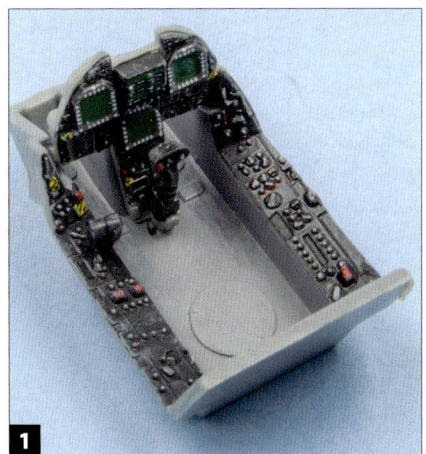

As with most builds, the starting point was the cockpit. Even though this kit was produced in 1980, it has one of the best out-of-the-box cockpits seen in a kit. With some careful painting, it can look every bit as good as a resin aftermarket replacement.

The wings were integral with the fuselage parts and there was a missing detail on the kit that I couldn't pass on making better. One of the hallmarks of the F/A-18 is that the leading and trailing edge flaps droop when it's parked. I started by using a scribing tool to thin the panel lines between the flaps and the wings. I used a piece of tape to guide the scriber so I would get a straight cut.

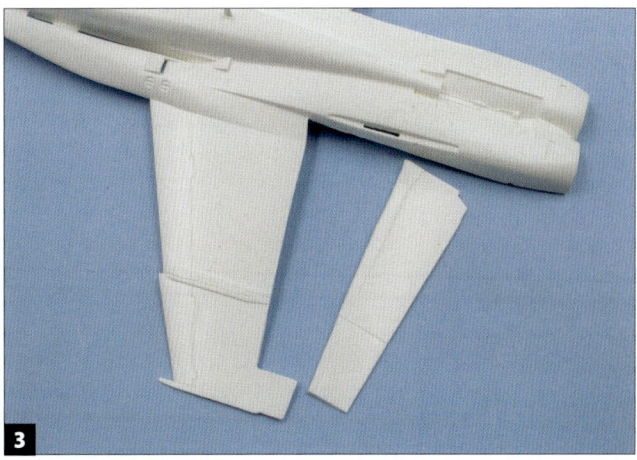

After thinning the plastic, I used a hobby knife to finish off the cut and remove the flap.

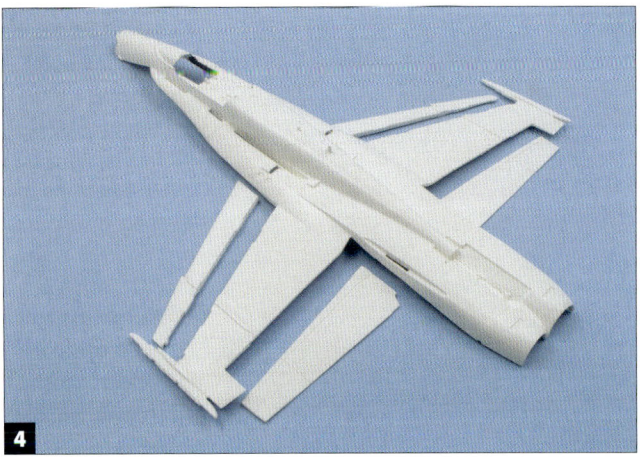

4 The same was done for the leading-edge flaps.

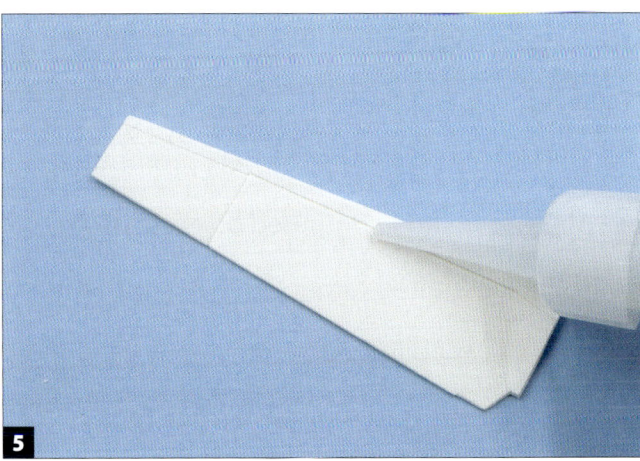

5 On the real aircraft, there is a narrow plate that drops down between the wing trailing edge and flap when it is in the lowered position to cover a gap and provide seamless airflow over the wing. This was included as part of the flap that I had cut off the kit wing and was represented by a panel line. I used super glue to fill in the line and smooth out the surface of the flap.

6 There is a small rectangular section of the underside of the flap that is molded onto the lower fuselage. I cut the pieces away …

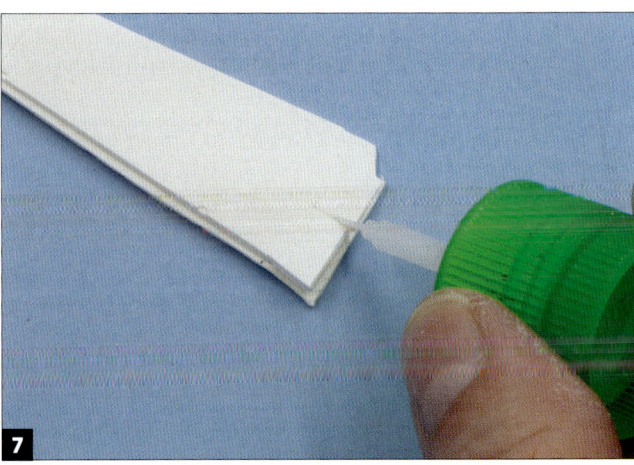

7 … and glued it to the flaps that had been removed.

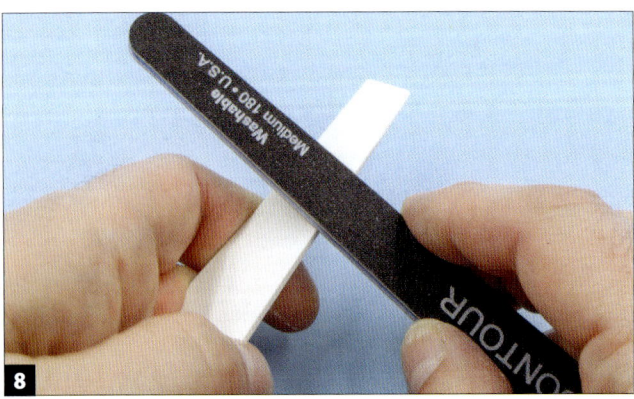

8 I finished it off by using a coarse sanding stick to round off the front edge of the flap.

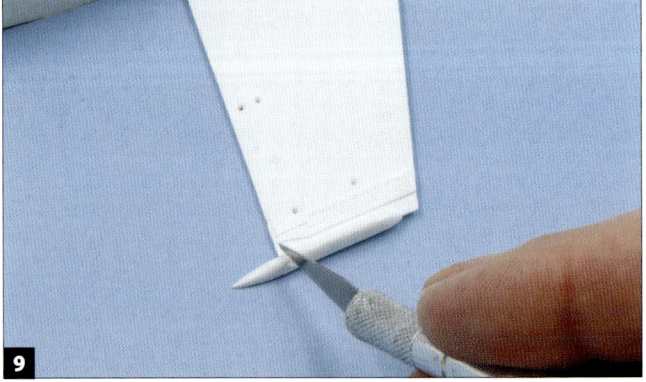

9 On the real jet, there are a set of hinges on the underside of the wings that raise and lower the rear flaps. Since the kit has the flaps molded in the up position, the hinges were up as well. To get them into the correct position required a simple cut and glue. I started by slicing away the hinge molded underneath the wing. Then, I glued the fuselage halves together and attached the leading edge flaps.

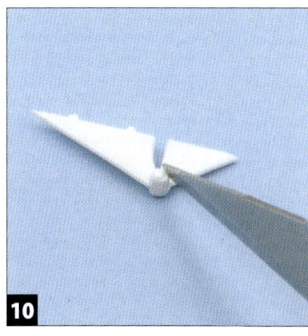

10

Then I turned my attention to the trailing-edge flaps. There are six hinges that are separate pieces. These were cut …

11

… and repositioned at about a 45-degree angle to match the position of the dropped flap. The modified hinge is on the left while the original is on the right.

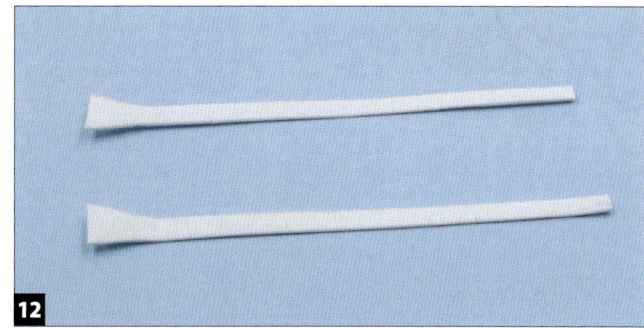

12

Using sheet styrene, I cut out two cover plates to go between the wings and the lowered flaps.

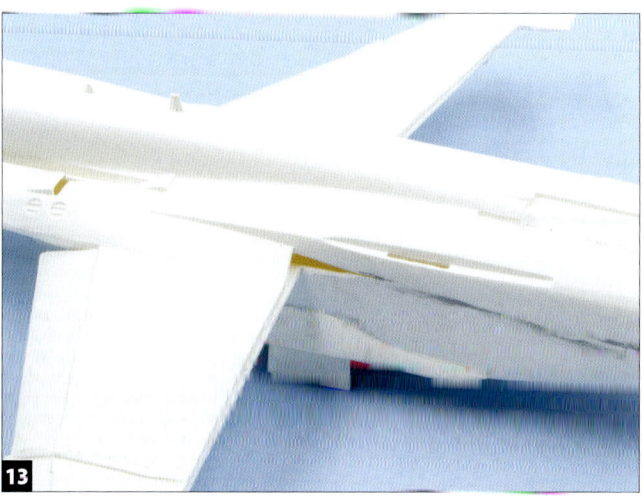

13

Removing the flaps left a triangular opening in the fuselage.

14

I covered the opening with a triangular piece of the sheet styrene, then glued on the cover plates. I used tweezers to hold the plate in position.

15

Next came the flaps. This is where I cheated just a bit. The flaps on the real aircraft, when in the lowered position, are supported only by the hinges. I was not confident my modified hinges would support the weight of the flaps, so I glued the flaps to the underside of the wing and then added the hinges to the appropriate position.

16

From the top, you can't tell at all.

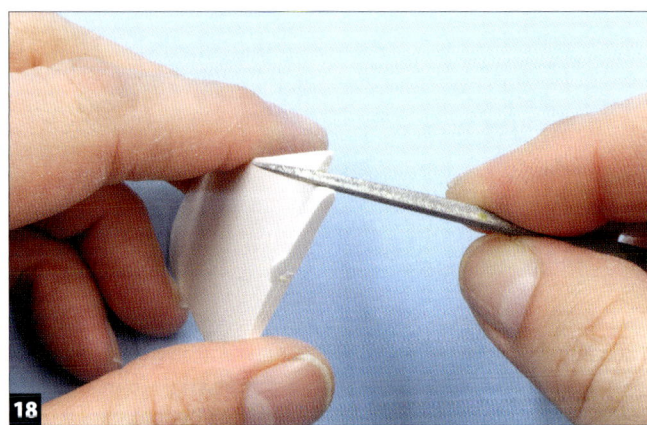

Another modification that needed to be made was on the horizontal stabilizers. The first FSD airframes had a notch, or dogtooth, on the leading edge. This was later filled in when it was discovered it actually slowed the airplane down. The Monogram kit has the later, complete leading edge. To backdate it to the original, I masked off the area I wanted to remove with tape and used a hobby knife to make the cuts.

I cleaned up the cuts with a metal file …

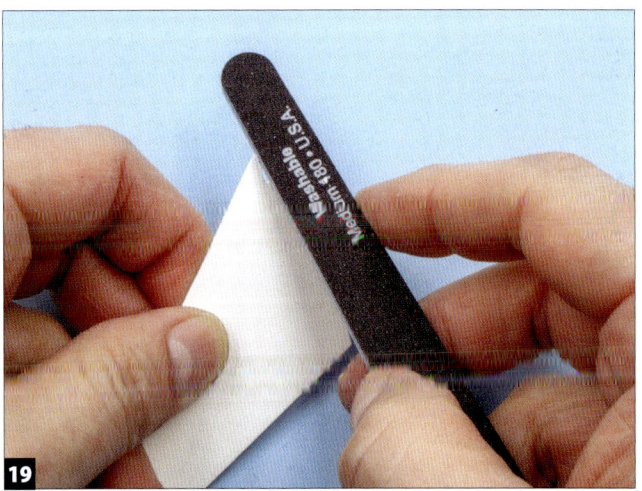

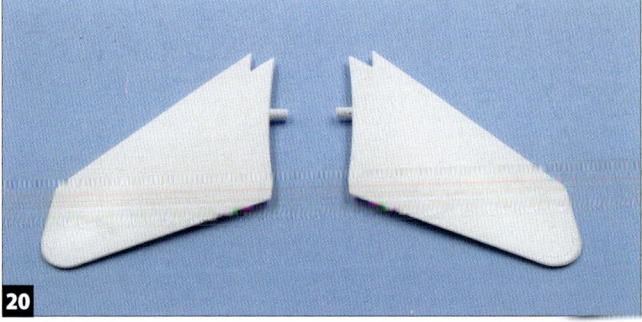

… then restored the airfoil shape using a coarse sanding stick.

The kit parts are actually connected by a plastic rod that allows you to position them. I cut this rod away, as I wanted to mount the stabilizers after the fuselage halves were together. Not wanting a simple butt joint, I enlarged the holes on the fuselage and glued styrene rod on the stabilizers. This allowed me to glue them on after construction.

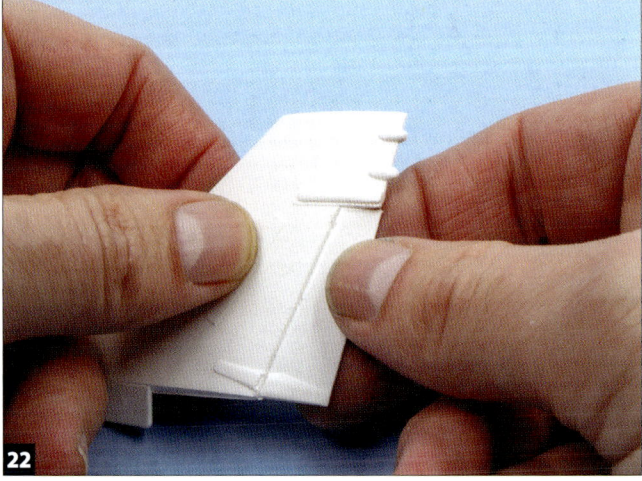

I also wanted to add a small detail to the tails. Because of the angle of the tails, it's not uncommon to see the rudders slightly askew. This was a simple, quick process that would add some "action" to the finished model. Using a hobby knife, I made a full cut at the top of the rudder, then gently ran the blade down the hinge line, making sure not to cut all the way through.

With the plastic weakened, I simply applied some pressure and bent the rudders, making sure they drooped in the correct direction, which would be toward the outside of each tail.

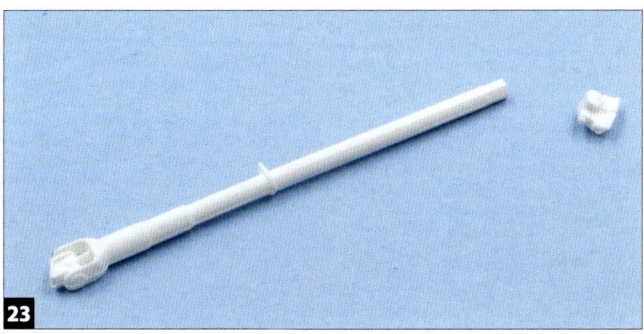

23 Continuing with the small details, the arrestor hook needed to be corrected. Strangely, Monogram molded the hook point upside down. That kind of makes catching the "3-wire" rather difficult. I cut off the hook point …

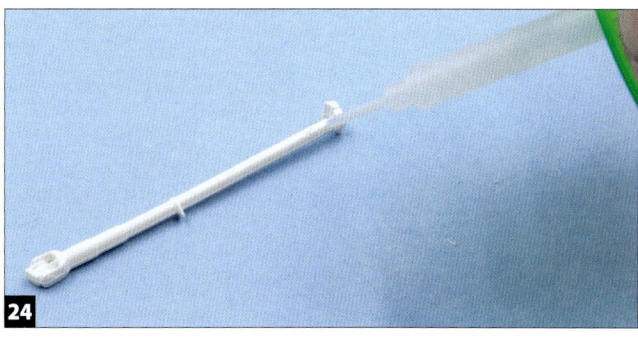

24 … flipped it around, and glued it back on correctly.

25 When it was dry, I painted it white and applied black stripe decals. It was an interesting look for a Hornet because the vast majority of F-18s have light and dark gray striped tailhooks.

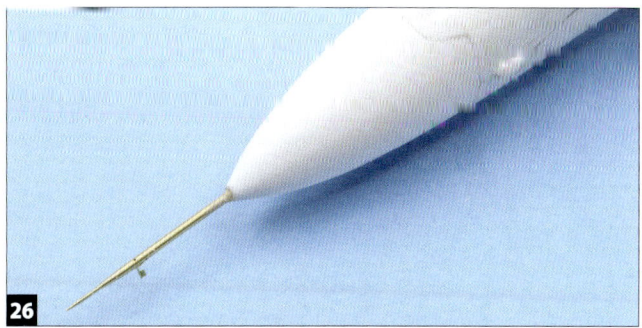

26 The final detail was to add the test probe to the nose. Master Model makes a turned metal probe for a 1/48 scale F-16XL that worked perfectly.

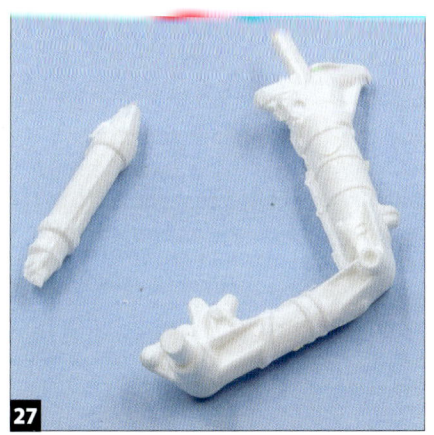

27 I replaced the simplified Monogram landing gear with metal legs from Scale Aircraft Conversions. These are designed for Hasegawa Hornets, but they worked with some extra detail, starting with removing the retraction piston from the Monogram kit part.

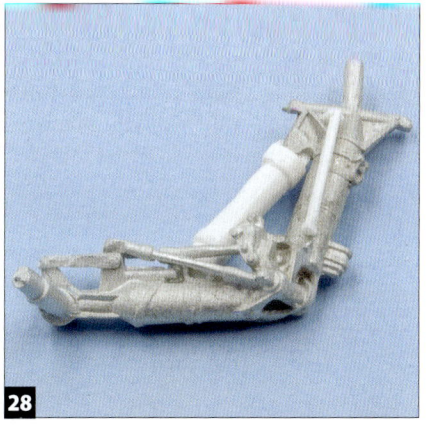

28 This was grafted onto the SAC part along with the short rod cut from the kit part.

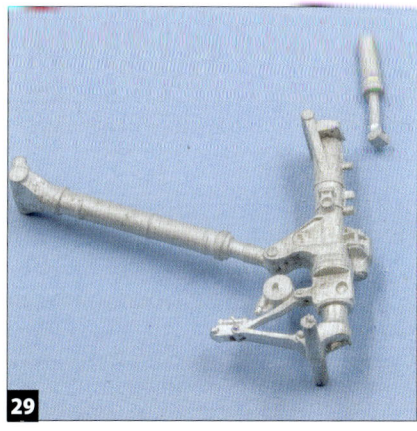

29 The front gear was a bit more involved. First, I removed the small hydraulic arm that was molded onto the SAC gear, as it interfered with the installation into the Monogram wheel bay.

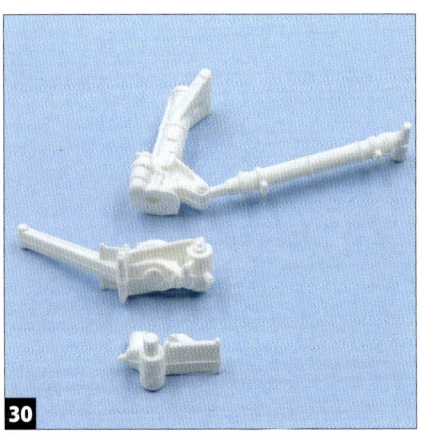

30 Then, I cut the Monogram gear leg into three sections and discarded the upper and lower parts.

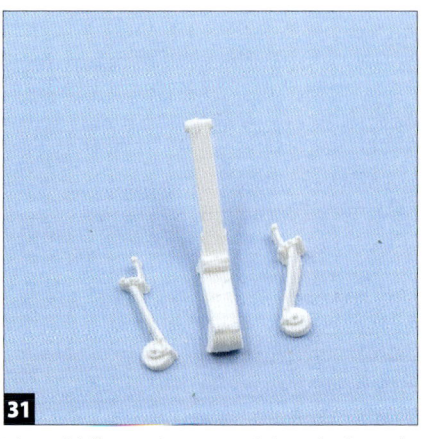

31 The middle section, containing the launch bar and cylinder, was used to fill in missing detail on the metal gear. The cylinder ends and retraction rods were separated from the launch bar …

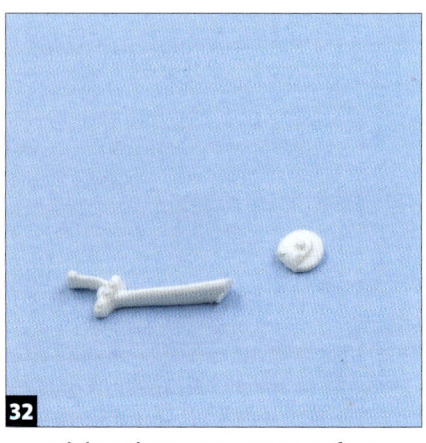

32 … and then those were cut apart from each other.

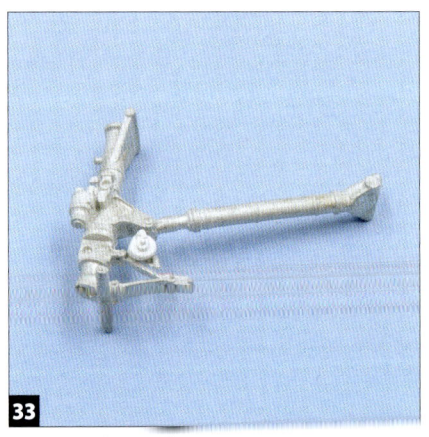

33 The cylinder ends were then glued onto the metal gear

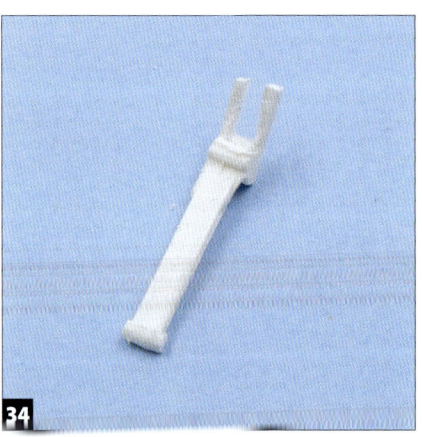

34 I cut a rectangular notch into the launch bar mount so that it would fit the metal gear.

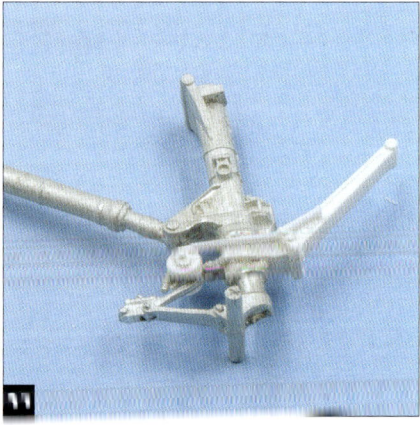

11 The launch bar was then added, along with the retraction arms. I wasn't happy with the look of the retraction arms, so I replaced the arms themselves with styrene rod.

36 With construction complete, I moved on to the challenging task of creating a painted finish that looked like it was unpainted. To make everything more uniform, and to ensure I had a smooth surface for the metallic colors, I sprayed the entire model with a coat of Alclad II gray primer.

37 Because of the multiple colors and patterns being used, I decided it best to map out a plan. I copied a 5-view drawing from the F-18 Walkaround by Squadron Publications, then, using markers, I color-coded each section of the various materials/colors that would be applied to the model.

38 Pictures showed this airframe's aluminum had a goldish hue, created when during alodining, a chemical application of a protective chromate conversion coating on aluminum. Alclad pale burnt metal was the perfect color for this, so I sprayed it over all the areas that were aluminum.

39 The front half of FSD 1 had more of the golden hue than the rear, so I masked off the front half to preserve the full color.

40 Then, I lightly oversprayed the remaining areas with Alclad aluminum, making sure to still keep a hint of the pale burnt metal visible.

41 Before moving on, I attached the landing gear to get the model up off the workbench. Then, all of the metallic areas were masked …

42 … in preparation for the spraying the black areas. I used Testors Model Master acrylic interior black.

43 Next, I masked the areas to remain black …

… before spraying Model Master acrylic yellow zinc chromate.

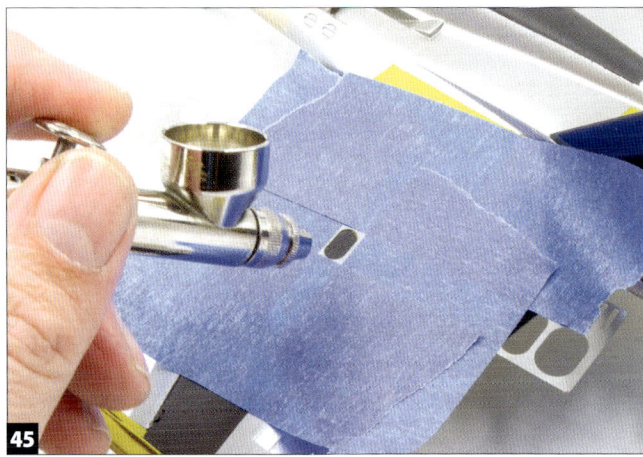

There were some black access panels on the wings. I used a metal scribing template that matched the panels on the wings, covering the remaining holes with tape. After matching the stencil and panel, I airbrushed it black.

My Hornet was looking more and more as I had I envisioned. Now came the small details. Using a fine-liner brush, I hand-painted the oddly-shaped areas at the base of the tail and stabilizers using Model Master acrylic dark green and engine gray respectively.

For straight-line details, I raided my spare decals to come up with stripes of various colors.

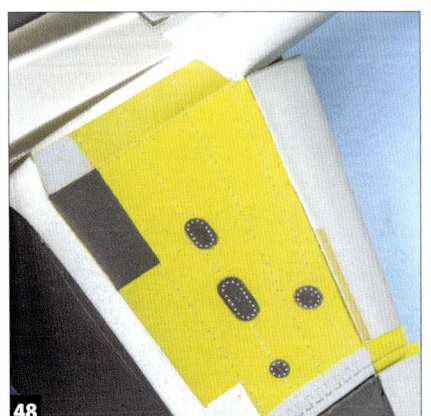

The wings were missing the riveting detail found on the Hornet, but I solved that omission with a combination of rivet decals from Superscale and Mike Grant.

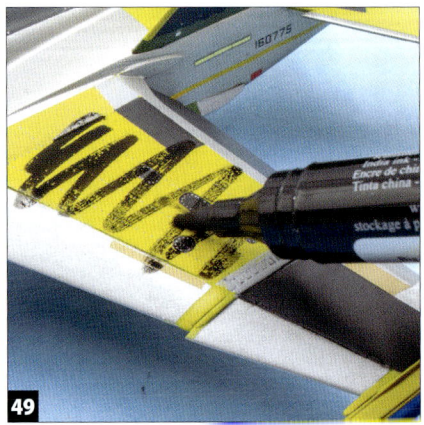

Even though the real aircraft was unpainted, it wasn't bright and shiny clean. After spraying a coat of Model Master acrylic clear flat, I used a Micron ink brush to "scribble" on the surface of the model.

I followed this up by spreading the ink over the wing using a soft, wide brush dipped in water. This stained the surface and produces a slightly grimy appearance.

51 Then, I removed excess ink by dabbing a paper towel over the surface, always sweeping towards the rear to replicate the airflow.

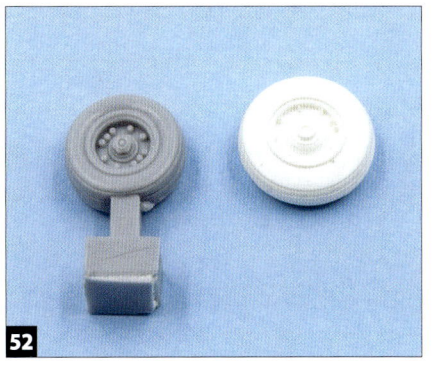

52 In the home stretch, it was time for the final small parts to be added. The front wheels from the Monogram kit are a bit too big, so I replaced them with parts from Royale Resin (R031). They looked much better and I was glad I chose not to use the kit wheels.

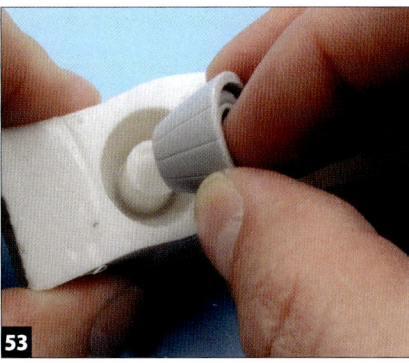

53 The kit nozzles are very plain, but a modeling buddy suggested I use the nozzle off of Monogram's 1/48 scale F-20 Tigershark, as it's more detailed. I copied it in a silicone mold—the Tigershark is a single-engined fighter—and cast a pair in resin.

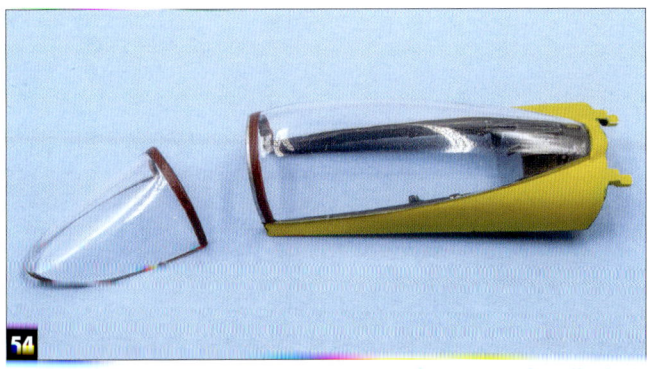

54 The canopy frame was dark red on the early Hornets. I replicated this with Model Master acrylic insignia red mixed with a drop of black.

55 While the kit's SJU-5 ejection seat was good, I replaced it with a resin seat that had the harnesses molded in and was more detailed. It finished off the cockpit very nicely.

56 The intake trunking on the Monogram kit is very shallow, so I covered the intakes with Steel Beach vinyl intake covers. I also added resin probe covers from Steel Beach. The red adds a nice touch to the metallic, black, and chromate colors. It definitely doesn't look like anything else that's sitting on my shelf!

9 Building *Queenie*

Kitbashing the first presidential jet in 1/72 scale

BY PAUL D. BOYER

To build "Queenie," all Paul had to do was shorten the Heller 707 fuselage, remove the wing root area from the 707 fuselage, remove the wing root area from the AMT/Ertl KC-135 fuselage, merge the KC-135 wing root with shortened 707 fuselage, modify the pylons to fit aftermarket engines, merge the KC-135 tailplanes with the 707 fuselage, shorten the vertical stabilizer, modify the nose-gear doors, open a new air-conditioning inlet, accomplish a difficult natural-metal, gloss-white, and Dayglo color scheme, and scrounge markings from his decal spares.

For my growing collection of U.S. presidential transports, I wanted to include the first jet in the series, the Boeing VC-137A. In 1959 the U.S. Air Force purchased three Boeing 707-153 airliners for transporting VIPs. Although not specifically set up as presidential transports, the trio became the primary aircraft for the president, especially for trips overseas. The new jets could leap the oceans in half the time as the VC-121E Constellation and VC-118A Liftmaster then in use.

The first of this trio, serial No. 58-6970, was dubbed *Queenie*, possibly because it was the "queen" of Military Air Transport Service's fleet. It was used by Presidents Dwight D. Eisenhower and John F. Kennedy.

There's no kit of the early 707 in 1/72 scale. But components to make one are available and that means it's kitbash time. This is a pretty involved operation with an extensive shopping list:

One Heller Boeing AWACS kit. The Heller 707 family of kits (707 Intercontinental, Air Force One, and AWACS) represents the late versions of the classic airliner with a stretched fuselage, a wing with wider span and greater area, enlarged tail surfaces, and "fan" engines. But it has the crucial "double-bubble" fuselage cross section of all 707s.

One AMT/Ertl KC-135A. The KC-135 Stratotanker has the same wing and wing-root structure as the early 707 versions, and that's just what I needed. The KC-135A kit also has the smaller horizontal stabilizers I needed, as well as the early nose-gear door arrangement and engine pylons that could be modified to fit the aftermarket engines.

One set of four resin JT3C engines with "organ pipe" exhausts from HaHen (No. 72006, hahen.de).

And there's a long list of "actions" that needed to be taken beyond basic assembly, all laid out on the following pages.

The President is aboard, so let's get into the air!

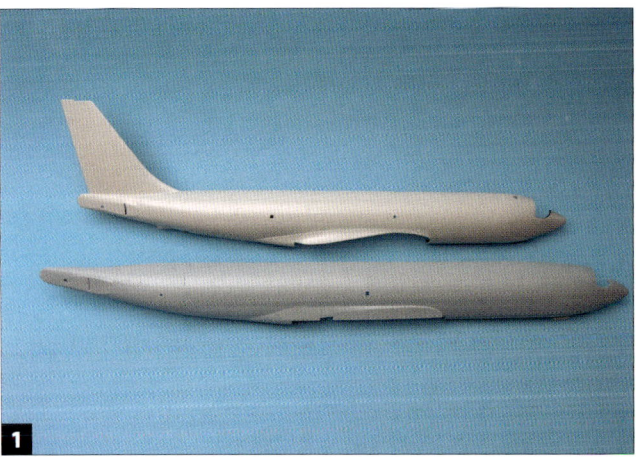

1 Here's a comparison of the fuselage sides of AMT/Ertl's KC-135A (top) and Heller's E-3 AWACS. The fuselage of the tanker does not have the double-bubble cross-section used on the airliners, so only the wing-root section of the fuselage will be needed. Heller's fuselage will be shortened and the wing-root section replaced.

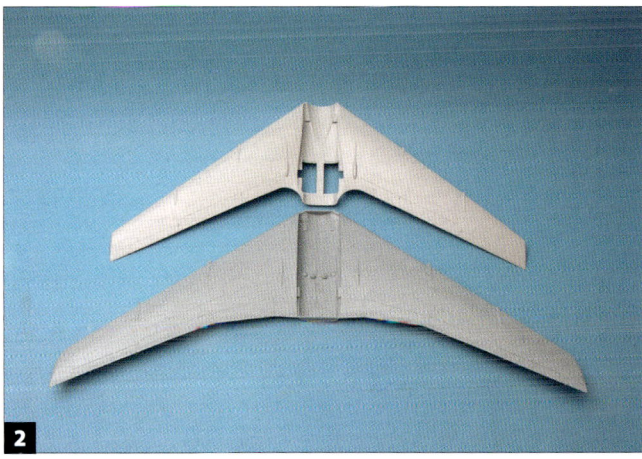

2 The KC-135 wing (top) will be used in the conversion. The Heller kit represents the larger wing of the intercontinental version of the airliner.

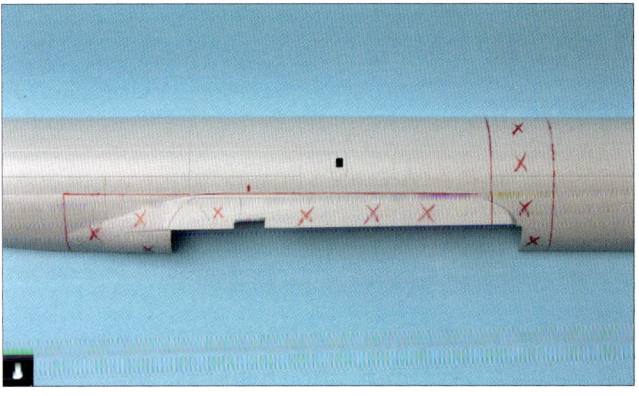

3 The Heller fuselage needs to lose 80 scale inches—approximately 1⅛-inch or 28mm—ahead of the wing. The red x areas are to be removed and repeated on the other half. The wing-root structure is removed up to the crease of the double-bubble cross-section in the fuselage.

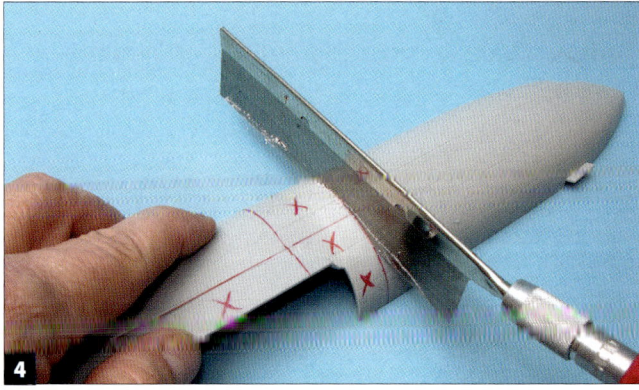

4 I used a razor saw to section the fuselage and to remove the wing-root structure.

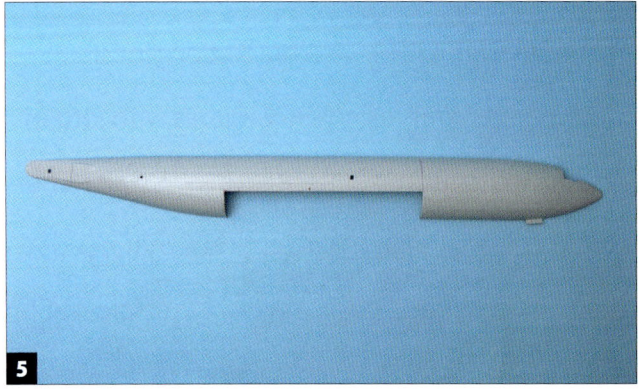

5 Here is the starboard half of the Heller fuselage with the wing root removed and the shortened forward end dry-fitted

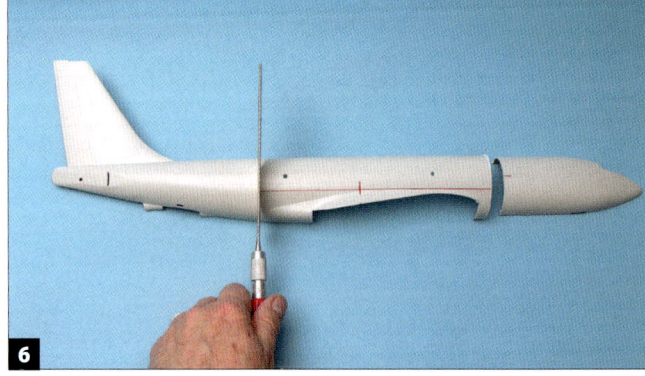

6 Only the wing-root areas of the KC-135 fuselage will be needed. Cutting the ends off first makes it easier to make the lengthwise cut.

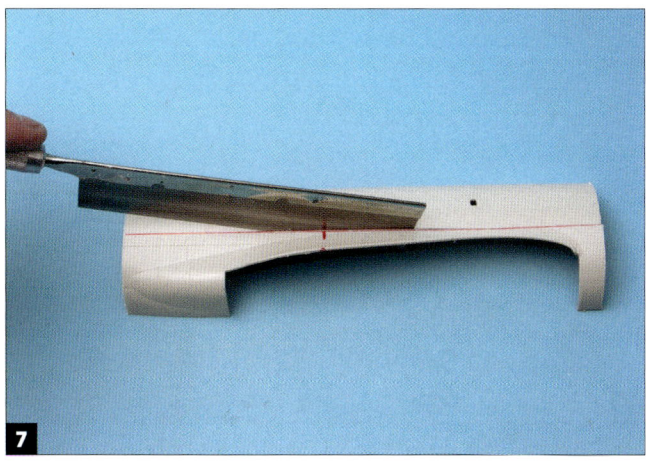

7 I drew a line level with the top of the wing-root fairing to establish the cut line. I purposely cut this section longer than needed so I could fine tune its longitudinal position on the 707 fuselage later on. I ended up removing the section of belly forward of the wing root.

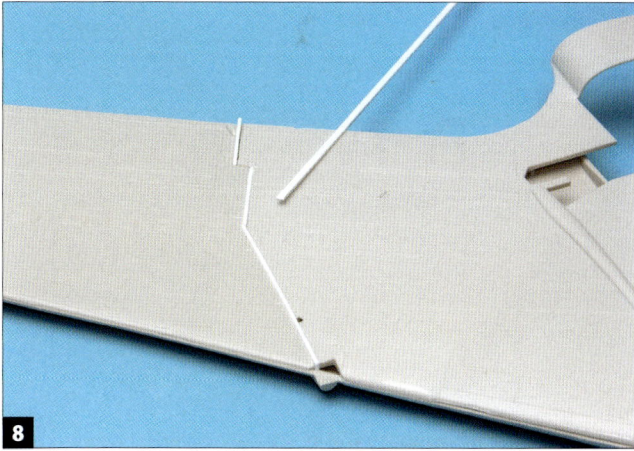

8 The wing of the AMT/Ertl KC-135 tends to droop, but it is fixable. First, attach the outer bottom surfaces to the left and right wings, concentrating on getting a good fit at the tips. When you attach the wings to the center bottom, don't force the assembly to close the seams underneath. Cement styrene strips into the gaps and sand the shims smooth; they will be hidden by the engine pylons.

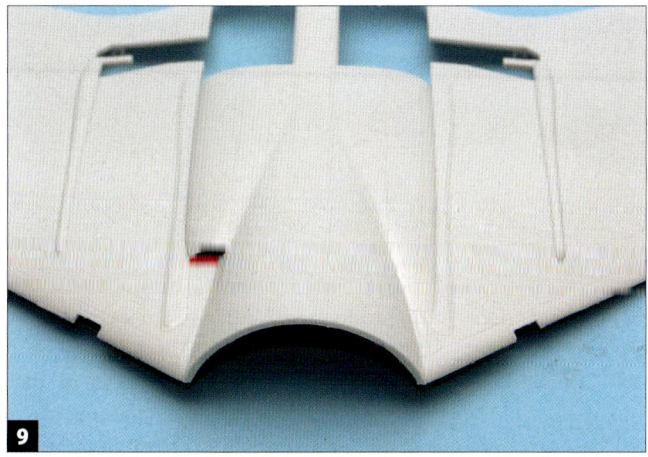

9 One minor detail that is easily corrected is adding a second air-conditioner inlet in the bottom center section of the wing. The left one is molded into the KC-135 wing, but I could see a way to open the one on the right side.

10 I used a razor saw to make a lateral cut, then four longitudinal cuts to form an open ramp for the inlet. After pushing the ramp down, the opening was revealed. I used gap-filling super glue to fill the kerfs and sanded them smooth.

11 Now there are two air-conditioning inlets as on the airliner. At this stage, I added the AMT/Ertl main gear struts and closed wheel covers to the assembled KC-135 wing assembly.

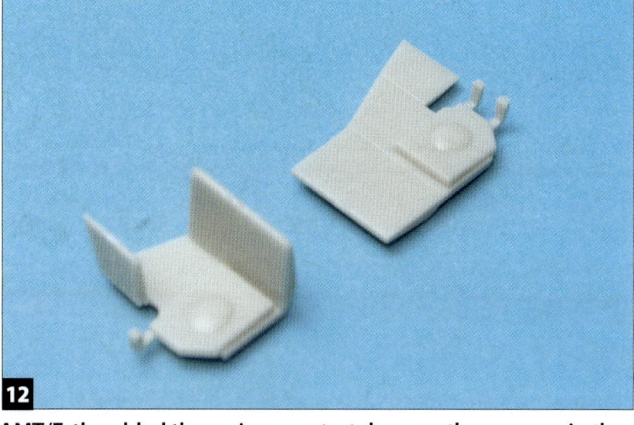

12 AMT/Ertl molded the main gear strut doors as they appear in the closed position (right). I cut apart the individual doors and reattached them as they appear when they are open. (Oops, broke off one prong there!)

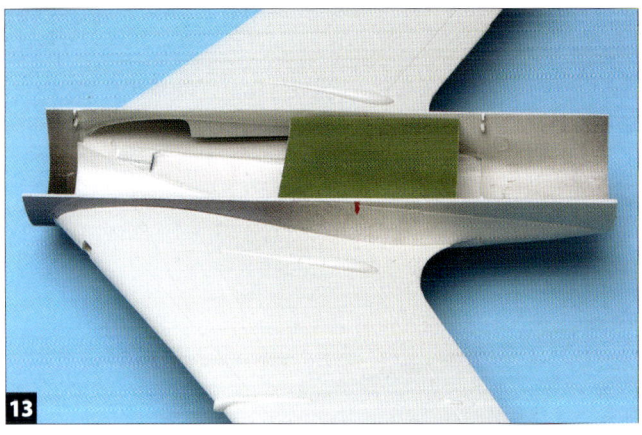

13 After attaching the wings to the KC-135 wing roots, I wanted to reinforce the assembly a bit. The AMT/Ertl kit has a long cargo-hold floor that stiffens the fuselage, but that wouldn't help in this kitbash. I inserted a piece of scrap .030-inch sheet styrene over the main wheel-well area to bolster the wing assembly.

14 Late 707s had side-by-side doors covering the nose-gear bay and they are molded in the opened position on the Heller kit.

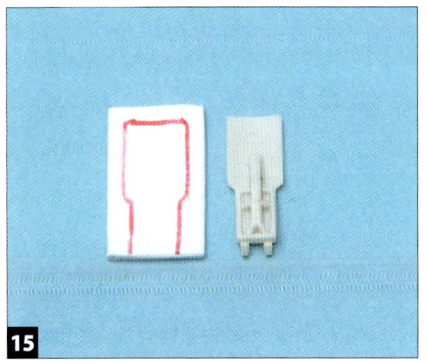

15 The nose-gear door on the earlier 707 was hinged at the rear as in the AMT/Ertl kit. I used it as a template to cut a new opening in a piece of sheet styrene.

16 After removing the Heller nose-gear doors, I fitted the Heller strut, the new sheet styrene opening, and the AMT/Ertl door.

17 To produce a stronger assembly, I glued styrene strips inside the fuselage halves. This increases the bonding surface for the cement and reinforces the joints. I used small clamps to hold the strips in place as the cement set.

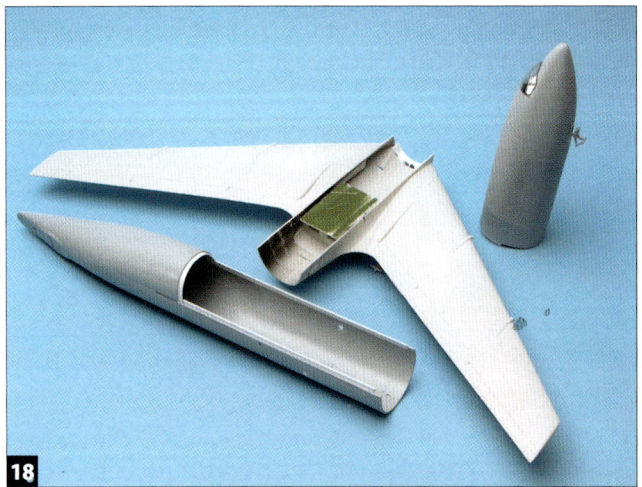

18 Here are the main subassemblies ready for the big merge!

19 And here they are dry-fitted with clear tape holding them together!

20 The early airliners had a shorter fin, so I sectioned the Heller fin and rejoined the large instrumentation mast to the leading edge.

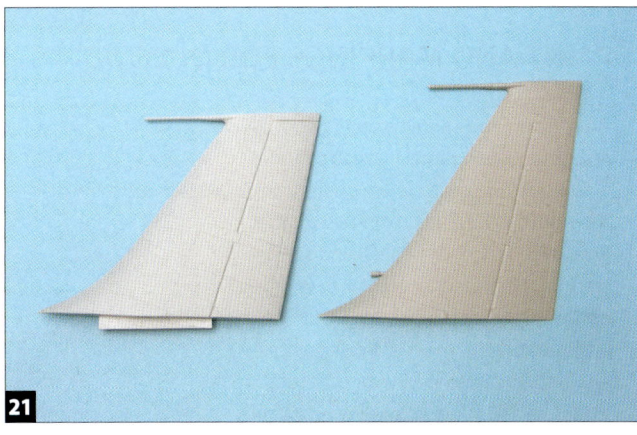

21 Here's the finished shortened fin next to a stock Heller tall fin.

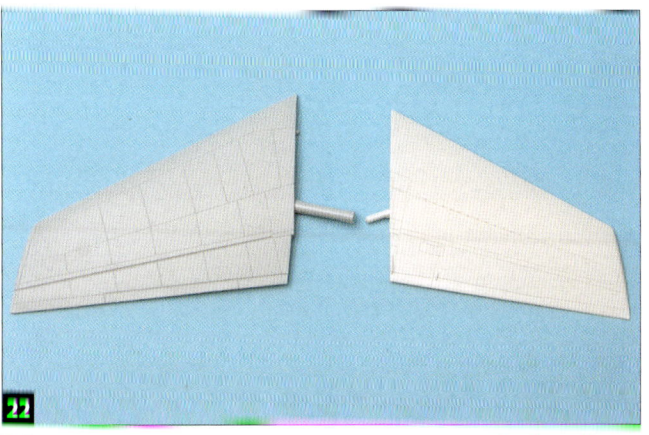

22 Before the "fan" engines were introduced, the 707s had small horizontal stabilizers. They come in the KC-135A kit (right) so we'll use them on this model.

23 The fairings around the horizontal stabilizer mounts were quite pronounced on the late 707s.

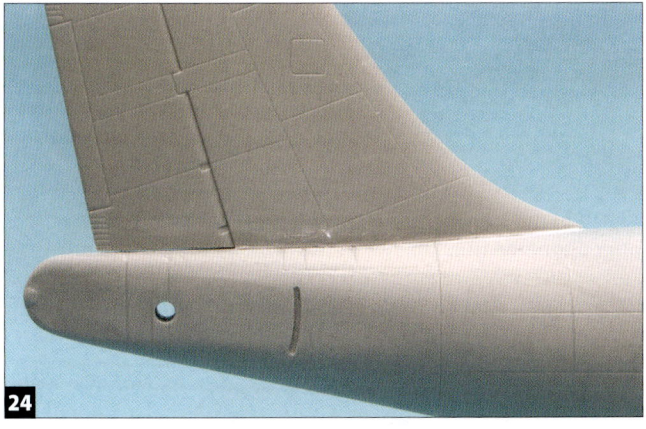

24 The early 707 fairings were subtle, so I sanded the Heller fairings down to the proper shapes.

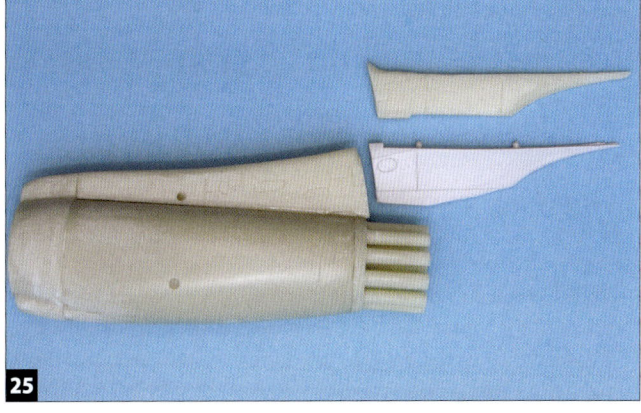

25 The HaHen resin engines come with pylons that are meant to fit the Heller wings. Since I used the AMT/Ertl KC-135A wings, I cut off HaHen's interface sections and replaced them with the interfaces of the KC-135A kit pylons.

PAINT AND MARKINGS FOR *QUEENIE*

After filling and sanding seams and rescribing a few panel lines, the model was ready for paint. Here's where using the AWACS kit has its main advantage: No windows to install or fill and sand smooth. I planned to use window decals on the complicated paint job.

Probably the most difficult paints to apply to any model are white, natural metal, and Day-glo colors. With *Queenie*, I had all three in abundance. The complicated layout of the Day-glo conspicuity markings (Testors Model Master fluorescent red FS 28915) was particularly vexing and had to be applied over flat white—I used Tamiya fine white primer in the spray can. The natural metal finish (several shades of Alclad) was applied over Tamiya spray can gloss black. I didn't take photos during the painting sessions, so you'll just have to take my word for it. It was a lot of work: spraying, masking, spraying, unmasking, masking, spraying ... rinse and repeat.

Once the paint was dry, it was time to decal. There's no decal sheet for any of the USAF 707s, so I relied on my collection of letter/number sheets, insignias, a rare Airway Graphics 1/72 C-97/KC-97 Stratofreighters sheet for lettering and command badges (No. AGM7-002), and Avigraphics sheet (No. AG7092) for window decals.

One problem to solve was creating the natural metal "halos" around the national insignias and the large USAF on the wings. For this, I applied the markings onto silver trim-film decal—that's right, a decal on a decal. As long as the paper of the underlying decal stays dry, this works! Once the insignias and letters were dry, I lightly sliced through the silver decal—but not through the paper—with a brand new No. 11 blade. I scored just outside the insignia and letters to form the silver outline or "halo." Then I cut around the scored item to separate it from the trim film sheet.

Next, I put a couple of drops of water in the bottom of a shallow plate, and laid each item on top of the water drops. I allowed the water to soak into the paper of the silver trim film sheet. When the haloed letter came loose from the paper, I carefully placed it on the model. I slid each onto a drop of setting solution on the model, but avoided getting water or solution on the top of the decal "sandwich." Once the decal began to soften, I used a hairdryer to aid in the softening and drying.

Queenie is ready for paint.

Decals were applied to decals to get a halo effect around the lettering and national insignia. Don't let the paper under the trim film get wet!

Just a few drops of water was enough to free the silver trim film from its backing paper before placing it on the model.

To most of us, a 707 is a 707, but once you put an early jet next to the later intercontinental version, the differences are obvious. And in its flashy military transport markings, Queenie really stands out!

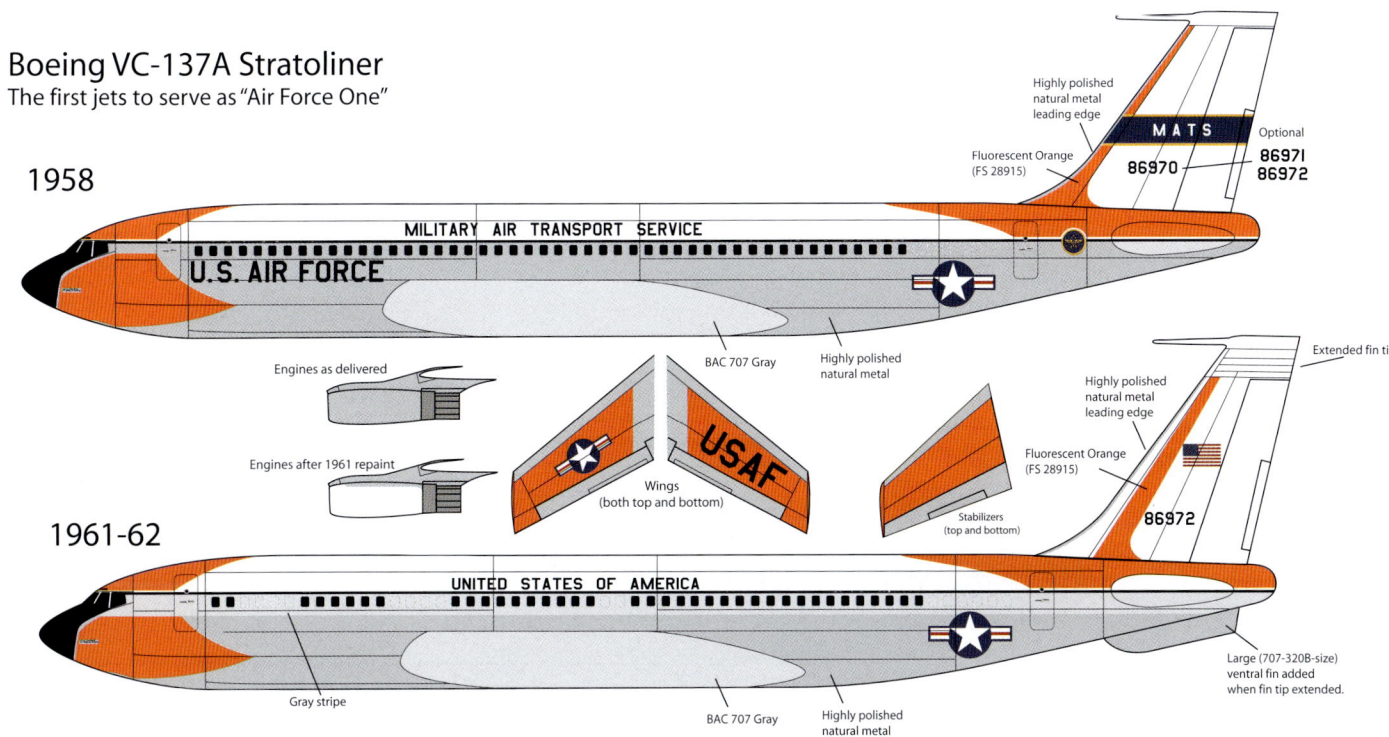

Boeing VC-137A Stratoliner
The first jets to serve as "Air Force One"

1958

1961-62

Wings are in standard 707 Coroguard/natural metal finish (except for day-glo sections).
These are non-turbofan 707-120s, with the small stabilizers and without the inboard wing glove.
Use the airliner-style JT3C engines with "organ pipe" sound suppressors.

VC-137C

Typical wing markings (both top and bottom, for both VC-137B and VC-137C). Wings in usual 707-320B metal/Coroguard finish.

VC-137B

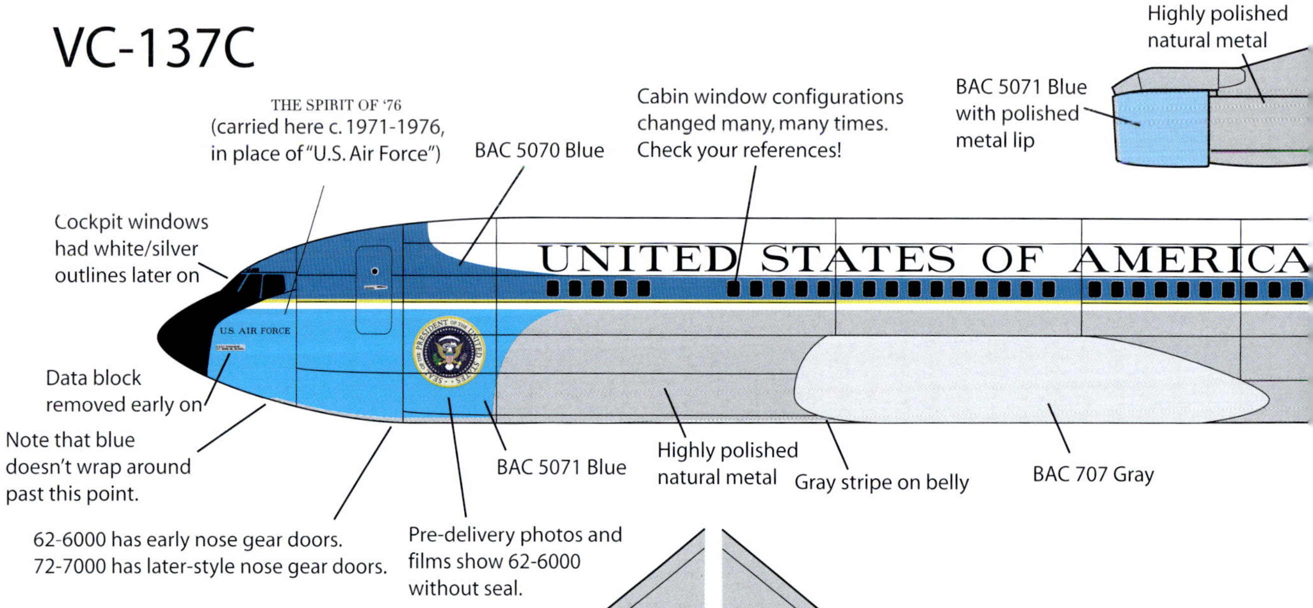

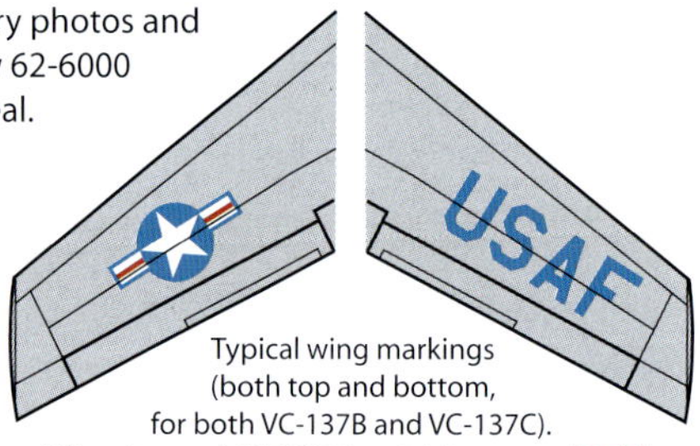

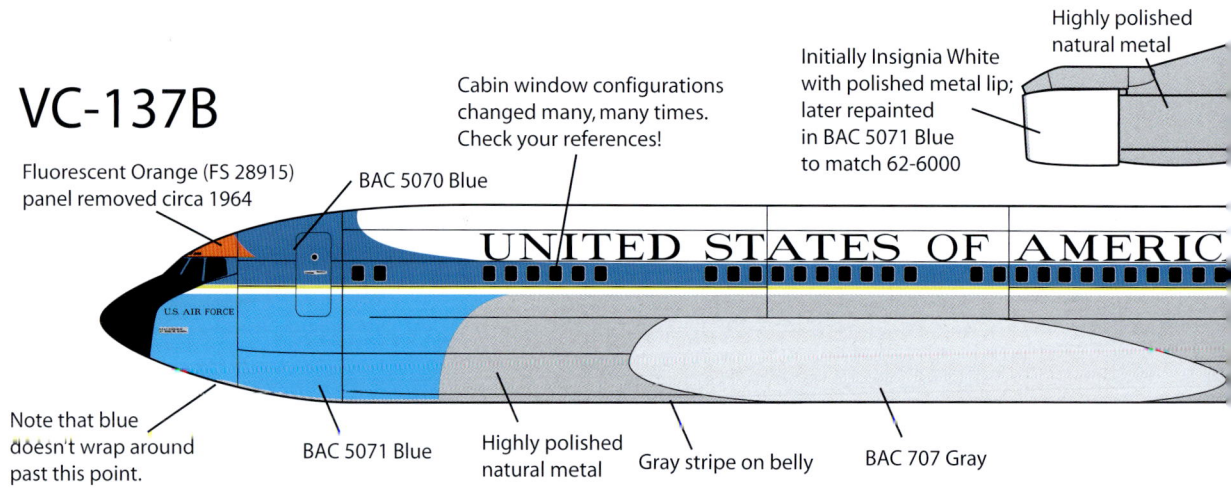

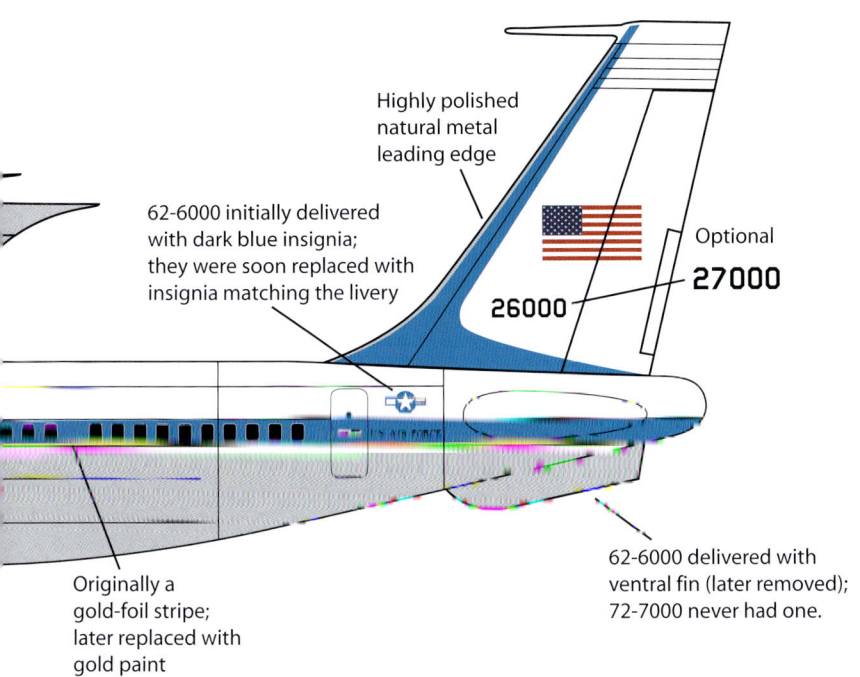

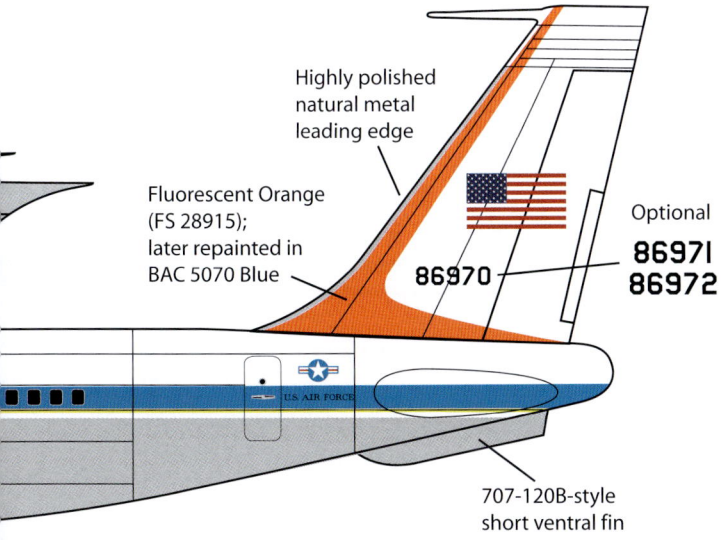

C-137B scheme (late 1970s-early 1980s)

Profile depicts 58-6971 as "Freedom One", January 1981.

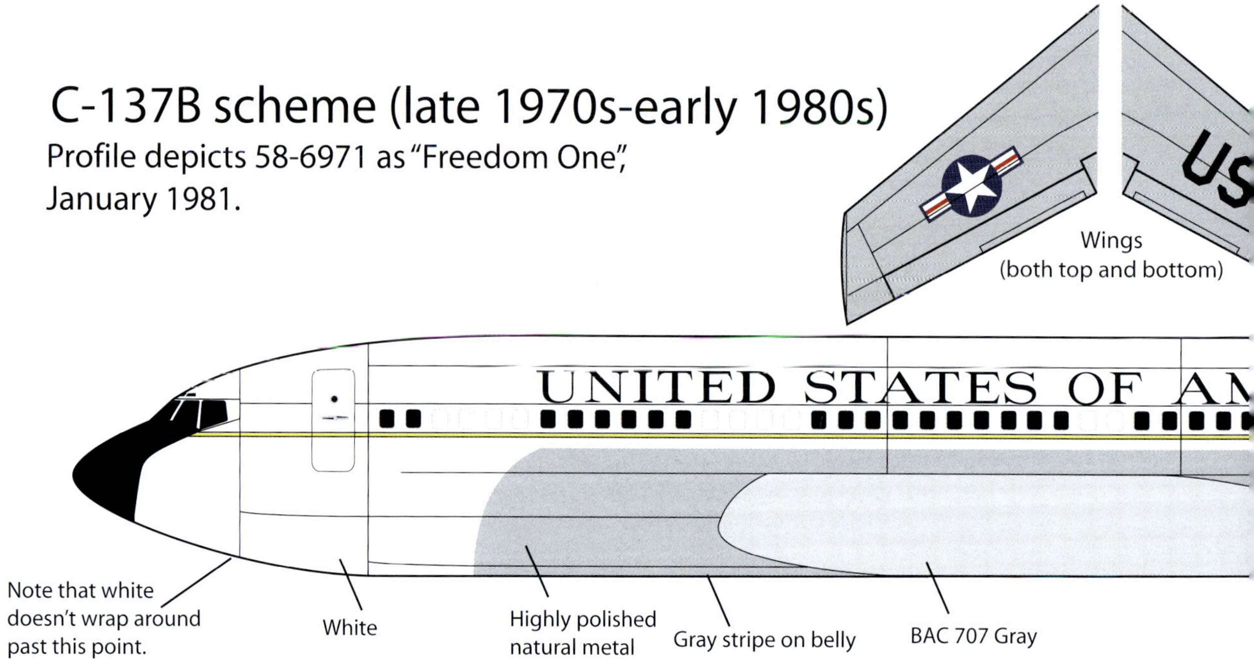

Wings
(both top and bottom)
UNITED STATES OF AM
Note that white doesn't wrap around past this point.
White
Highly polished natural metal
Gray stripe on belly
BAC 707 Gray

Final VC-137B/C scheme

62-6000 and 72-7000 also wore this scheme after the VC-25s were delivered.
Also worn by VC-137Cs 85-6973 and 85-6974.

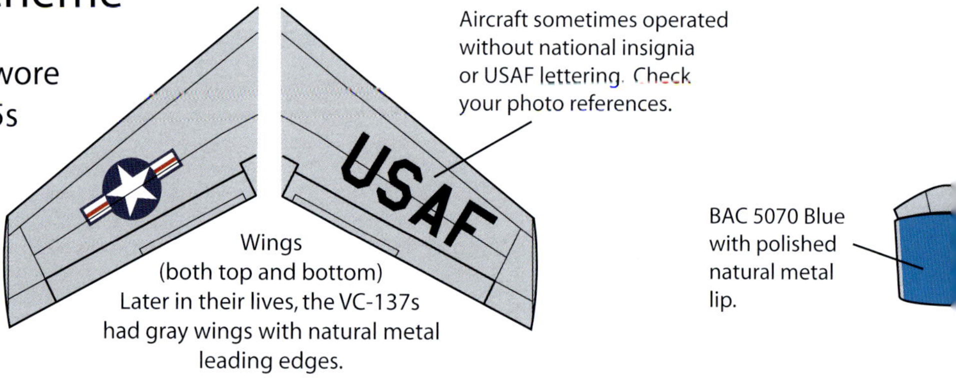

USAF
Aircraft sometimes operated without national insignia or USAF lettering. Check your photo references.
Wings
(both top and bottom)
Later in their lives, the VC-137s had gray wings with natural metal leading edges.
BAC 5070 Blue with polished natural metal lip.

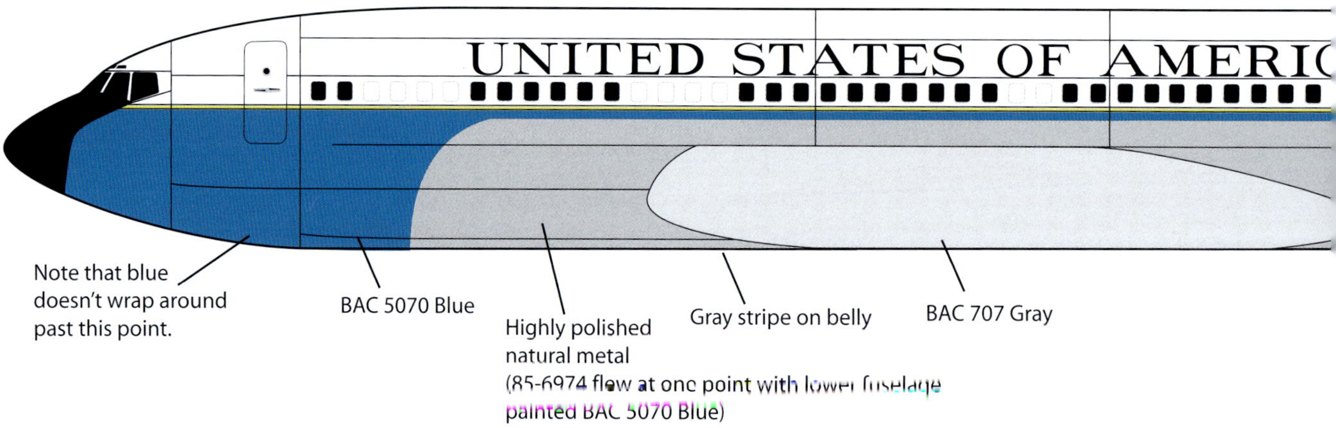

UNITED STATES OF AMERIC
Note that blue doesn't wrap around past this point.
BAC 5070 Blue
Highly polished natural metal
(85-6974 flew at one point with lower fuselage painted BAC 5070 Blue)
Gray stripe on belly
BAC 707 Gray

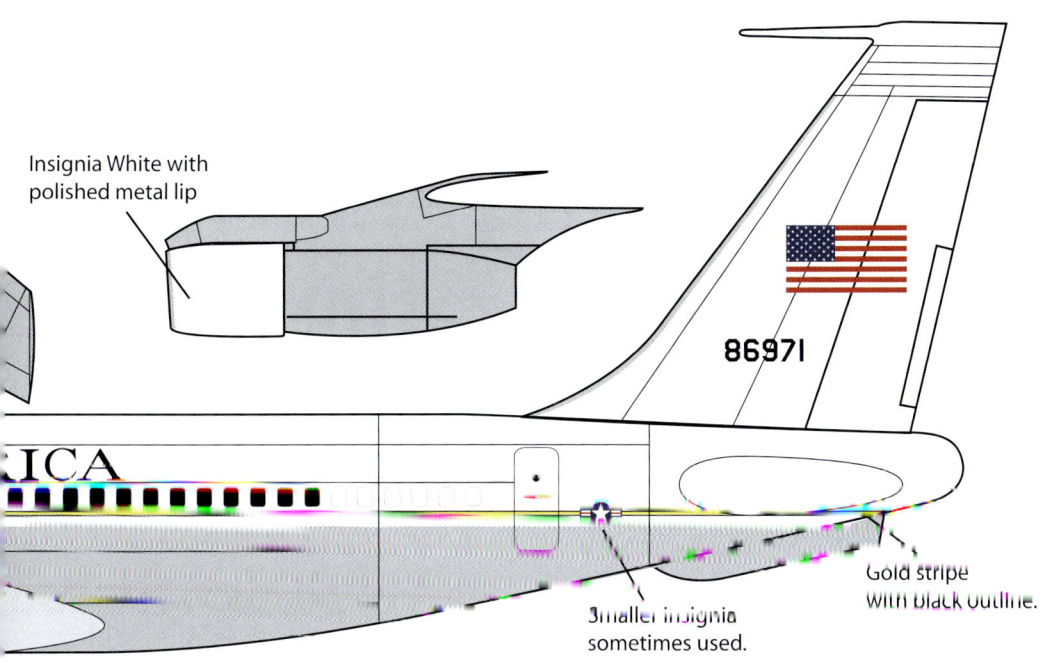

Insignia White with polished metal lip

Smaller insignia sometimes used.

Gold stripe with black outline.

86971

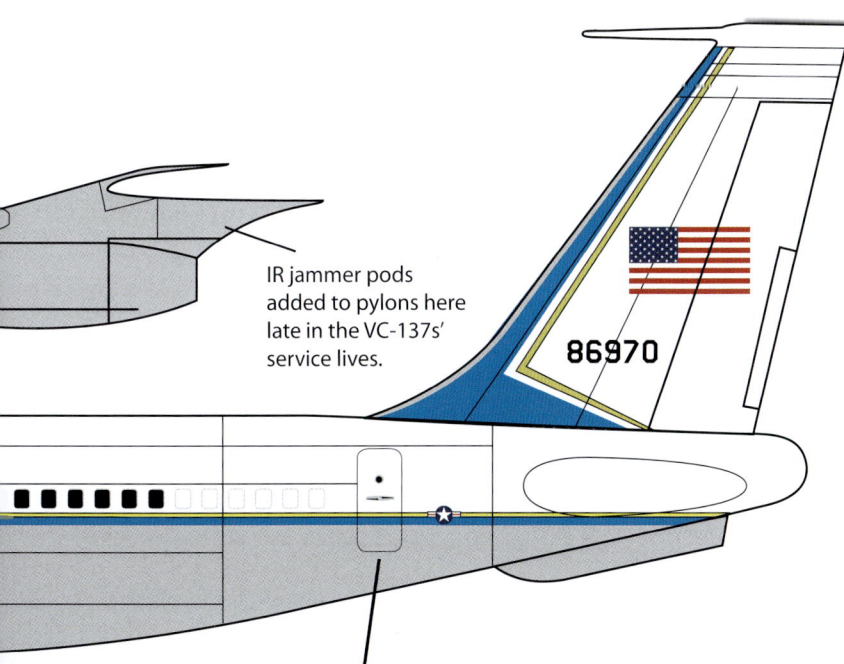

IR jammer pods added to pylons here late in the VC-137s' service lives.

86970

Door outlines not usually painted on the VC-137Bs or ex-AF1 VC-137Cs, but were sometimes painted on the "supertube" ex-commercial VC-137Cs. Check photo references.

10 Finishing America's first operational jet

Refining Sword's 1/72 scale Lockheed P-80A

BY VLADIMIR KAFKA

The P-80 is easily the most beautiful early jet that still had the graceful shapes of World War II dogfighters. While it wasn't a first American jet fighter—this honor belongs to P-59 Airacomet—it was a first to have real combat value, claiming a first U.S. jet kill as well as several speed records.

The early production machines were given to the 412th Fight Group, an elite unit consisting of pilots with rich WWII experience. They transferred their kill marks to rudders of their new steeds, giving them a bit of a what-if look to an unknowing eye of a present day viewer.

This particular machine was flown by Bruce Holloway, a veteran of the legendary Flying Tigers. The name *Rhapsody in Rivets* was inspired by a 1940s Disney cartoon. Ironically, there are no rivets visible, as early P-80s were puttied, polished smooth, and sprayed with gloss, light gray paint called pearl gray. This presents a modeling challenge: How do I make it look interesting and not like decals are put directly on top of a polished Mr. Surfacer layer. Fortunately, apart from the nose art and some yellow trim common to all of this squadron's machines, this one is decorated by colorful boss bird stripes, which help a lot to make it "pop" in a display case.

Given its historical significance, it is surprising how little attention the P-80 gets from kit manufacturers compared to its Korean War brothers in arms, the F-86 and F-84. In 1/72 scale the only options are Sword and an ancient kit from Airfix. The Sword kit suffers some accuracy flaws. But on a positive note the Sword parts are well molded with fine panel lines. There are several boxings available, including different nose wheels, pitot tubes, and seat. The one thing that doesn't change is cockpit placement, although it differed between the A, B and C versions. More on this later.

Vladimir Kafka took care of fit and accuracy issues to finish Sword's model of this early American jet fighter.

1 Based on prior experience, I knew cramming everything into the fuselage—cockpit, wheel wells, intake inner walls and splitter plates, and of course nose weight—was problematic. This time I glued fuselage halves together first figuring I could fit most of the parts through the wing opening.

2 The small, oval landing light in the nose is provided as a larger clear insert. The kit guns look OK, but I drilled out the opening to replace them later with brass tube.

3 The molded bleed-air vents on the intakes are shallow, so I rescribed and reshaped them with a scalpel. They will be one of the details on an otherwise almost smooth surface.

4 The excellent resin wheel wells have large pour stubs that require extensive sanding for proper fit. I recommend working in a sink with running water to not end up covered in drifts of resin dust.

5 To avoid my Shooting Star being a tail-sitter, I glued five 1 gram ball lead fishing sinkers into the cramped nose, half of which will be occupied by the resin wheel well.

6 The kit cockpit doesn't look bad. Apart from the pedals and some little bits for the side consoles, I used original plastic parts throughout, although I removed the lower half of the rear bulkhead. I also installed the plastic seat; there is a resin ejection seat in the kit, but it is appropriate for later versions only.

7 There is not much extra space in the fuselage, so successively inserting all the pieces felt like playing Tetris. Instead of using the thick, poorly fitting kit parts, I made the intake inner walls and splitter plates from thin plastic card. To limit visibility through the intakes, I painted the insides black.

8 The kit windshield doesn't fit its cutout on the fuselage. To fix this, I started by extending the cutout aft slightly so I could move the windshield back to the correct position for the P-80A version. I filled the resulting gap with styrene strips.

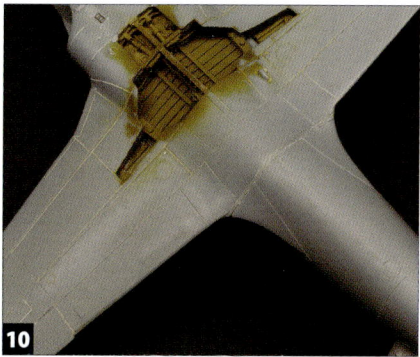

9 I thinned the canopy and refined its shape, then polished it with a cotton swab in a motor tool and Tamiya polishing compounds. I drilled a tiny hole for the antenna wire, which goes through the canopy on its way from the headrest to the rudder leading edge. I also removed a raised rectangular shape depicting a canopy sliding rail behind the cockpit.

10 The seam between the rear fuselage and wing required extensive filling, but sanding was easy as there are no details around it and no rescribing was needed as no panel lines run across the joint.

11 I didn't use the kit's two-part jet pipe, but did install the rear bulkhead to set the depth for a styrene-tube replacement. I also found the vertical stabilizer tip to be a bit anemic so I reshaped and bulked up the outline with thin styrene strip.

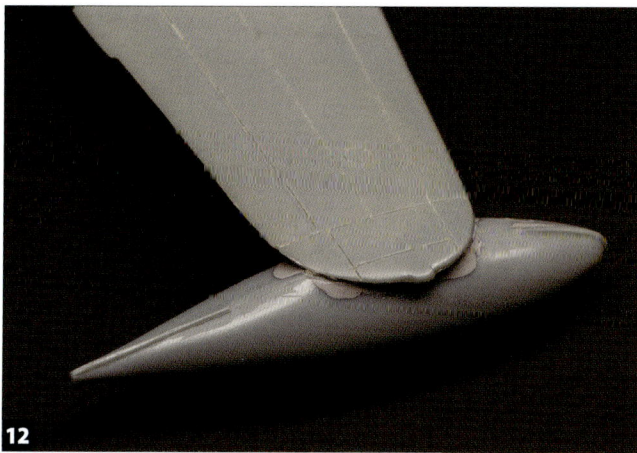

12 Sword did a nice job on the early Lockheed wingtip tanks. Before installing them and filling gaps between them and the wings with superglue and Mr. Surfacer, I removed part of the raised centerline ridge as it didn't extend all of the way around the tank.

13 Gaps and a step marred the wing root. I applied a lot of superglue then sanded the area smooth.

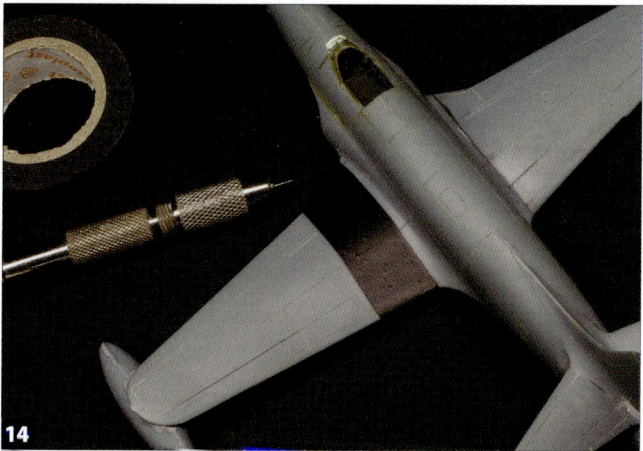

14 To replace panel lines lost to sanding and filling, I rescribed them with a sewing needle using black electrical tape as a guide.

15 Sword's P-80 intakes have been criticized for fit and shape, with them appearing too large and drooped. I dealt with the former with patient sanding and applications of superglue and Mr. Surfacer with a toothpick to seams. I tried to improve the shape of the intakes with careful sanding referring to photos.

16 My last improvement for the intakes was new splitter plates made from thin sheet styrene.

17 New guns, made from thin-walled brass tubes by Albion Alloys, give more scale finesse to the Shooting Star's distinctive armament.

18 I primed the airframe with an overall coat of Mr. Surfacer, which revealed several seams underneath …

19 … and on top that needed repair before painting could commence. Sanding and superglue took care of most of them.

20 The final color, pearl gray, looks very similar to the color of Mr. Surfacer and revealed a couple more problems I needed to fix. I used Mr. Color FS26440 gray (No. C325) as a close match; the tone of the actual color has been the cause of much debate.

21 Masking, masking, masking. Fortunately, Mr. Color paints are durable enough to stand up to repeated handling and taping. Interestingly, even the gun blast tubes were painted yellow, which makes for an interesting detail.

22 I had to repaint and re-mask the color stripes that marked this commander's aircraft several times.

23 The final thing I masked and airbrushed were the black wing walkways on either side of the cockpit.

24 After attaching the windshield with HpH epoxy, I painted it first black, then gray to match the rest of the plane.

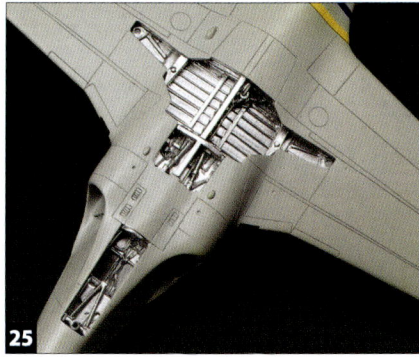

25 My research indicated the wheel wells on the P-80A were silver rather than zinc chromate green or yellow.

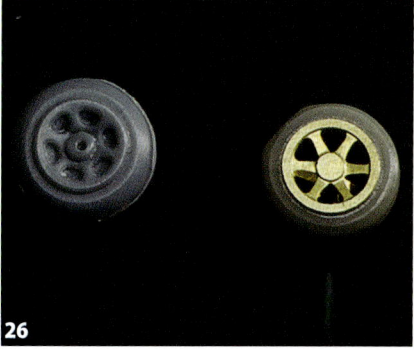

26 I replaced the kit's main wheels with Aires resin parts designed for 1/72 scale F9F Panthers. To improve the kit's front wheel, I made photo-etched (PE) metal open six-spoke hubs that I fitted after drilling the center of the plastic part. The PE hubs are now available from Airone Hobby.

27 Nearing completion, I prepared to attach the small parts and details, including gear doors, struts, and legs, and speed brakes. I thinned all of the doors and struts for a better scale appearance.

28 The kit's beautiful decals are thin and prone to folding and breaking so I handled them with care and applied a lot of water to the surface to prevent them sticking too early. Note the antenna wire made from Ushci van der Rosten rigging thread going through the canopy.

I kept weathering to a minimum as photos showed **Rhapsody in Rivets** was kept clean. The only thing done was a light panel wash before I called my early jet done.

11 Folding the wings on a Cold War sub hunter

Get Classic Airframes 1/48 scale Gannet fit for a hangar

BY ANDY COOPER

Described by some as ugly, the Fairy Gannet's squat and ungainly silhouette gives it the purposeful look of an aircraft designed for a specific mission—submarine hunter/killer. It served with the naval air arms of the United Kingdom, Indonesia, West Germany, and Australia.

I have always thought it an interesting aircraft and the first to be powered by twin gas turbine engines with each unit driving one of two contra-rotating propellers. My interest was piqued by a visit to the Australian Fleet Air Arm Museum in Nowra, New South Wales, where there is a Royal Australian Navy Gannet on display. It is a large, complex and impressive airplane up close. So, I just had to model it—and replicate the distinctive double wing fold.

Only two 1/48 scale Gannets exist—Dynavector's vacuum-formed kit and Classic Airframes injection-molded plastic and cast resin offering. Out of the box, the latter builds with the wings extended. Since I was unable to find any aftermarket wing-fold sets, I would have to scratchbuild the folds.

Andy Cooper's Fairy Gannet is ready to be stowed aboard an aircraft carrier. Folding the wings added another dimension to this build.

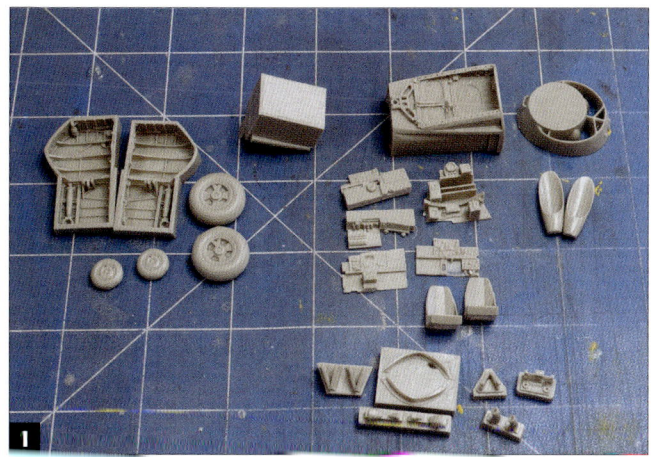

1. While pondering how to approach the wing fold, I prepped the kit's resin, which includes wheels and gear bays, cockpit parts, exhausts, and the nose. A rinse in warm, mildly soapy water will remove any mold release agents that can interfere with glue and paint.

2. The wings won't affect the cockpit, so I assembled the crew sections. After gluing the major parts together, I painted them dark gray. Seat belts were added with thin strips of masking tape and scrap photo-etched metal (PE) for buckles.

3. No decals were provided for the instruments, so I carefully painted the side consoles and panel based on photos. I intended to pose the canopies closed, so much of this detail would be invisible once the model was finished.

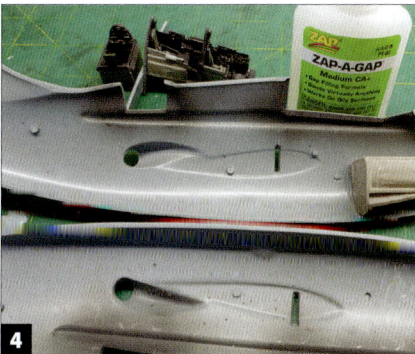

4. The nose and air intake are molded as a single resin piece that mates with a resin nose-wheel bay. Sanding and repeated dry-fits soon had these parts ready to go into the port fuselage half with a dab of thin superglue. The kit instructions indicate installing the gear leg now, but I left it off for painting.

5. Despite all that resin up front, I was not confident the model would sit on its tricycle undercarriage. So, I added several small fishing weights. But that wasn't nearly enough ballast, which eventually forced me to turn to another solution as I will explain later.

6. With the nose parts in place, I finished off the crew stations and mounted them into the port fuselage half.

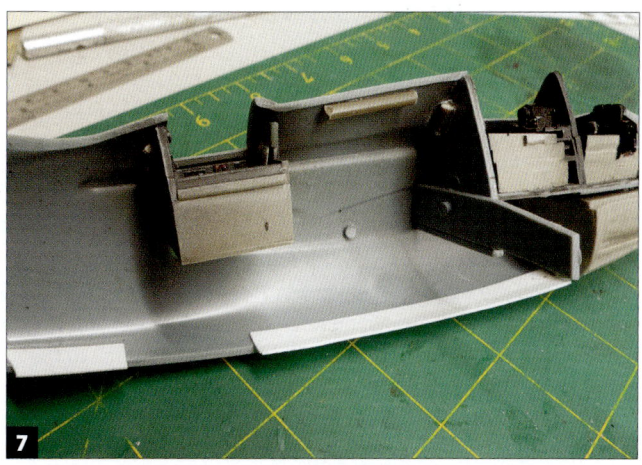

7. The large fuselage relies on a butt joint with no locators, so I added some scraps of styrene along the main joints to bolster the seams.

8 Working from the tail forward, I aligned small sections of the joint and applied glue. Tape and clamps held everything together as the glue dried; then, a little filler took care of minor gaps.

9 The canopy sections were too narrow, so I added styrene rails inside the lip of the cockpit to improve the fits.

10 Even with the rails, one canopy had to be spread with a piece of stiff wire until the glue holding it to the fuselage set. Then, I carefully removed the wire with small pliers.

11 Once the canopies were ready for dry-fitting, they looked ill-fitting and somewhat agricultural. But, that's just how they appeared on the real aircraft—so success! I masked the frames and glued the sections in place.

12 To blend the windshield, I glued on a thin strip of styrene followed by Tamiya putty. Careful sanding took care of the rest.

13 In preparation for cutting the wing-fold lines, I taped the upper and lower wing halves together. Then, based on references, I marked the fold lines on both lower and upper surfaces, then drew a new hobby knife blade along the lines repeatedly, scoring the thick plastic.

14 Judicious use of a razor saw completed the separation and left me with three sections top and bottom—the wing stubs that attach to the fuselage, the middle that will bend up, and the outer that will bend back out.

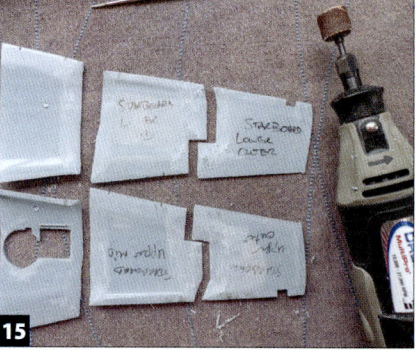

15 Before adding detail to the ends of each section, I thinned the cut edges with a sanding drum in a motor tool. The resin main wheel wells still need to be attached to the openings on the lower halves.

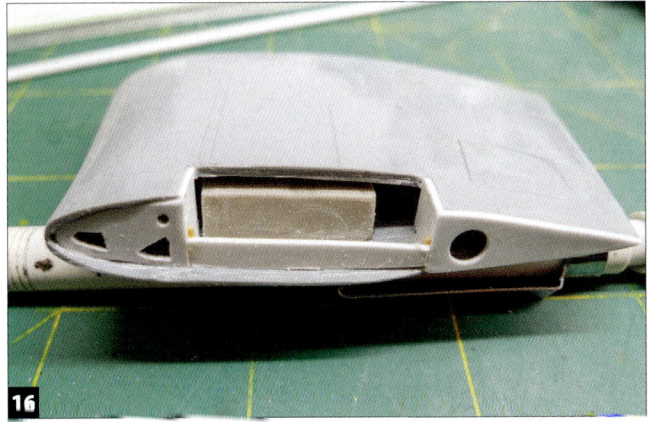

16 Using photos, I built representations of the wing spars and ribs in the separated sections with sheet styrene and scrap. A punch and small files opened and shaped the various holes revealed when the wings are folded.

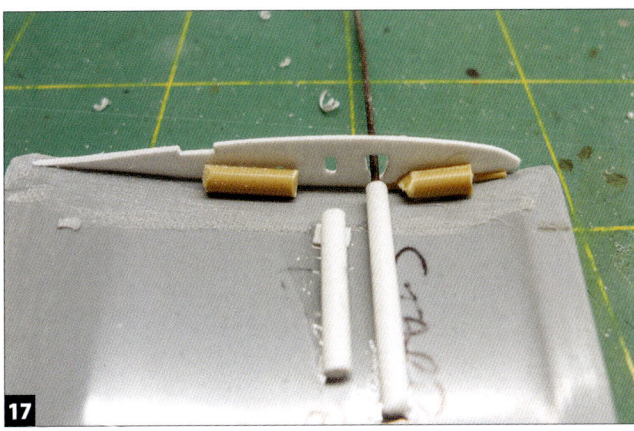

17 At this point, I built only the basic structures to see how the middle section would sit before adding the details. To support the relatively heavy wing parts I planned to embed stiff wire in the middle section, so I glued styrene tubes into the stubs to fit them. The wires could be bent as needed to refine the position of the sections before gluing them.

18 I attached the completed wing stubs to the fuselage, filled the seams at the root, and left the parts to dry

19 The middle and outer sections of the wings were detailed the same way using photos to detail the ends with sheet styrene and surplus PE from my spares box. I periodically test-fitted each section to ensure it would all fit at the end.

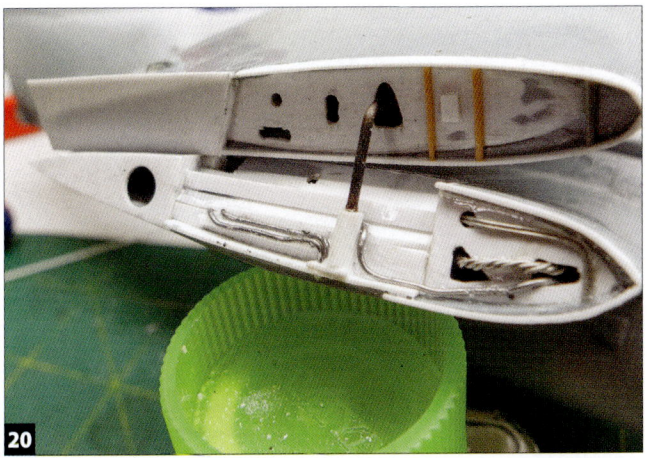

20 A length of stiff wire embedded in the sections will hold them in their final positions. Further detail was added at this stage, such as the prominent hydraulic cylinder on the stub that will anchor the wire holding the middle section. I added cable, fuel, and hydraulic lines using thin solder and fuse wire.

21 A dry run proved that the sections would sit just right and with a few minor adjustments my idea looked like it was going to work.

22 My chosen subject was an RAN aircraft aboard the carrier HMAS *Melbourne* in the mid-1960s. To prepare for paint, I separated the components and sprayed them with Tamiya gray primer.

23 Then, I pre-shaded panel lines by airbrushing thin black paint along the recessed details.

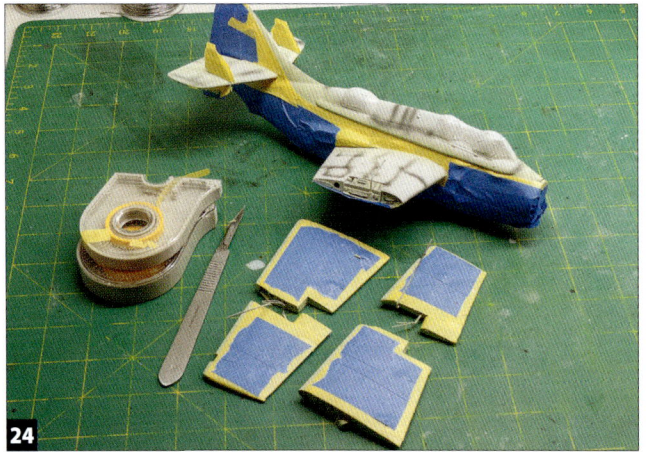

24 The scheme of dark sea gray over sky was common to nearly all Gannets in service including the Australian bird I was building. I airbrushed light coats of Tamiya sky (XF-21) over the undersides and most of the way up the fuselage and the vertical tail allowing some pre-shading to show. Then I masked in preparation for painting the upper surfaces.

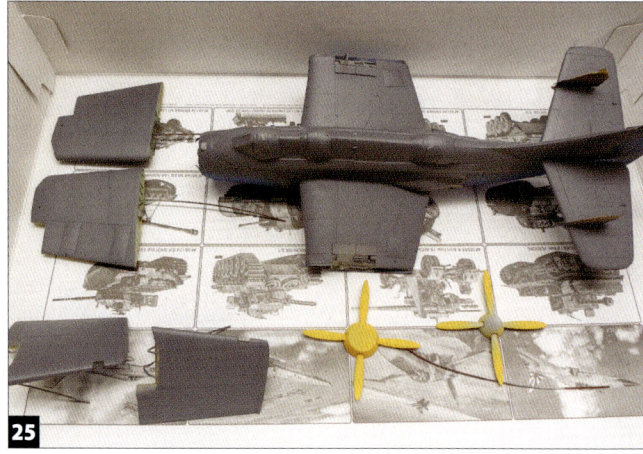

25 I painted the upper surfaces with Hobby Color H331, a good match for dark sea gray.

26 Once this was touch dry, I removed the masks and left the model to completely cure. Then, I airbrushed a protective layer of Alclad II Aqua Clear in preparation for the decals.

27 The kit-supplied Cartograf decals for an RAN Gannet went on with no problems. I took extra care to align the wing markings as the wing-fold makes things a little confusing.

28 I did not use the yellow Rescue placards as my references did not show these on Australian aircraft. I painted the spinner yellow and propeller tips yellow, then masked and painted the spinner mid green and the blades black. Another coat of Aqua Clear sealed the decals.

29 Using a brush, I applied a light gray wash, mixed from white and black artist oils and thinned with mineral turpentine, to panel lines. The wash was allowed to dry for an hour or so, then I wiped the excess away with a soft rag and cotton swabs damp with mineral spirits.

30 Employing the same technique, I used a black artist oil wash to deepen panel lines on the dark gray areas.

31 The result was subtle effect of weather and shipboard operations on an otherwise well-maintained aircraft. I sealed this work with acrylic clear flat to dull the gloss coats applied earlier.

32 Weathering done, I started to bring the subassemblies together, starting by joining the outer and middle section of both wings. Matching the angle of the sections to each other and test-fitting them with the stubs ensured alignment before the parts were glued.

33 Supporting the model with discarded packaging from a laptop, I added the assembled wing sections to the inboard wings. Adjusting the stiff wire in the embedded tubes and the angle of the fold with small pliers got everything lined up just right. A small dab of quick-drying glue on the inner edges of the outer wing ailerons held everything in place while superglue was applied to the wires.

With the wings secured, I used photos to build a representation of the intricacies of the fold mechanisms with scrap styrene and PE. Bolt and rivet heads were punched out of sheet styrene.

To strengthen the folded wings, I made the red poles seen in many pictures of the stowed Gannets using styrene rod wrapped in lead foil to represent telescoping sections. These were painted and put aside to add in the final stages.

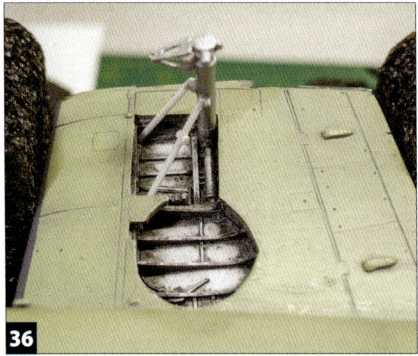

While assembling the main undercarriage legs, I discovered that the kit's retraction struts were too short. So, I replaced them with styrene rod.

Initially things looked good—until I added the nose wheels. They were just enough to shift the center of gravity and turn my Gannet into a tail-sitter.

Unable to add weight to the nose, I turned to another solution—anchor the model on a base that looked like a carrier deck section. A small section of craft wood was cut to size and I glued a piece of 120-grit wet-and-dry sandpaper to it using PVA glue.

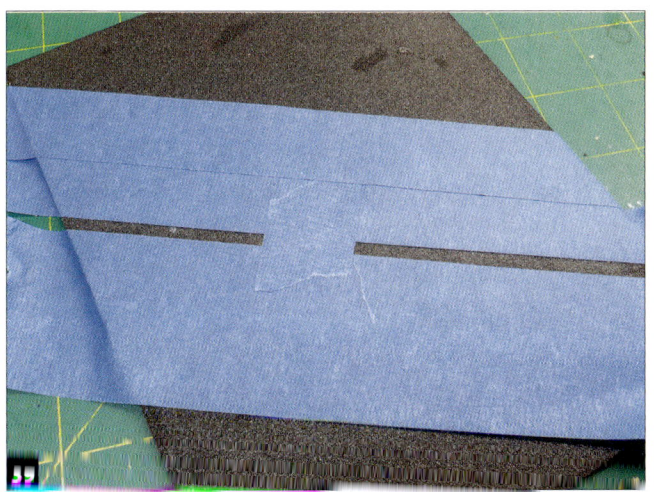

Then, I masked and sprayed a white line to break up the monochromatic surface. The base was coated with an acrylic clear flat.

I glued wire pins into holes drilled into the bottom of the wheels. These pins were matched to holes drilled in the base and the model secured with superglue. This made the model easy to handle during final assembly.

I finished the Gannet with the wing support poles, propellers, and an antenna wire. Overcoming the challenge of the wing fold made this build special.

A gaucho dressed as a pirate

Building Hasegawa's 1/48 scale Sea King for Argentine service

BY RICARDO DACOBA

During the 1982 Falklands or Malvinas War, the Argentine navy operated from EAN Calderon, a small airfield on Pebble Island on the archipelago's northwest side. British SAS commandos disabled the field and many of the aircraft stationed there in a raid on the night of May 14-15, stranding 10 Argentine personnel. Rescuing those aircrew became a focus of Argentine naval command. On June 1, two Sea Kings, designated S-61D-4 in Argentine service and normally assigned to antisubmarine warfare, took off from Rio Grande in southern Argentina bound for Calderon. One, designated 2-H-233, had been hastily repainted with dark blue over its white upper surfaces as camouflage, but there was not enough paint to cover both helicopters.

Carrying extra fuel, fighting poor weather and flying low to avoid British radar, the two Sea Kings made it to the airstrip, picked up the 10 crewmen, and returned to Rio Grande without a major incident.

I wanted to build one of the two copters involved in the mission so I turned to Hasegawa's 1/48 scale SH-3H. The kit was first produced in 1991, but I used Revell's 2001 reboxing for my build. It is an excellent kit with fine recessed surface detail but there's not much to see inside. I faced two big challenges: First, backdate the SH-3H to D configuration and, second, try to reproduce the interior and engines.

Ricardo Decoba shares how he filled his Argentine SH-3D with interior and engine detail.

1 One of the most noticeable changes for Sea Kings operated by Argentina are the side pods, which are shorter and rounder. I used 2-part epoxy putty to build up the center and form a new rear section, modifying the length.

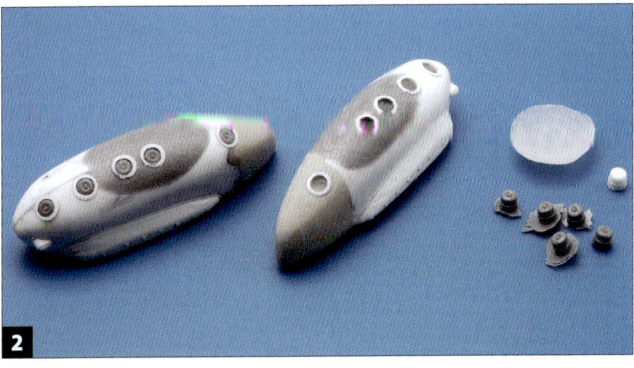

2 I scratchbuilt a master for the access covers along the top of each pod, then reproduced it with a silicone mold and resin.

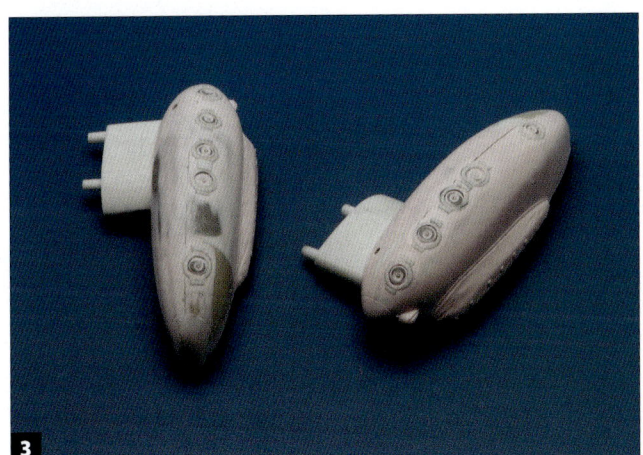

3 After spraying the pods with a layer of gray primer and correcting revealed blemishes, I finished the side pods with a layer of Mr. Base White 1000.

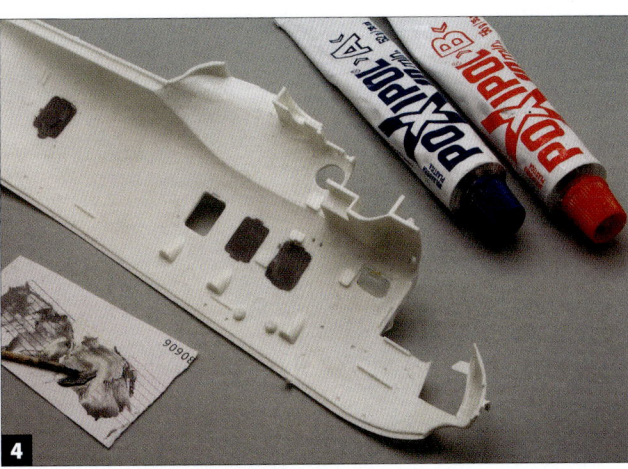

4 Some of the window openings aren't appropriate for Argentine SH-3Ds, so I filled them with 2-part epoxy glue.

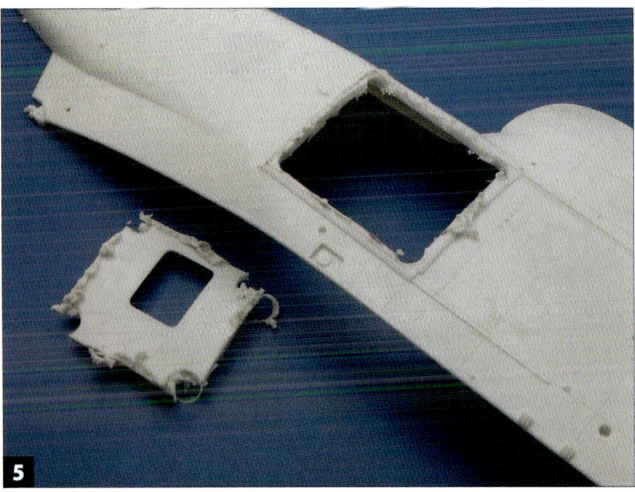

5 I wanted to pose the side door open, so I carefully removed it by drilling holes at the corners and then cutting between them. Flat and round files refined the shape of the opening.

6 I made a new sliding door with sheet aluminum and detailed it brass and styrene.

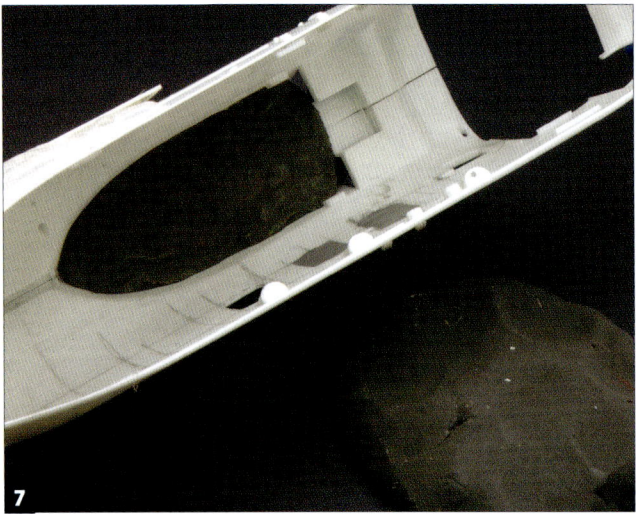

7 The ceiling of the cabin is open to the engine compartment. To fill the void, I first pushed the fuselage halves together then filled the space with clay up to a level 5mm shy of the lip.

8 Then, I applied a layer of epoxy putty and, using a wet finger, smoothed it a much as possible until it was level with the ceiling's contour.

9 Once the putty was dry, I separated the fuselage and removed the putty and clay plug.

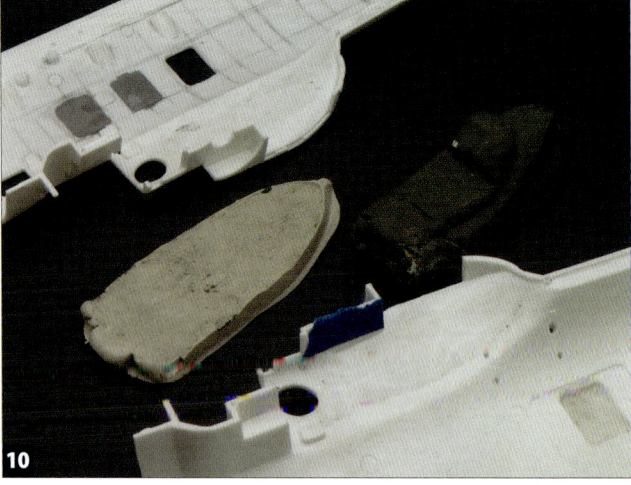

10 Then, I discarded the clay keeping only the epoxy; it was glued to the port fuselage half.

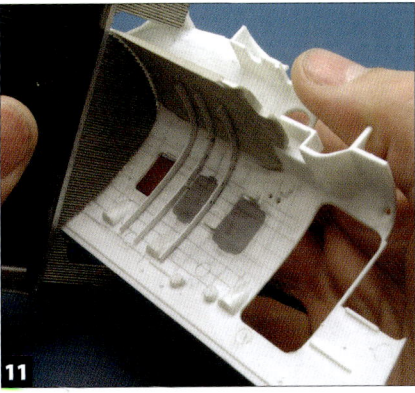
11 I placed a contour gauge at the locations of frames inside the fuselage,

12 Transferring those shapes to sheet styrene …

13 … and using a pair of dividers, I made each rib.

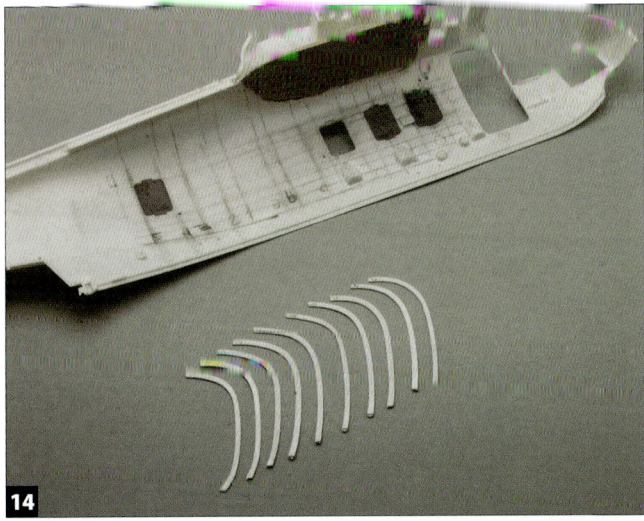
14 High dosages of patience and several sessions over a few days were required to complete all the necessary ribs.

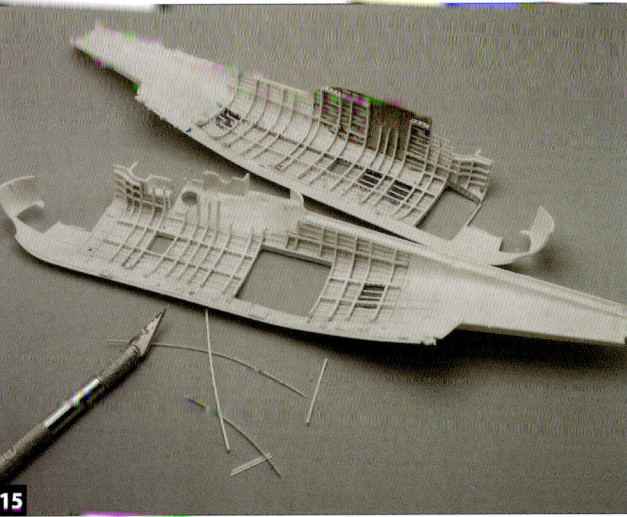
15 I used several thicknesses of strip styrene to add longerons and other structural details inside the helicopter.

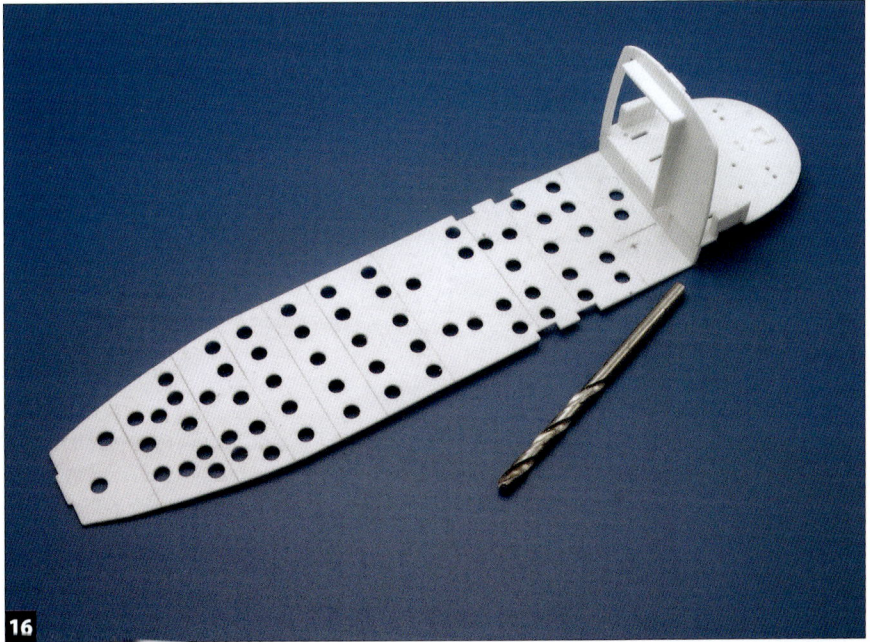
16 The cabin floor was devoid of detail. To rectify the omission, I drilled holes where each of the equipment and seating mooring brackets should be.

17 I heated a piece of kit sprue, then pushed it into the head of a Torx screw wrapped in brass tube. Repeating this process multiple times produced enough copies …

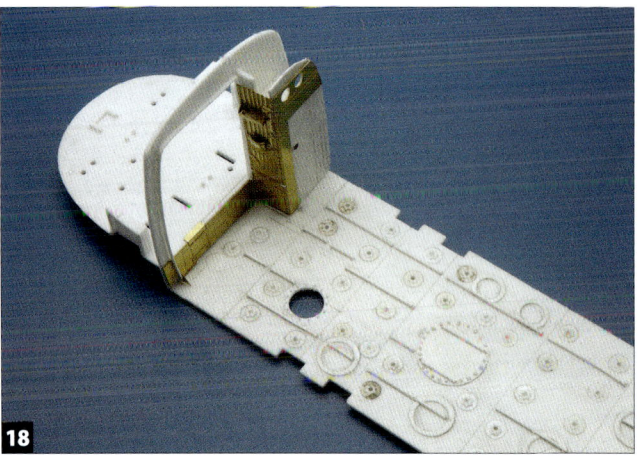

18 … to fill the holes in the floor. I also added access covers, braces, and rivets.

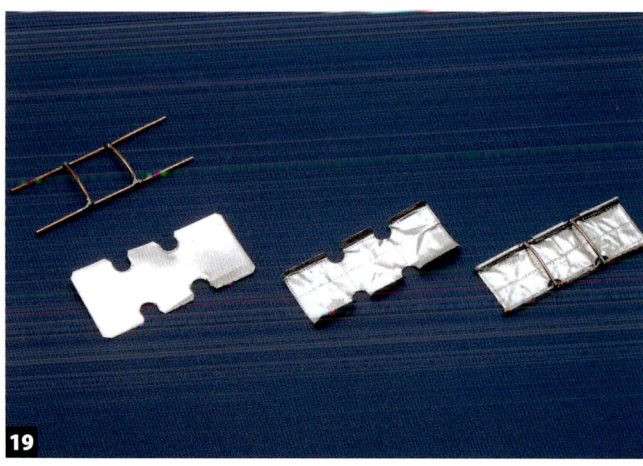

19 For seats in the cargo area, I made frames from copper wire soldered together. Thin aluminum sheet shaped and bent, then embossed with stitching reproduced the seat bottoms.

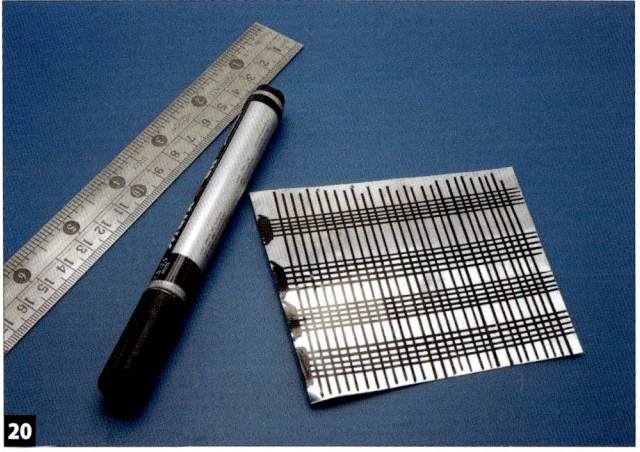

20 The webbing backs needed a different approach. First, I drew the pattern on aluminum sheet with a permanent marker.

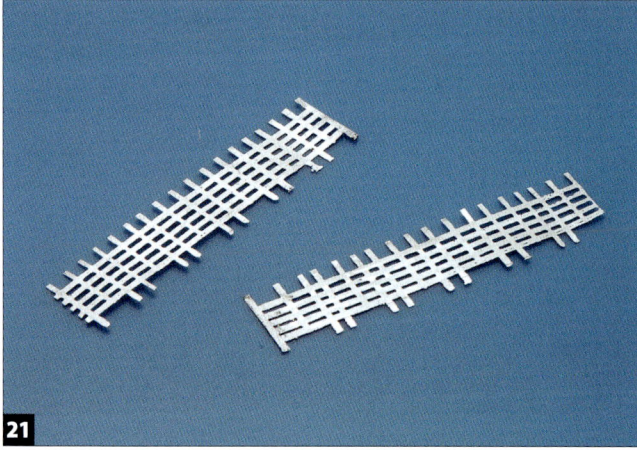

21 Then I dipped the sheet in ferric acid for a few moments. It ate away the bare aluminum producing thin, flexible webbing for the seats.

22 Before adding more details, I painted the interior with Tamiya neutral gray (XF-53).

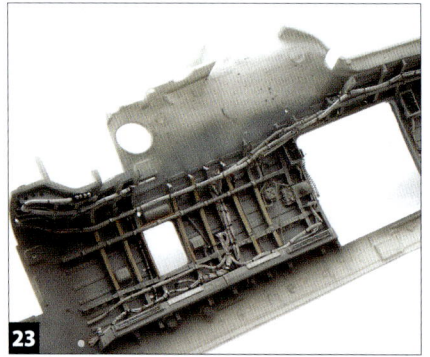

23 Solder grouped into bundles added electrical wiring to the walls. It is always more convenient to paint them before gluing them in place.

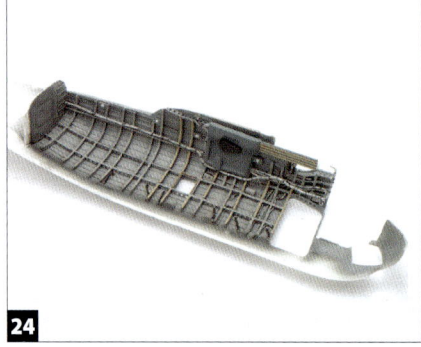

24 I made the interior cover for the main rotor with sheet styrene and resin. After painting it, I attached it to the ceiling.

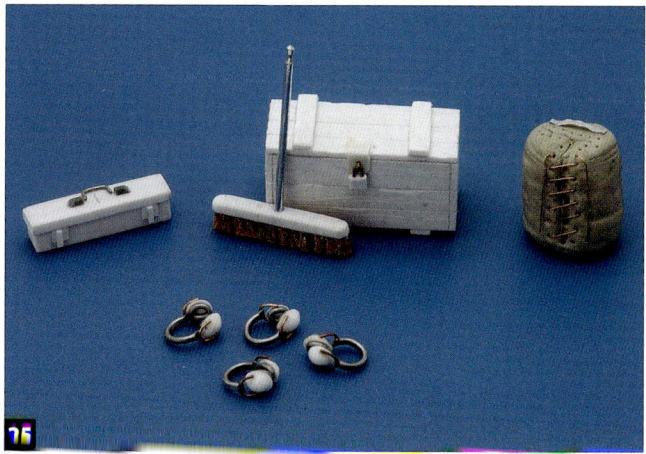

25 Using styrene and wire, I made accessories to detail the cabin, including a tool box, broom, crate, bagged rafts, and headphones.

26 Painted with reds and yellows, these items add color to the interior.

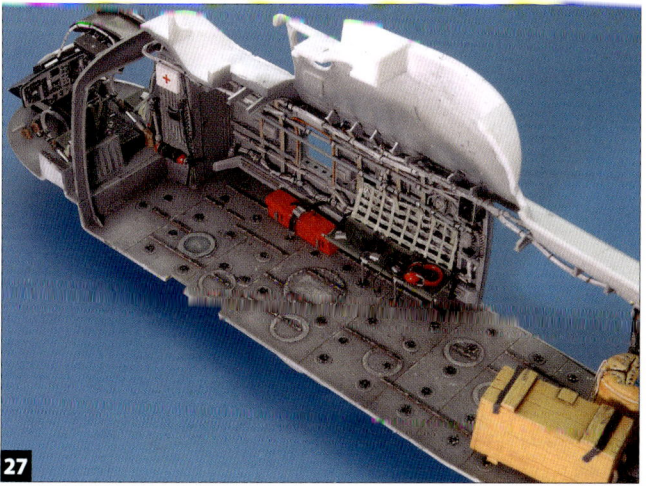

27 With the details, including the cockpit, in place, I was ready to close the fuselage.

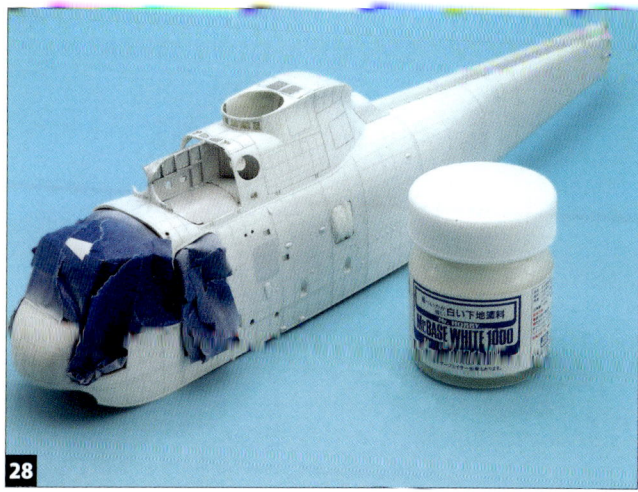

28 After gluing the airframe parts together and masking the openings, I applied a generous layer of Mr. Base White.

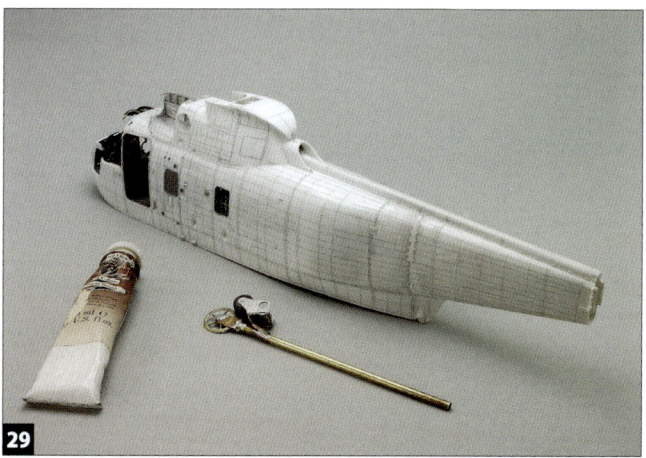

29 Using a pounce wheel made from a watch gear, I reproduced rivets over the fuselage. Dark artist oils confirmed their placement and consistency.

30 I made details for the engine bay with aluminum and sheet styrene.

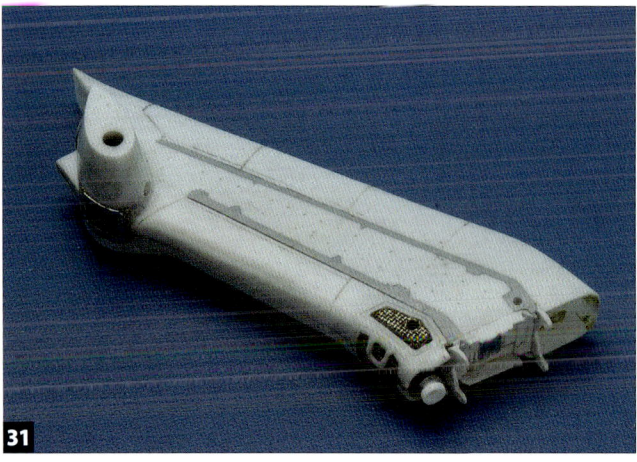
31 The tail section was improved with the addition of brass mesh screens. I made the internal structure for the folding section from various plastic parts.

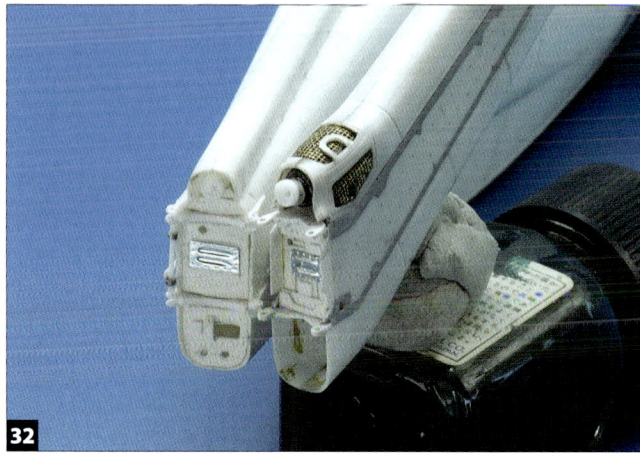
32 I test-fitted the folding mechanism for the tail boom before painting.

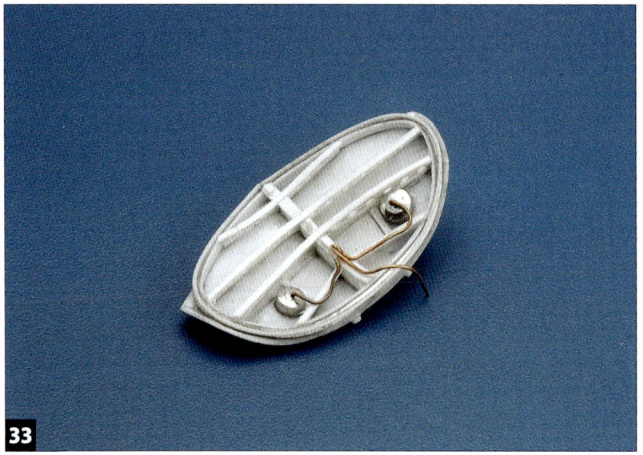
33 To pose the nose avionics bay open, I cut away the forward section of the belly.

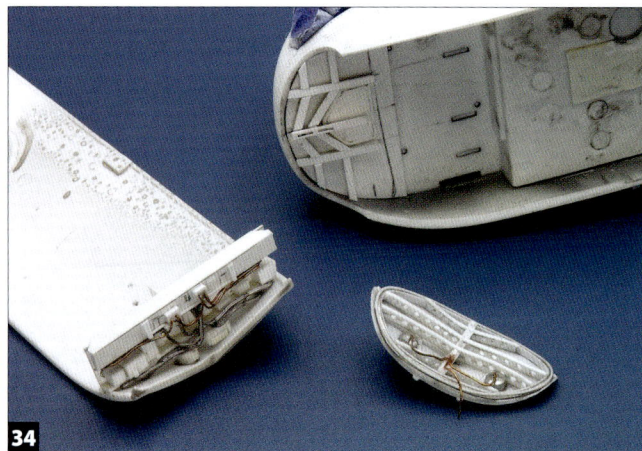
34 I detailed the inside of the hatch, bay, and its ceiling with bits of styrene and wire.

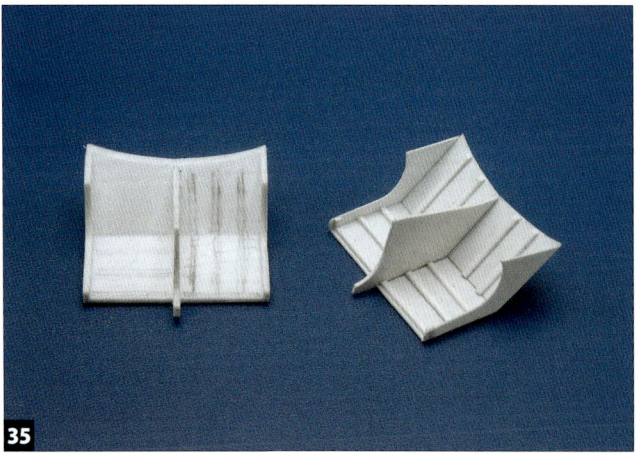
35 The kit's protective cowling for the intakes was overly thick and lacked internal structure. I replaced it with a guard scratchbuilt from styrene.

36 The main rotor is a focal point, so I scratchbuilt many details and modified others with styrene and resin.

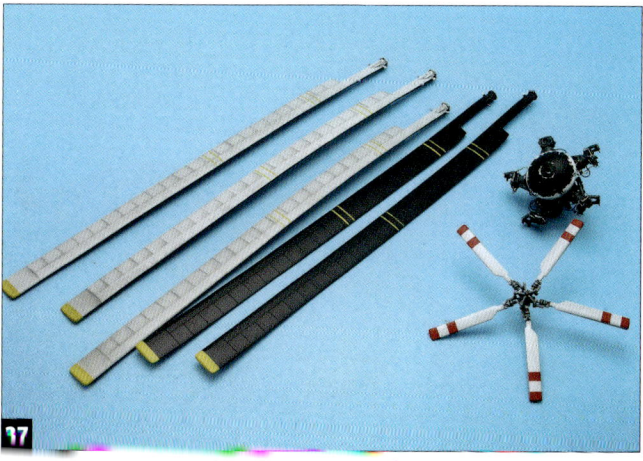
Here are the main and tail rotors painted awaiting final assembly.

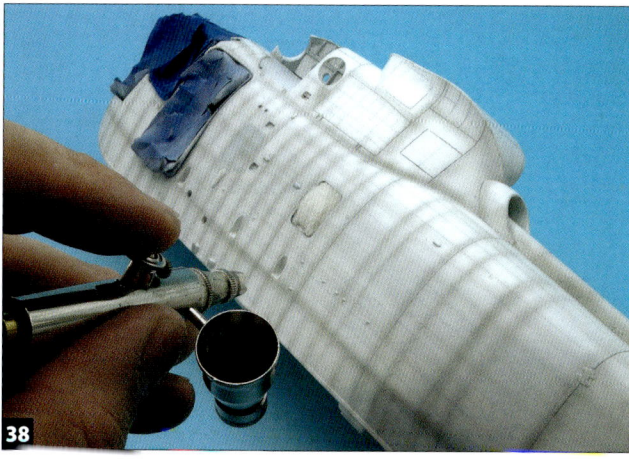
Once the base coat was dry, I airbrushed medium gray pre-shading along panel and rivet lines.

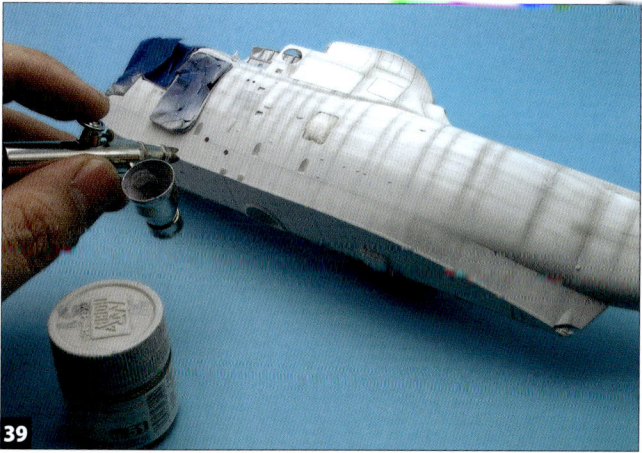
I started the camouflage by spraying the lower fuselage with Hobby Color gloss light gull gray acrylic (H51); thin layers left the pre-shading slightly visible.

Using paper masks and worms of poster putty, I painted the upper fuselage with Tamiya acrylic flat sea blue (XF-17). I wanted an irregular edge between the colors typical of field-applied camo.

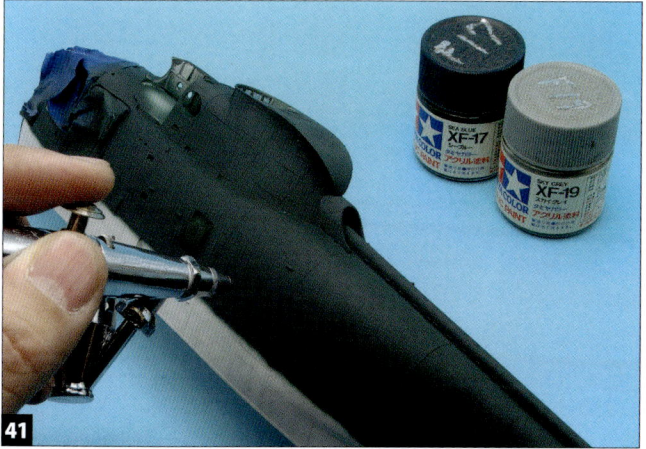
Then I sprayed sections of the upper surfaces with a lightened version of sea blue to add variety to the finish.

I cut blue tape masks to paint the exhaust panels with Tamiya acrylic semigloss black.

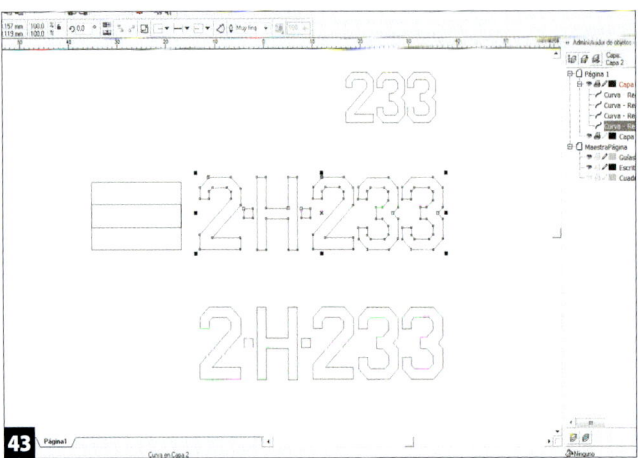

43 I prefer to paint markings rather than use decals, so I drew them using vector software, and then made the masks with adhesive film.

44 After transferring them to Frisket self-adhesive film, I sprayed the aircraft's IDs first with light gull gray …

45 … then with thin layers of white. Removing the masks revealed the sharp numbers.

46 I used a fine brush and Humbrol brown yellow (94) to add profuse chipping over the aircraft. Note the white showing through under the rotor, and area of extreme wear.

47 Next, I brushed on a layer of black watercolor mixed with extender for acrylics. After it dried, I wiped away excess with a cloth damp with water, before sealing everything with clear satin varnish.

48 This image shows the finished and weathered main rotor and engine bay.

49 The kit supplied engine intakes and exhausts, but I scratchbuilt everything between and around them.

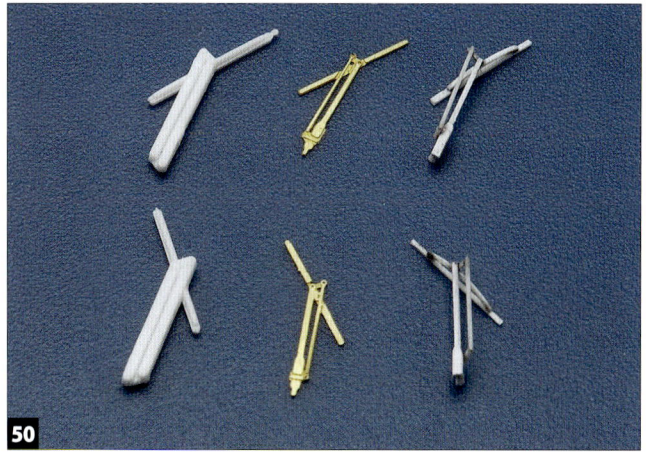

50 After looking at my options for wipers, including the kit parts (left) and Flightpath photo-etched metal (center), I chose to scratchbuild them instead.

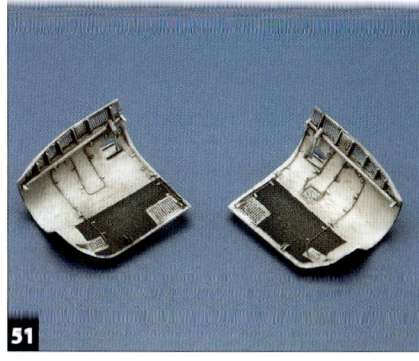

51 I thinned the kit engine access covers, then detailed the inner faces with copper mesh and wire.

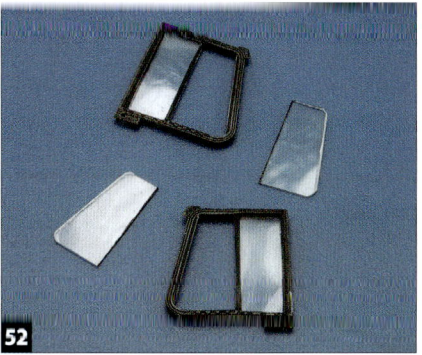

52 To pose the side windows open, I removed the transparent sections and replaced them with thin acetate.

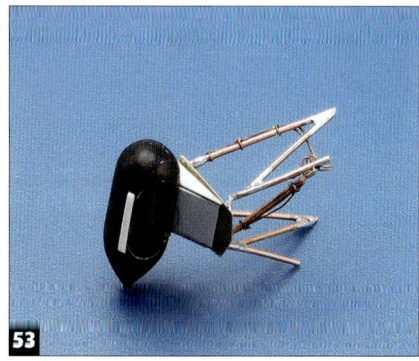

53 The side winch was modified to match the one used on the SH-3D, then I scratchbuilt a new support made of copper wire soldered together.

54 To improve the main landing gear, I deepened the tire tread and added Flightpath PE.

After attaching all of the subassemblies, I added antennas and wires to finish my Argentine Sea King.

13 Mastering biplanes

Special techniques bring early planes to life

BY CHUCK DAVIS

Building biplanes, especially those from the World War I era, calls for a handful of special techniques, such as painting fake wood, applying lozenge decals, and adding the dreaded rigging. Taken together they inspire fear in modelers not familiar with treading these mysterious waters, but the techniques required are relatively easy with the tools and materials available today. A standard WWI German two-seater like Wingnut Wings' Halberstadt CL.II (Late) provides a straightforward experience for practicing these special techniques.

The Halberstadt CL.II was a two-seat combat aircraft performing what we would today call battlefield interdiction along with escort for other two seaters. Armed with both forward and

Chuck Davis conquered lozenge decals with heat and wing rigging with Berkshire Junction E-Z Line. Tips for dealing with photo-etched parts and for creating wood grain detail with paint take the pain out of building this 1/32 scale Wingnut Wings kit.

rearward firing machine guns and a plethora of grenades and other nasty droppable items, the CL.II was also able to carry a radio for contact with the troops. Fast and maneuverable for the day, the CL.II was not an easy foe to tackle. Wingnut's 1/32 scale version, though, is easily brought to bay with a few simple tricks, taking the mystery out of biplane building.

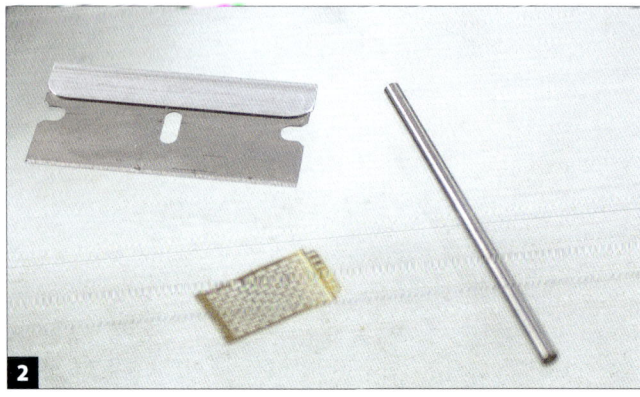

1. Machine guns are one detail that stands out on a WWI kit, so it pays to make them look as good as possible. Wingnut Wings includes photo-etched metal (PE) cooling jackets, but before using them, it's a good idea to anneal the brass—make it softer—so it will bend around a radius gently without kinks. Heat the brass using a butane torch until it glows red evenly, then let is cool.

2. The easiest way to form the cooling jacket is to find a rod with a diameter slightly smaller than the jacket—in this case a gauge pin. In addition, you'll need something to trap the PE part against the pin and a firm surface to do the forming. A trusty razor blade and an old glass bathroom scale work nicely.

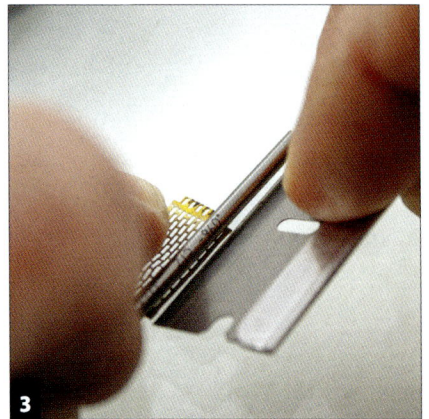
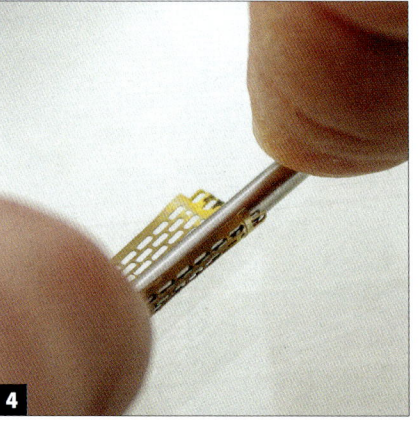
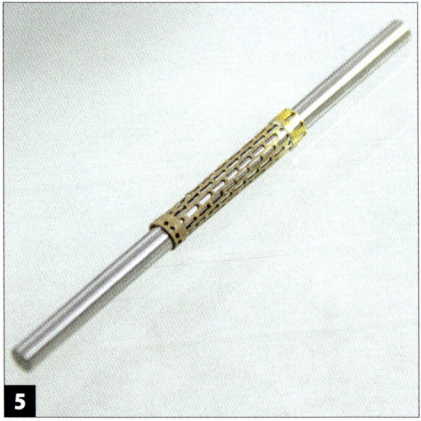

3. Place the pin as close to the edge of the jacket as possible, making sure it is parallel to the long edge. Then slip the blade under the lip of the brass jacket.

4. With the blade, lift the edge of the brass jacket tight against the pin and then hold the brass in place against the pin, rolling the pin over for a complete circle.

5. You should end up with an evenly rolled circular jacket formed around the pin.

6. The jacket can be installed carefully over the part supplied in the kit, and the front sight assembly glued on. The muzzle can be opened by carefully spinning the tip of a knife blade in the center of the opening.

7. As good as the details are in Wingnut Wings kits, there are some things that can be improved upon, like the rear-mounted LMG 14/17 machine gun. The barrel, jacket, front sight, and barrel-changing handle have all been replaced on the lower weapon by a set from Master Model.

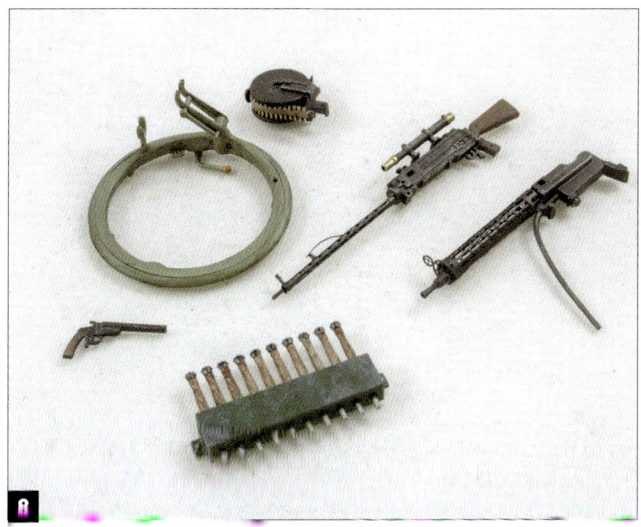

A The full weapons load for the C.II is shown completed — including a flare gun and a rack of grenades.

9 Assembling and painting the landing gear can be accomplished as a subassembly. The first step is painting the tires — usually a shade of gray, since rubber was scarce. I find the quickest way of easily painting wheels is to use a circle template as a reusable mask. Simply find the appropriate diameter, mask the adjacent circles to prevent overspray, and …

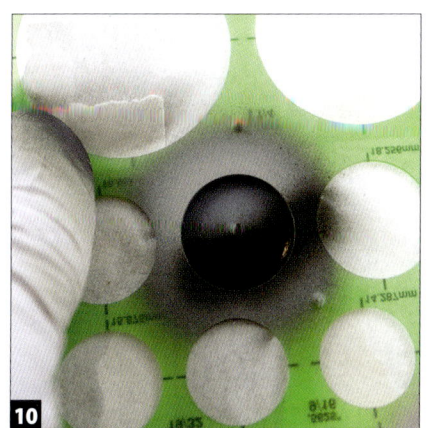

10 … paint the center wheel color. A hint — always use one side of the circle template to mask and the other side to spray paint against. That way you don't risk transferring paint from a previous model to the current wheel while you hold it in place. Ask me how I figured that one out …

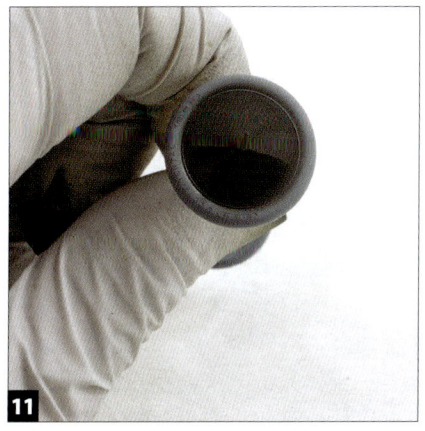

11 *Voila*! A complete, painted wheel. Simple and fast. Any minor overspray can be hidden with a wash around the wheel or other weathering.

12 The fully assembled and painted landing gear, with a generator mounted to the strut. The instructions didn't call for it, but since I mounted the optional radios I had to provide them with some electrical power. Pictures provided in the instructions showed the engine-mounted generator was not an option, so I went with the landing gear mount — conveniently hidden in the same photographs.

13 Wingnut Wings' engines are fully detailed kits by themselves. Here is the 180-horsepower Daimler-Mercedes D.IIIa engine for the marking option I was building. Many of the parts have been assembled prior to painting. Only the cylinders, intake manifold, and rocker arms were left off.

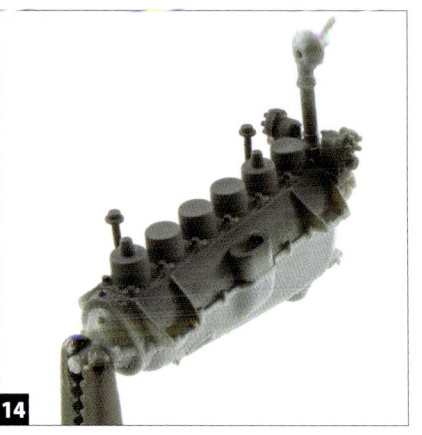

14 Wingnut molded the base of the cylinders on top of the engine block, posing a difficult masking job. First, I painted the cylinder bases Tamiya NATO black.

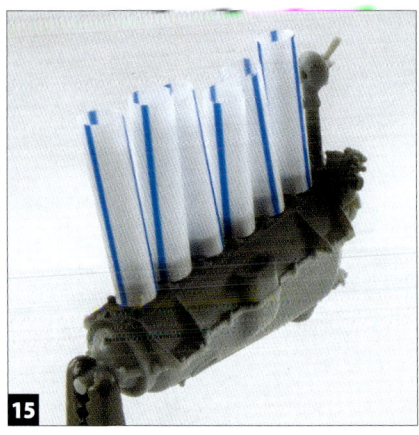

15 Next, I stole a straw from the kitchen and cut it up. The sections fit perfectly over the cylinder bases and took seconds to install.

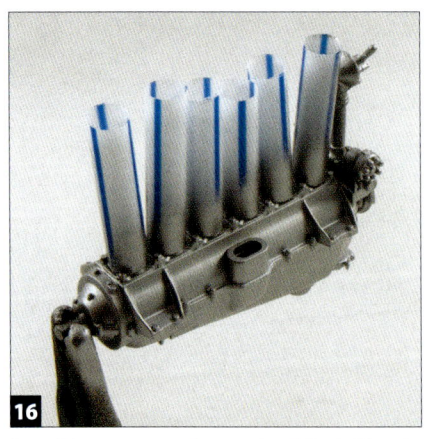

16 I could now spray the engine block Metalizer aluminum with impunity.

17 A few seconds to remove the straws and a perfectly masked set of cylinder bases was revealed.

18 The rest of the engine details can now be painted and added. Weathering and the included decals finished the powerplant. Thanks to the kit design, the engine can be installed after fuselage painting and decaling.

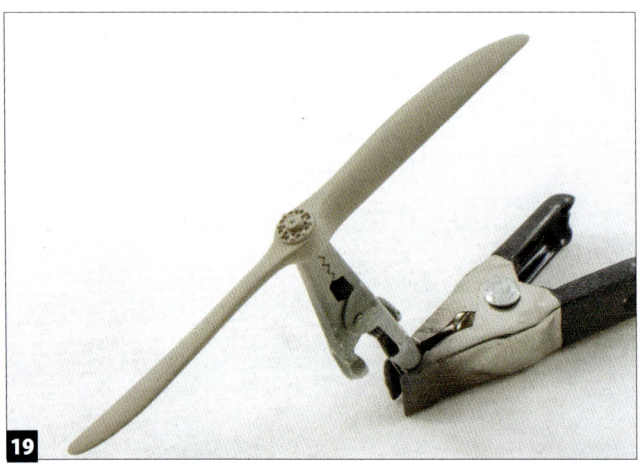

19 Wooden propellers are a focal point. First step in my wooden prop process is to paint a light tan; I used Tamiya deck tan (XF-55).

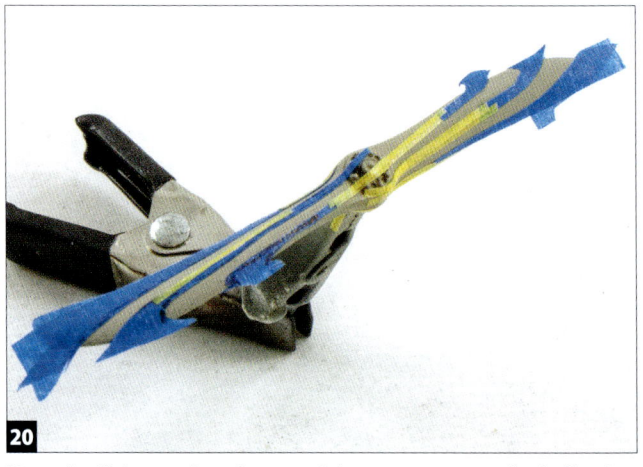

20 Next, the lighter-colored areas of the prop were masked off referring to pictures for the general appearance, and …

21 a coat of a medium brown was applied—Tamiya linoleum deck brown (XF-79) works.

22 Removing the masking reveals the beginnings of a laminated prop. I sealed the acrylic base coats with clear gloss.

23 To add wood grain, burnt umber artist oil paint thinned with Turpenoid—an odorless thinner—was brushed on. Thicker paint produces darker, more pronounced wood grain; I thinned the paint to about the same consistency as paint for airbrushing since I was looking for a mild grain.

24 After letting the oil paint sit for about four hours, I used a stiff brush to stroke a grain pattern into the oil paint.

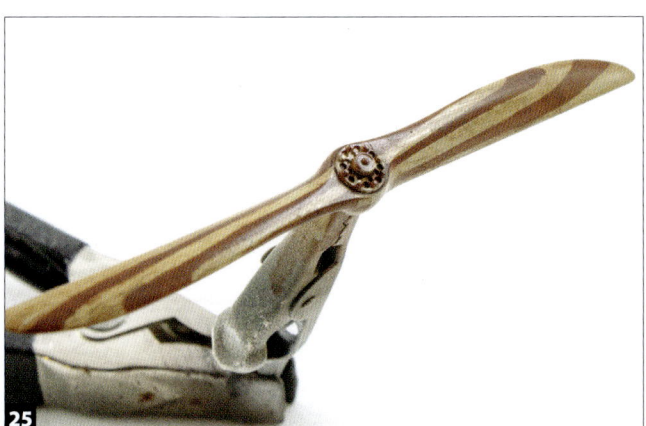

25 Here is the prop with the grain finished.

26 For a bit of extra flare, I coated the prop with Tamiya clear orange (X-26) to deepen the wood color and seal the oil paint.

27 Manufacturer labels and a final semigloss clear coat finished the propeller, which I set aside to dry.

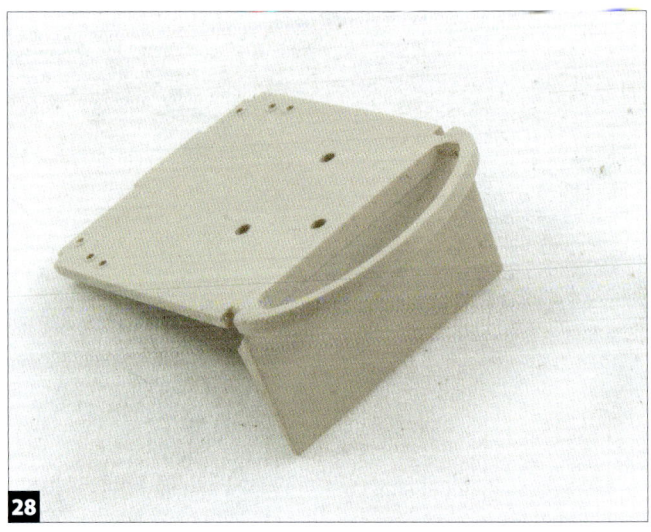

28 The prop wasn't the only wooden part on the Halberstadt, the interior has its share too. I used the same process as the prop starting with a layer of deck tan.

29 Next, oil paint was thinned and applied in the direction of the grain. The consistency of the oil paint is thicker this time to produce more pronounced grain.

30 After waiting at least two hours, I worked the grain into the part with a stiff brush. Get artistic: Twirling the brush adds knots in the wood and using different parts of the brush bristles can add unique effects. Oil paint allows plenty of working time, so your first effort doesn't have to be the end result.

31 The finished wood grain just needs a clear coat to seal it. Remember to vary the grain direction for effect. Differing levels of gloss, as well as clear yellow or clear orange overcoats can add variety as well.

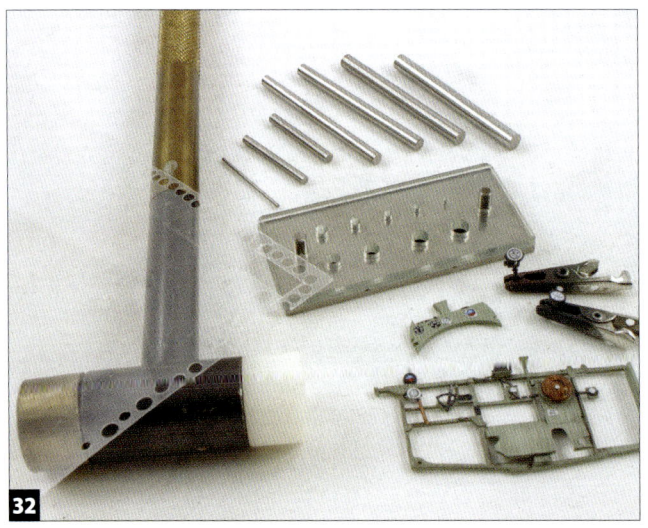

32 Wingnut Wings provides comprehensive decals for its kits, including stenciling and instruments. An easy way to add detail is to complete the instruments with glass using thin, clear plastic discs. I made several using a simple punch-and-die set and .005-inch clear styrene sheet.

33 Select the appropriate punch and give it a sharp tap to create a cover sized to the instrument.

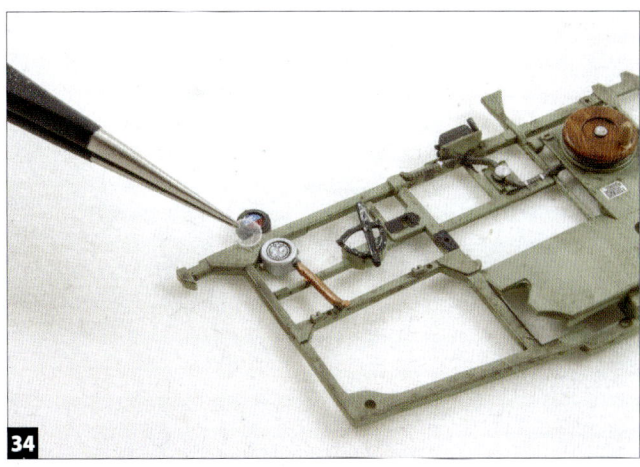

34 Good tweezers allow careful placement of the clear disk using a drop of Pledge Floor Gloss (PFG) or clear part cement. I find this method easy and faster than applying multiple drops of clear gloss on top of the instruments and I think it simulates the detail better.

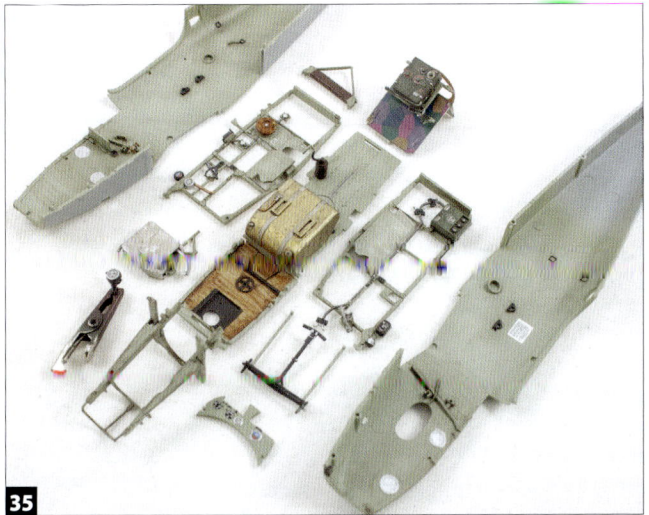

35 One thing about WWI aircraft—their interiors are multicolored! Often, items were left in the natural color of the material from which they were made.

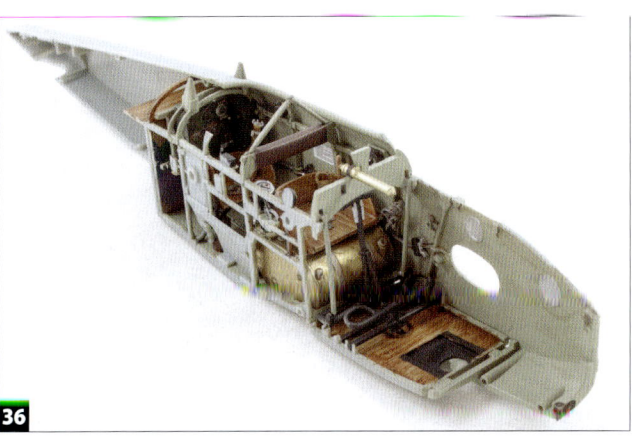

36 Usually, the fit of the interior in a Wingnut kit is so tight that glue is not necessary. That's the case for this kit as well.

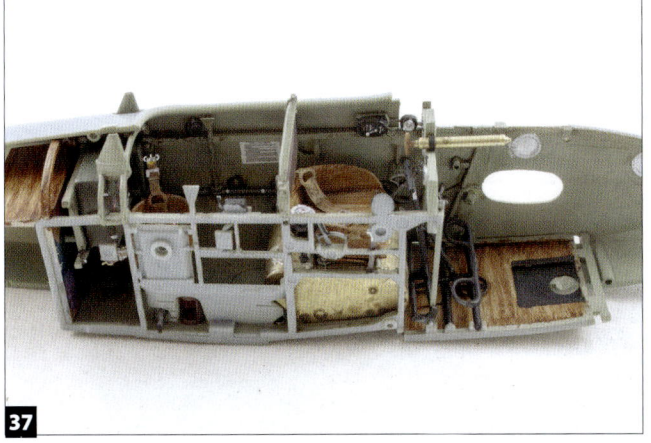

37 Here's another view showing stenciling and other details packed inside. Thanks to precise engineering the fit is perfect—but proceed carefully to make sure everything is aligned before attempting to close the fuselage.

38 The Halberstadt carries a subtly complex paint scheme—sort of a random "cloud" pattern of five colors with an overall stippling of a yellowish tan. Looking like a *Scooby Doo* sea monster, all five colors have been mixed and applied per the clear kit instructions. The pattern is completely random—I was trying to approximate the appearance since it's nearly impossible to discern an actual pattern.

39 I mixed the cloudy yellow stippling color as directed in the instructions. Referring to the hints given on the Wingnut Wings website, I thinned the mix to normal airbrushing consistency, and then dialed the air pressure back until I managed a consistent spatter pattern—about 5 psi in my case. I then carefully overcoated the entire fuselage.

40 The hints on the website worked! You can see the stippled overspray in this close up. It completely changed the look of the model from a vibrant sea monster to a camouflaged hunter.

41 To apply lozenge camouflage, the kit provides one-piece decals that have cutouts for features, like strut attachments, where needed. Notice the footrest panel missing on the decal. Decals must be applied over paint; I use Tamiya gloss black (X-1), which hides minor dings and imperfections in decal application.

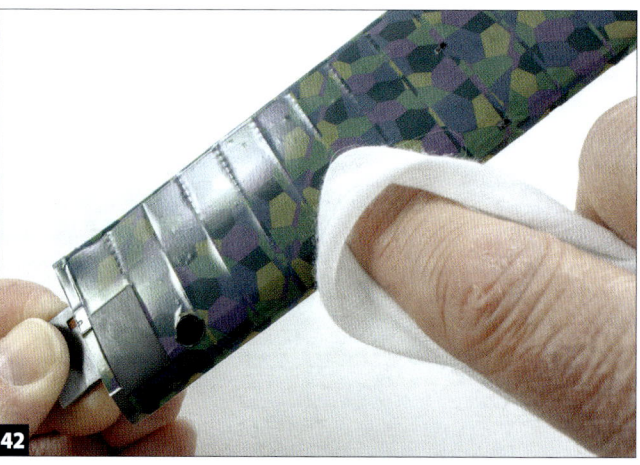

42 The process starts like any other large-area decal application, with careful placement and alignment, followed by pressing excess water from the decal with a soft cloth or cotton swab, taking care not to move it.

43 Instead of decal solvents, I use heat to get the decal to settle into the wing's surface detail. A hair dryer passed across the surface does the trick.

44 If necessary, a little help from a scalpel blade can help settle the decal around the wingtips and other complicated surfaces.

45 Here you can see that the decal has settled pretty well, but it's still a bit rough around the edges.

Another quick hit with the hair dryer conformed the film around the edges.

Then, a touch of decal solvent applied to the ribs and other openings and edges ensure a tight fit and the wing was finished.

All the various subassemblies are complete and ready for final assembly: Building biplanes is marked by many seemingly independent build-paint-assemble sessions. It all comes together at the end though. Then there's rigging …

Rigging is essential for building biplanes. It is not hard with the proper tools and materials, but requires patience and a good rigging diagram, something supplied in the kit instructions. For this model, I used E-Z Line—an appropriately named elastic material marketed by Berkshire Junction for model railroad use. Tools include fine tweezers, a glue applicator, a pair of "squizzers" for trimming, and accelerator for the superglue with an old brush to apply it.

First, I superglue one end of each of the lines to its anchor point. Typically, I start by attaching the lines to the upper wing first, sometimes before it's even attached to the model. Here, I've left the landing gear and rudder off to ease handling and minimize the potential for damage.

To finish the attachment, each line is trimmed about 2mm or so shorter than needed and then stretched to the end point. A drop of glue placed at the attachment point is "kicked" to a fast cure by applying some accelerator fluid to the line using the old brush. Touch the wet line to the attachment point and poof — it's attached.

14 Building Hasegawa's 1/8 scale Fokker Dr.I

A very large scale static display model

BY BOB STEINBRUNN

Every so often we look at our stash and ruminate on what we should be building next. Having had Hasegawa's Museum Model Series Fokker Triplane reposing on a shelf for several years, I thought it was time to attempt the build.

This is a fascinating airplane kit—one of four in the series—and is produced to a very high (and large!) standard. No kit, however excellent, is without its faults of omission and commission, and this one is no exception.

1. This multimedia kit has been around since 2001 and comprises 858 pieces in wood, polystyrene, ABS resin, aluminum, white metal, rubber, and brass. The discriminating modeler striving for more accuracy, like me, can more than double the parts count with scratchbuilt and aftermarket bits.

2. The kit's plastic propeller doesn't really capture the look of the original made from laminated walnut and birch. To replace it, I laminated seven alternating layers of cherry and basswood with Titebond, an aliphatic resin adhesive that can be sanded, drilled, and carved, unlike rubbery white glue.

Big kits lend themselves to lots of detail. Controllable flight surfaces, anyone? Bob Steinbrunn wasn't satisfied with using just what came in the box, adding fine wire for rigging, and lacing his own wire wheels, among other upgrades.

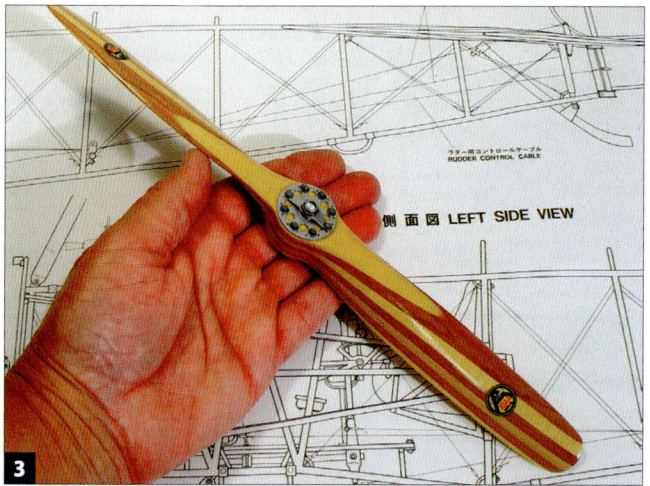

3 Using a sanding drum in a motor tool, I first roughed out the shape. Then I slowly and carefully shaped each blade, creating the twist in them as the pitch decreased toward the tip. The blades needed to be scale thin, but I didn't want to sand through the wood. Three coats of Minwax Helmsman urethane spar varnish, lightly sanded between coats with a fine foam sanding block, created an authentic finish.

4 The prop maker, Axial, stamped each blade with data. I re-created this with decals made on my computer using Microsoft Word and Copperplate Gothic Bold in a 4-point font that closely matches the original. This was printed on clear decal paper, then given several coats of Testors clear gloss lacquer. I also replaced the kit Axial labels with homemade decals made from a photo.

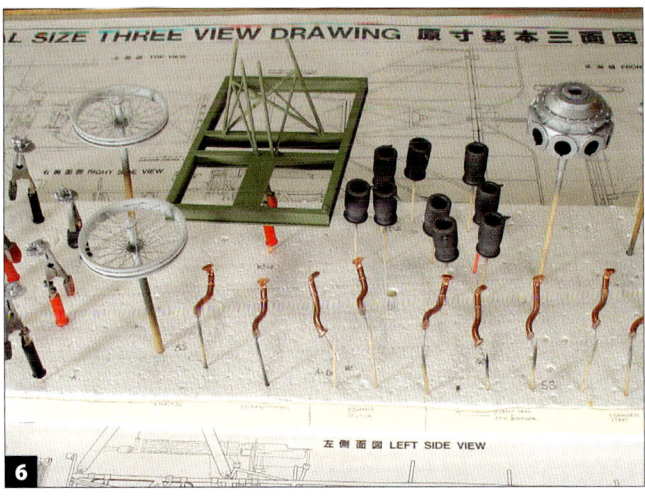

5 When building the engine (left), I used Kagero's CAD images for detail and color reference to ensure accuracy. The instructions show the engine bearing plate being assembled upside-down, with the oil pump on the right side and the magneto on the left, when the opposite is correct; simply spin the plate 180 degrees for the correct position. Having a Williams Brothers 1/8 scale Le Rhone 80 rotary engine (right) on hand was also useful.

6 A large piece of 1-inch-thick styrene foam holds parts for painting and drying. The parts were secured either by small clips attached from the underside where the lack of paint won't show, or by .015-inch steel rod inserted in holes drilled into the part where the attachment won't show. The rods were glued into drilled holes in toothpicks that were pushed into the foam.

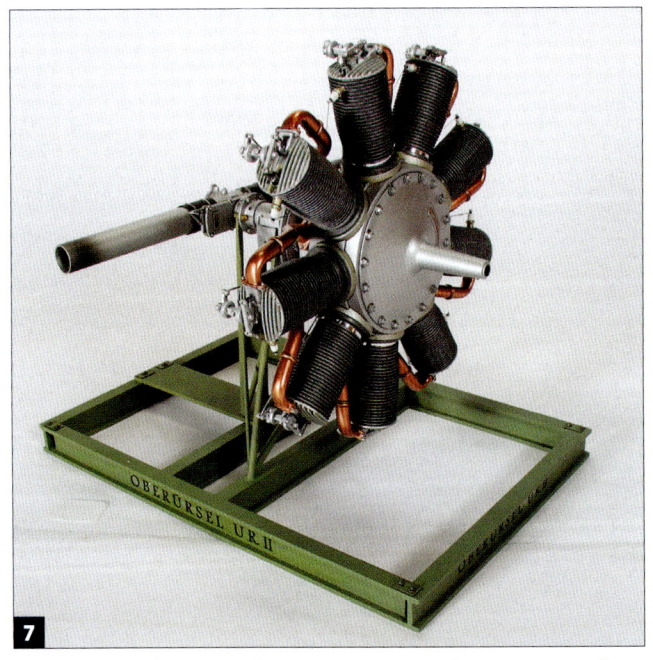

7 The completed Oberürsel engine sits on a maintenance stand made of Plastruct girder and Evergreen styrene rod. The crankcase was airbrushed Spray 'N' Plate Hard Non-Buffing Metalizer, the cylinders were painted with a mixture of Floquil old silver and engine black, the intake pipes with Alclad II copper, and the stand with Floquil ocean green (5-OG), a good match for RAL 6003, also used for the fuselage frames. Silver metallic tape was used to make the clamping rings at the bases of the cylinders.

8 The cylinder heads were airbrushed Floquil old silver and had their thick solid valve springs replaced with HO scale train coupler springs. I made valve pushrods from .019-inch brass rod painted silver to replace the overly thick brass rods in the kit. The spark plug wires were strung with EZ Line.

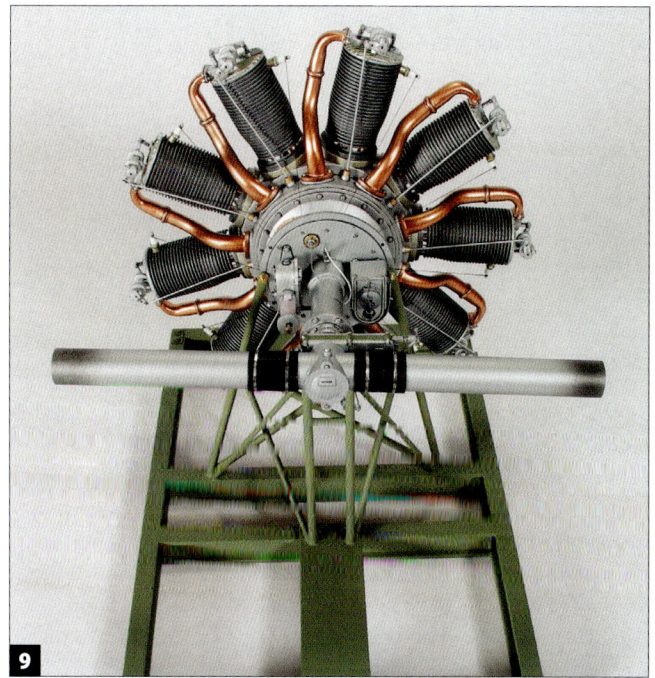

9 The engine air intake tubes were provided with electrical heat shrink to replicate hoses and photo-etched metal (PE) hose clamps from Detail Master secured them. Mig Productions dark wash popped details, including nuts, bolts, and seams.

10 During assembly, the instructions show the engine bearer plate (the circular disk that the forward stand supports are attached to) going in upside-down. It should go in as seen here so the oil pump is on the left looking forward and the magneto is on the right. The ends of the air-intake pipes show an accumulation of castor oil flung from the rotating engine.

11 The small, compact engine was dwarfed by the propeller. The 110-horsepower Oberürsel UR.II engine weighed only 330 pounds wet and was 37.7 inches in diameter, the Axial propeller was 8-feet, 7.15-inches in diameter.

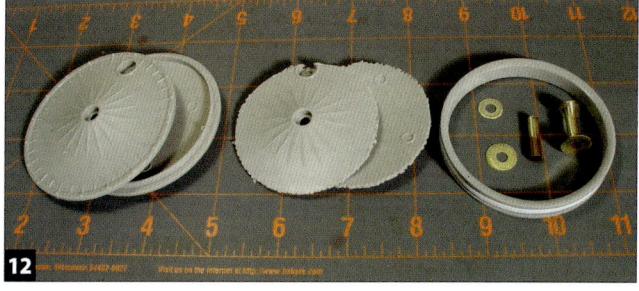

12 To make the wheels more authentic, I removed the solid disc centers by first drilling a series of holes around the inside of the rim, then connecting them with a ½-inch circular saw in a motor tool. After thinning the rims, I cut hub plates from .010-inch brass, then drilled holes to receive .015-inch steel spokes; there are 16 on the outboard face and 32 inboard on each rim. Pieces of ³⁄₁₆-inch brass tube soldered to the hubs will fit over the kit's brass axle.

13 Key to making spoked wheels is to fabricate a jig which locates the rim concentric to the hub. I used .020-inch sheet styrene for the base, then raised four locating mounts built up from .080-inch strip styrene. Stops were glued on the ends of the mounts after careful measuring with a compass. The hub sits on a 5/32-inch brass tube, the same diameter as the axle in the kit, and it stays centered as the rim turns.

14 I cut the spokes from .015-inch K&S steel wire and the spoke nuts from .030-inch brass tube. To keep the rim level and straight, install several spokes on one side of the rim, then the same number on the opposite side. Next several were installed at the 90-degree position, then several at the 270-degree position. After that the gaps in between can be filled in. The inboard row of 32 spokes is now complete.

15 Each finished but unpainted wheel has 107 pieces in it, including a valve stem made of .030-inch brass tube with a .010-inch brass needle valve inside. To accurize the kit hub covers, I removed the four molded-on nuts, then thinned them. They were the final touch on the wheel project that consumed over 30 fun hours.

16 I airbrushed the wheels Alclad II chrome without a gloss black base coat that made the finish look more like steel. The tire was painted medium gray, more authentic for a World War I tire than black. The rubber tires were too flexible and looked floppy, so I cut 3/8-inch widths of black foam and inserted it inside each tire to support them. The spoke locator diagram on the right was drawn up using plane geometry and a compass to accurately mark spoke holes.

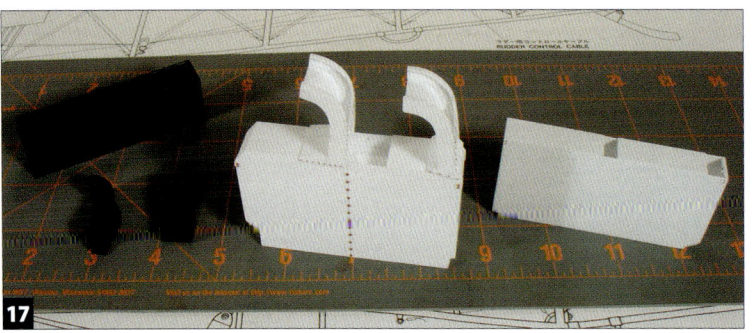

17 The kit's black ammunition container (left) is a too-shallow rectangle without the original's complex shape and has poorly shaped ammo feed chutes. And the kit omitted the container that collected the cloth ammo belts after the rounds were fired and the spent shull casings were ejected. This container was situated forward of the ammunition container in the airframe. I made both items with Evergreen .020-inch sheet styrene detailed with .020- and .040-inch diameter Tichy Train Group rivets.

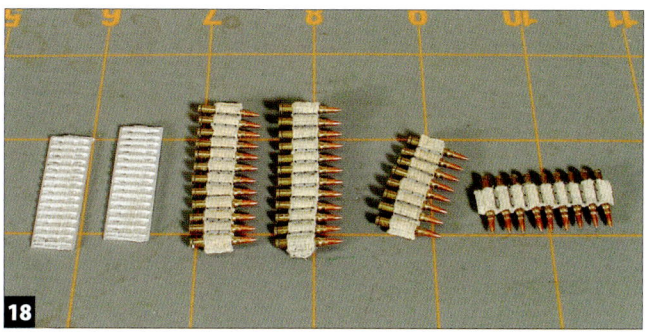

18 The kit provided two metal ammunition belts that lacked detail in this large scale. Plus, the rounds were molded as halves, not circular or three-dimensional as seen on the left. I replaced these with DiD larger caliber ammunition belts; I painted the bullet portion of the round with Testors copper. The belts' metal reinforcing plates between each round were made from .010- x .020-inch strip styrene with three rivets added with a technical drawing pen.

19 I needed 64 turnbuckles to rig the fuselage framing as well as the few external runs. After cutting the bodies from .040-inch brass tube, I tapered the end of each one. The rings at each end were made up from a single piece of .015-inch stainless-steel wire. I used round-nose pliers with one tip ground down to a smaller diameter to create a small ring. First, one ring was shaped, then the wire was threaded through the tube, and the opposite ring shaped. I painted the wire with Testors silver after filling the gaps at the end with superglue. I hoped 64 turnbuckles was enough since they consumed 18 hours of mind-numbing work in a Zen-like trance that I'm not anxious to repeat.

20 Here's the frame painted with Floquil 5-0 ocean green, with a bungee-sprung tailskid added. I cut the wood floor into two sections before installing it and the control stick, rudder bars, and hanging scratchbuilt ammunition container. I loosely strung control cables for the rudder, ailerons, and elevators with Beadalon .018-inch bright beading wire, which has 49 strands covered with an extremely thin transparent nylon. It is easy to work with using superglue, and looks exactly like full-size control cable.

21 I dressed up the fuel tank with two rows of Tichy .020-inch styrene rivets. A second filler neck and cap has been added for the castor-oil section. I thinned the metal filler cap and added proper finger grips, and added a valve and sump on the bottom, mounting flanges with rivets, and a fuel-gauge mount in the center with Tichy bolts and standpipe.

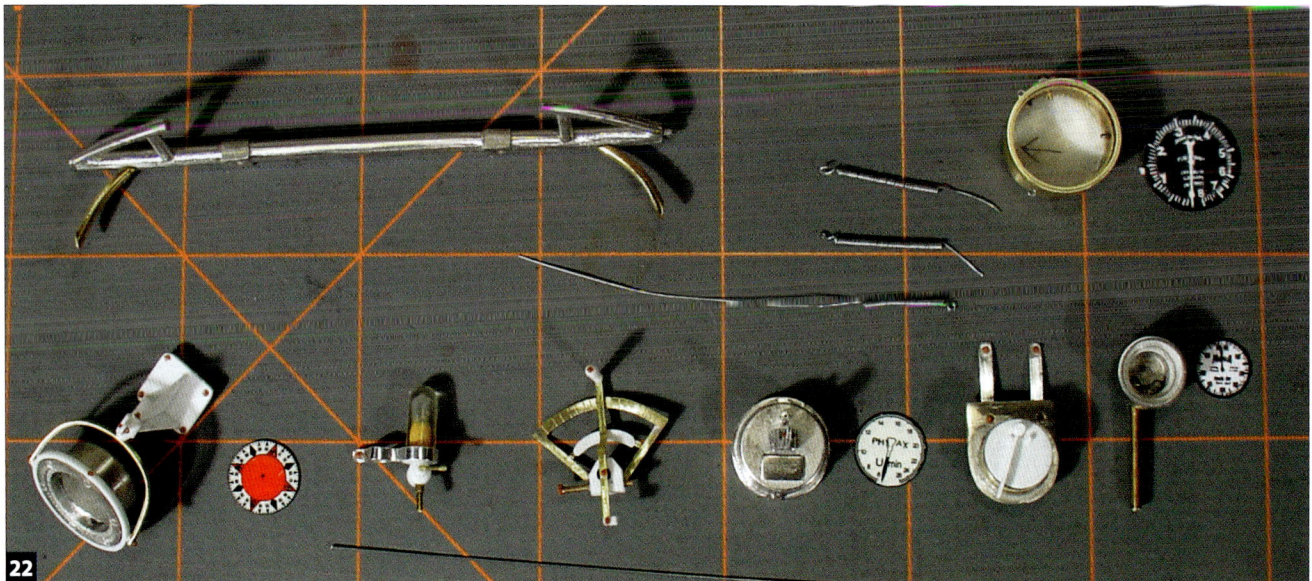

22

Here's an assortment of cockpit instruments and devices. Top row: a cross member with its solid triangular aft supports replaced with brass rod; a scratchbuilt altimeter made from two sizes of brass tube and suspension springs made from .010-inch wire wrapped around a .015-inch mandrel. On the right is the altimeter's face copied from the internet, printed to size, and touched up with black and white paint. Lower row: the compass with scratchbuilt mount and gimbals and its kit dial. Next is an oil pulsator made from a clear handle of an eye-shadow applicator, brass tubing, and aluminum sheet. It was drilled out and painted inside to depict the castor oil level.

Next is the scratchbuilt engine fuel mixture regulator quadrant, made from brass strip and styrene rod that replaced the inaccurate cast-metal kit part. To the right is a tachometer with an instrument face taken from the internet. To its right is the magneto switch, which the kit calls a 'thermometer'. The mount was rounded on the bottom, and the housing was made from brass tubing and sheet styrene with a strip styrene handle. Next is the fuel gauge, not given in the kit, but one unused instrument case in the kit was utilized to make this. The instrument face came from the internet, printed, sized, and touched up with black paint.

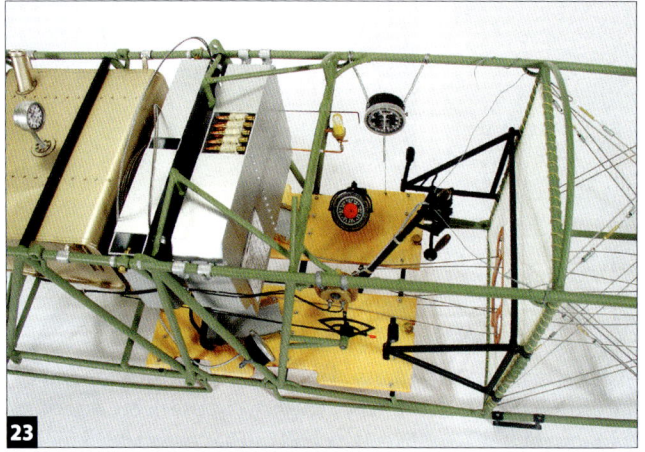

23

A view of the right side of the cockpit showing the altimeter suspended from springs. To the left of it sits the oil pulsator, and above that is the emergency fuel shut-off handle. Below these sits the compass on its scratchbuilt mount. On the far left sits the scratchbuilt fuel gauge mounted on top of the fuel tank. Behind the seat mount is a fabric bulkhead laced to the framework that prevented the rear fuselage fabric from being blown out by the air blowing into the cockpit. This was made from a section of a faded tan bed sheet with reinforcing strips glued around its perimeter. Thin wood veneer was applied to both sides to replicate the leather protector which has the control cables for the elevators and rudder running through it.

24

The left side of the cockpit with the Bosch magneto switch at the top, and the fuel regulator quadrant with control rods leading forward to the fuel tank valve. To the right of this is the tachometer.

When rigging the fuselage, I started with the center frames, then the upper, lower, and side frames in that order, and alternating from side to side working from front to rear to avoid twisting the fuselage. Working in this manner keeps equal tension on every part of the framework. I rigged the aircraft with the same Beadalon .018-inch wire I used for the control lines.

A close-up view of the rigging illustrating how realistic the Beadalon beading wire looks. It doubles back through the ends of the scratchbuilt turnbuckles and was locked in place with a touch of superglue. The large coil of wires at the rear of the frame are control cables for the rudder and elevators.

Diverging from the instructions, I added the landing gear at this stage. The aluminum firewall was bolted on after I airbrushed the outer edge red. It and the landing gear struts were attached with brass bolts, washers, and nuts from Micro Fasteners. The struts were attached to the fuselage on the real aircraft with ball and socket joints. Using the hex-head bolts is artistic license and certainly is more realistic and less obtrusive than the unauthentic and unappealing large slotted machine screws and nuts the kit provided for most attachments.

I detailed the axle wing ribs with extra pieces of .010-inch basswood and bored out fore and aft lightening holes. The kit's wooden axle housing should represent metal, so I clad it with .010-inch sheet styrene with brass angles along the upper fore and aft edges. Over 100 Tichy .020-inch styrene rivets were superglued on based on references before the axle box was airbrushed with Alclad II aluminum. I replaced the kit's wood dowel traverse braces with K&S ⅛-inch aluminum tube.

This rear view of the axle wing shows the extra wood strips detailing the ribs. A sharp draftsman's pencil was used to lightly outline the structural details, then the wood was given a brushed-on coat of polyurethane varnish colored with a bit of Floquil Daylight orange for a warm honey color. As molded, the lower bracing wire attachments were semicircular chunks at the base of the struts. I replaced them with two steel wire rings blended into the struts with J-B Weld. The white bungee shock cord provided in the kit is excellent; realistic and functional.

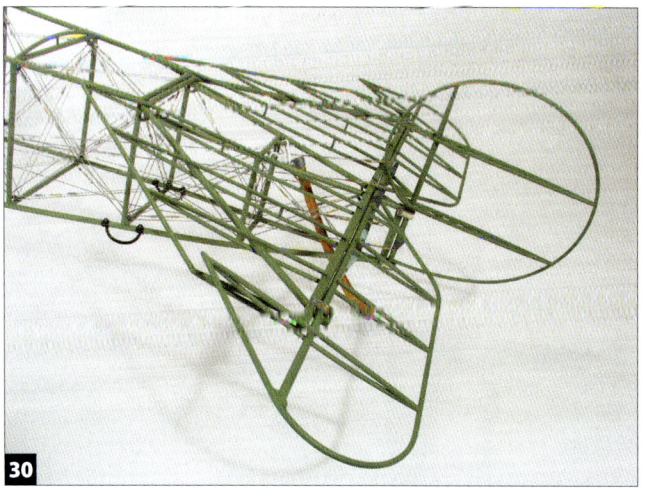

30 After cleaning up and priming the horizontal stabilizer, elevators, and rudder, I airbrushed them with 5-O ocean green. The elevator hinges and hinge housings were cut down since they were oversized and caused a sloppy fit. I detailed them with .010-inch brass strip and Tichy bolts, then attached the control cables with scratchbuilt turnbuckles and swages. Moving the control column moves the control surfaces. Great fun!

31 I formed the aluminum seat back around a paint bottle and attached it to the aluminum seat pan, then painted the seat cushion with Floquil mud followed by burnt umber artist oils to give it a leather look. A thin piece of mahogany was shaped to the seat pan under the cushion, varnished, and two mounting brackets for the seat belts were bent to shape from brass rod and cemented into holes drilled in the mahogany. The seat belts were made from Tamiya masking tape painted Floquil panzer yellow, then grimy brown pastel dust was brushed over them to give them a dirty, worn look. Stitching on the belts was created with a sharp draftsman's pencil and the metal buckles were cut from .010-inch sheet brass and filed to shape. I slit a piece of USB cable lengthwise and removed the wires, then slipped it along the edge of the seat back and painted it with tan acrylic and two coats of burnt umber oils.

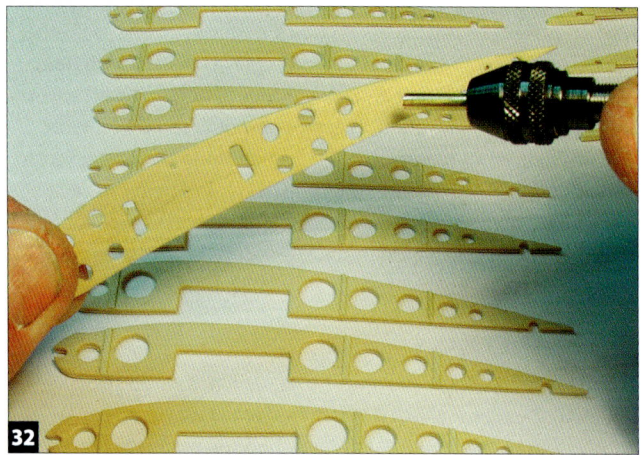

32 The main wing ribs lack the aft-most lightening hole, and the wingtip ribs had none. Fearing that drilling would split the wood, I made a hole cutter from a section of 1/8-inch brass tube. The inside edge was chamfered with a No. 11 blade to create a sharp circular edge, then a cutting disc in a motor tool cut teeth around the perimeter. In this photo I'm finishing up one wingtip rib. I added vertical stiffeners to each rib with .015-inch strips of basswood.

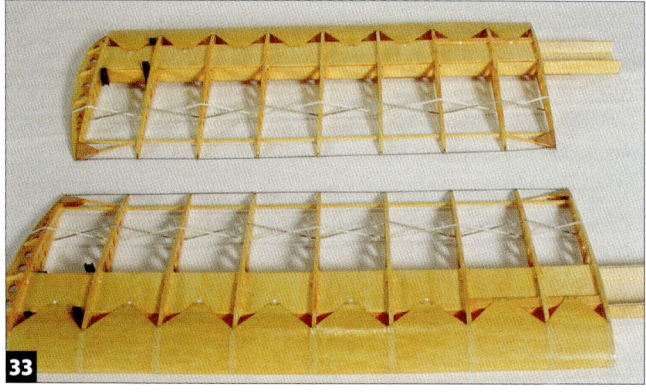

33 I spent a month completing the two sections of the lower wing. The saw-tooth leading edges were fashioned from .010-inch birch veneer from realwoodpaper.com and have reinforcing tape over the rib noses made from 3M Fineline tape. I also added wood stiffeners, gussets, angles, and reinforcements before painting the parts with polyurethane varnish tinted with Floquil Daylight orange.

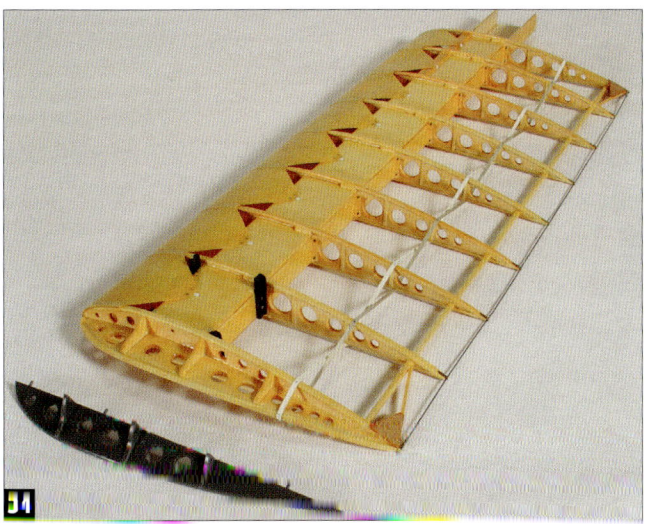

34 The plastic kit end ribs needed to be painted to look like wood. Instead, I cut new ribs from excess wood stock in the kit, then steam-bent them to an airfoil shape by wetting them with water, then used a soldering iron with a wood-bending tip to steam them to the proper curvature. The six gussets on each rib were made from .070-inch basswood.

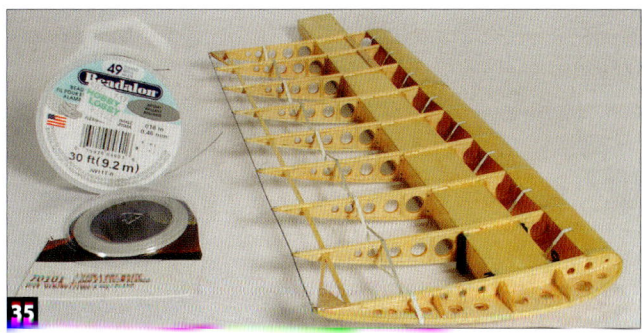

35 On the real Dr 1, white cloth strips secured the plywood leading edge cladding under the wing and reinforced the ribs to prevent them twisting. The kit provided black crinkle tape, so I replaced it with 3M 1/16-inch x 40-foot white tape (No. 70101). I also replaced the kit's scalloped wood trailing edge with an authentic wire trailing edge made from Beadalon .018-inch beading wire held to each rib with annealed .010- x .030-inch brass strips.

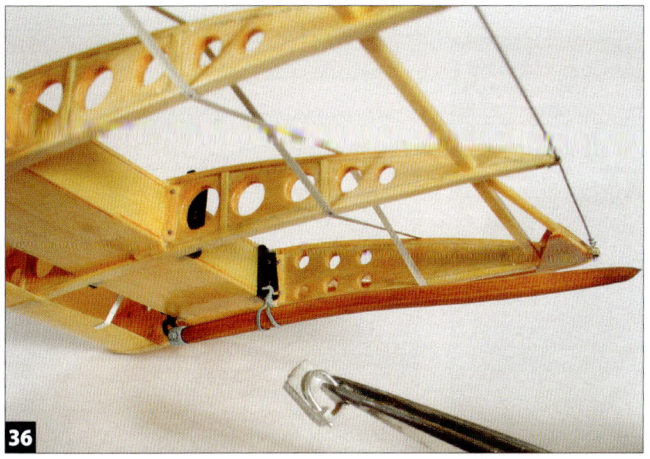

36 After carving the wingtip skids to shape, I introduced a gentle S curve with the wood-burning tip in a soldering iron. The skids were stained with burnt umber artist oils. I cut off the unrealistic white-metal rear bracket saving the upper portion. Two .010 x .030-inch annealed brass strips were formed into a cradle, superglued to the each of the top sections and the joint reinforced with a dab of J-B Weld. The discarded portion of the white metal bracket is shown below.

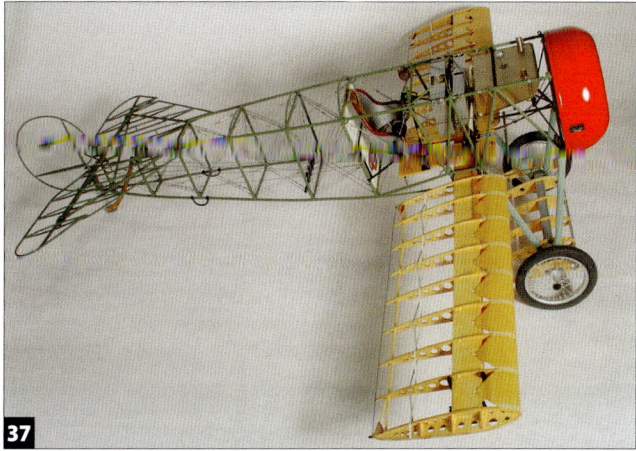

37 Lower wing on, I was ready to start on the middle wing. I worked in reverse of the instructions, which start with the upper wing. In terms of complexity, the lower wing is the simplest and any mistakes will be less obvious. By the time I got to the upper wing—the most difficult of the three since it has the complexity of the ailerons—my skills and experience were up to the task. Coincidentally, this sequence matches that used to build the full-size fighter.

38 I removed the engine from its display stand and mounted it on the airframe. The carburetor intake pipes, carburetor, and adapter collar were removed from the back, and the mounting plate was superglued to the front of the aluminum firewall from the front. Then the other components were threaded into the airframe and glued to the engine from behind.

39 Then, I wired and plumbed the engine, with a fuel line from the tank to the carburetor, an oil line from the oil section of the tank to the oil pump, a metal coil-wound tachometer cable from the tach to the magneto, and two electrical wires from the magneto switch in the cockpit to the magneto and engine mounting plate.

40 This right-side view shows the oil line from the oil pulsator in the cockpit running to the oil pump, a metal coil-wound cable from the gun triggers in the cockpit to the synchronization fitting on the magneto, the rod connecting the emergency fuel shut-off lever in the cockpit with the carburetor linkage, and two metal coil-wound machine gun synchronization cables from the magneto fittings leading back to the cockpit to be later attached to the underside of the machine gun breeches. The loose cables aft of the fuel/oil tank will be connected to the ailerons later on.

41 The cowling snapped on without needing the obtrusive kit-supplied screws thanks to three styrene nubs inside that engage female fittings on the firewall. I filled the holes in the cowling with J-B Weld sanded smooth, then primed and painted it. The propeller has an internal brass strip acting as a key which engages a slot in the engine crankcase nose shaft so that when the propeller is turned the engine turns with it as well.

42
The wing ties required some work. (They were not really interplane struts since they offered no structural support. Rather they "tied" the wings together to keep them from oscillating up and down under aerodynamic loads.) I sanded the laminated wood ties smooth, then, using a cut-off wheel in a motor tool, cut a groove into their upper and lower edges to accommodate the brass pins that attach the ties and the wing. I folded the fittings in half with a 5-Speed Hold & Fold, then, using a piece of .065-inch brass sheet and the nylon end of a jeweler's hammer, I squared the ends of the brass fittings. The full-size fittings were solid on their fore and aft edges, so these openings in the model fittings will be filled with J-B Weld.

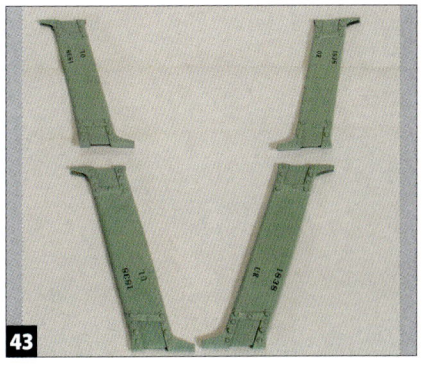

43
The wing ties were airbrushed, then detailed with four additional rivets on the fittings since the kit's stamped brass pieces had too few. These extras came from Tichy .070 inch styrene rivets. The wing ties were labeled with Woodland Scenics dry transfer lettering for their position on the aircraft: OL = Oben Links (upper left); UL = Unten Links (lower left); OR = Oben Rechts (upper right); OL = Unten Rechts (lower right), and the serial number which was #1838.

44
The middle wing was mounted and is awaiting installation of the lower wing ties. The loose cables are for the ailerons on the upper wing and the cabane strut braces.

45
The aluminum cabane struts required filing, sanding, and polishing to remove their length-wise striations. I accurized the upper attachments, removing a large block from between the collars for the screws with a steel cutter in a motor tool. The aircraft serial number appeared on the forward cabane strut and more dry-transfer lettering was used here.

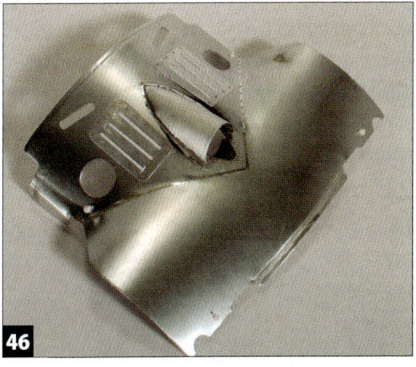

46
To detail the aluminum fairing between the engine and cockpit, I drilled and filed a hole for the oil filler on the right side across from the fuel filler opening. Using .005-inch thick aluminum foil, .010- x .030-inch styrene strips for stiffeners, and Tichy .020-inch styrene rivets, I made two blast plates to fit under the machine-gun muzzles. To replace the kit's undersized white-metal fuel gauge hood, I used a drill and steel cutters to open a tear-drop shaped opening. Aluminum foil was used to make the new hood, which was formed around a small flashlight to shape.

I still wasn't satisfied with the Axial logo on the propeller. Some were cream, but further research showed most logos were black and white. I found a large high-resolution image on the internet and copied it to a Word document. I reduced it to 15mm in diameter, and made multiple copies on one row. I printed this on white decal paper with an inkjet printer. After allowing a day for the ink to dry, I sprayed three light coats of Testors Dullcote from an aerosol can. I used light coats to ensure the ink would not run or craze. The decals were applied over the cream colored ones. Walthers Solvaset was used lightly, and when dry the flat finish decals were given a gloss coat. The new decals are clear and sharp and I'm finally happy. And so it goes with a long-term model. As your skills improve over the months or years, you find you aren't entirely happy with things you've done earlier, so you go back and re-do them. This adds time, of course, but it also builds satisfaction in your work.

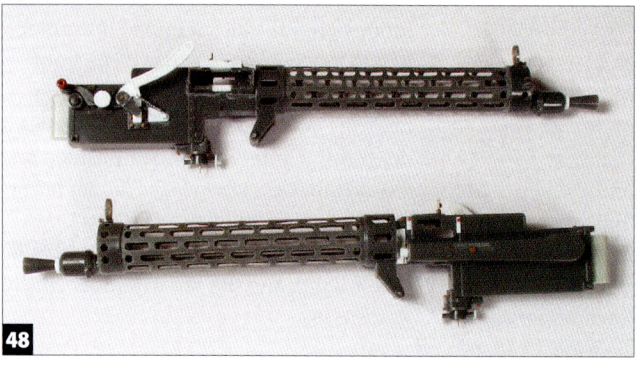

My extensive improvements to the two Spandau machine guns include: Tichy nuts and bolts; brass rear sight, thinned front ring sight with .008-inch brass crosshairs; drilled out muzzle booster with new barrel and nut; and the cocking handle was reconfigured to the later type with a Kingstrom device. The last involved a scratchbuilt extra handle with .010 x .020-inch edging, a toothed-gear segment, and a toothed gear on the cocking handle end. The simple blob on the end of the cocking handle was cut off and replaced with a .040-inch shaft with a bead on the end, which is much more realistic. There are 192 pieces in the two guns.

I airbrushed the guns with a mix of 85 percent Floquil engine black and 15 percent Floquil dark blue for a blued finish. Then, I rubbed the weapons with graphite dust for a realistic gunmetal. Colour Shapers, a handle tipped with a rubbery compound, are perfect for applying powders like graphite or pastels.

I painted and installed the fuselage top deck; the kit's wooden side panel were replaced with .010-inch aluminum as they were metal on the real aircraft. All three panels have turn fasteners made from punched styrene discs and styrene rod. Then, I attached the guns and ammunition feed chutes. Note the scratchbuilt windscreen made from clear acetate, brass angle, strip styrene, and Tichy nuts and rivets.

The coaming was painted with Tamiya desert sand acrylic, then brushed with burnt umber and raw sienna oil paints. Rubbing this with a cloth after the paint dried produced a distressed and worn leather appearance. I made the two-piece turtledeck with .010-inch Real Wood Paper and it extends farther aft than the kit's paper-backed wood part. The cabane struts were fitted without glue; they'll be secured when the top wing is attached.

A made the cowling hold-down cable with Beadalon wire and its anchor tab with .010-inch brass sheet drilled out to receive a 00-72 brass bolt. After cutting the hex head off that bolt, I squeezed the end with pliers to produce an elliptical flat, which I drilled out to accommodate the cable; a nut and washer secure the other end. Four tabs with Tichy bolts and strip styrene hold the cable in place. Tichy .020-inch styrene rivets detail the cowl.

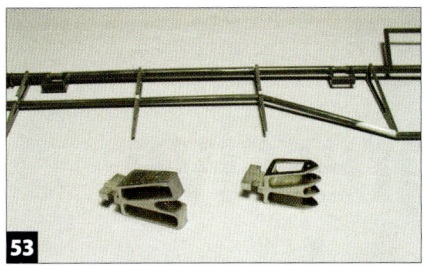

53 Since I was not going to use the scalloped-edge wood pieces for the aileron trailing edges, strip and half-round styrene filled the notches to attach it. Real wire trailing edges will be added later. The aileron pulley brackets were rather clunky, so I reshaped them with a cutting disc in a motor tool, files, and sanding strips, and carved a lightening rectangle top and bottom.

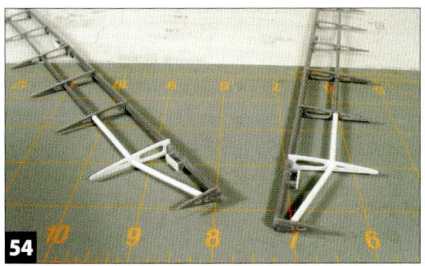

54 The ailerons were converted from the kit's early style—tapered on the inboard trailing edge—to the later version by replacing the short rib, second from the inboard end, with a longer one matching the other aileron ribs. After attaching the rib to the aileron leading edge, styrene rod replaced the kit spar. I trimmed the rectangular hinge fittings and capped the rear end of the hinge box with .020-inch sheet styrene.

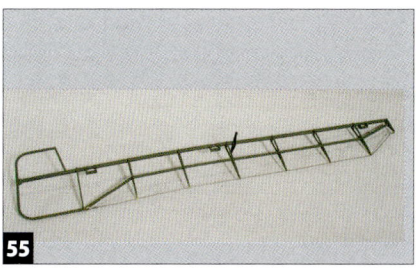

55 Here's the completed port aileron with its control horn, wire trailing edge, and rib clips holding the wire in place. Each clip has a Tichy .020-inch rivet on the top and bottom to represent the clip's fastener.

56 In this close-up of the hardware involved in the trailing edge, you can see how the Beadalon .018-inch 49-strand Teflon-coated wire shows its strands. Brass strip was fashioned into end and rib clips, and .010-inch beading wire was used to make the coil fasteners at the ends of the wire.

57 The top wing is now on and it seems that the model has outgrown my small photography booth. This is a good illustration that large models require large display spaces.

58 Once the aileron pulleys and brackets were in place, I threaded the Beadalon control cables from the fuselage, up along the wings out to the tip. The cables will be tensioned once the ailerons are installed and will move differentially with control column lateral movement.

A left rear view of the aircraft at Land O' Lakes Aerodrome, northern Wisconsin.

15 Going aggressive with an Eagle

Improving Tamiya's 1/32 scale F-15

BY CHUCK SAWYER

Chuck Sawyer re-scribed every panel line, and added many panel lines that were missing. He also placed a few thousand new rivets and fasteners to make the surface detail really pop, all with the goal to make the most accurate F-15C he could.

I love the F-15 Eagle, but my favorite versions were the F-15Cs and F-15Ds painted in desert brown or Flanker blue camouflage of the 65th Aggressor Squadron at Nellis AFB. Sadly, this squadron was disbanded on Sept. 26, 2014, after almost a decade of service, as were all aggressor F-15s in the USAF. Thankfully, I have hundreds of pics of these jets when they were in service, having attended many Aviation Nation airshows at Nellis each November. Most of my photos are of AF800010, an F-15C painted in Flanker blue that always seemed to be on the tarmac.

I started with Tamiya's 1/32 scale kit (No. 60304). It's pretty good for a 1994 vintage kit, although there are some fit problems and it shares many parts and details with Tamiya's earlier F-15E (No. 60302) some of which are wrong for an F-15C.

I set out to fix these issues as well as go all out with many, many aftermarket parts, especially for the cockpit and engines. Armed with my own photographs and the *Modern Eagle Guide, 2nd Edition* by Jake Melampy (Reid Air, ISBN 978-0-9888529-5-2), I spent 22 months and several hundred hours' work making it as accurate as possible. I used Testors Model Master enamels unless otherwise stated.

AFTERMARKET KITS
In most cases, Chuck only used a few parts from each kit:
Aires F-15C Resin Cockpit Set (Late), No. 2063
Avionix F-15C Resin Cockpit Set, No. AV32023
Wolfpack F-15C Update Set, No. WP32025
Wolfpack ELTA 8222 ECM Pod Set, No. WP32053
Eduard F-15C Eagle PE Set, No. 32056
Eduard F-15E Ejection Seat PE Set, No. 32601
Eduard F-15E Strike Eagle Exterior PE Set, No. 32169
GT Resin F-15 Seamless Intake Set, No. GTR32003
GT Resin F-15 Seamless Exhaust Set
GT Resin F-15 Antenna and Vent Set, No. GTR32015
GT Resin F-15C Wheel/Tire Set
Two Mikes F-15 Corrected Exhaust Nozzles, No. 32014
Zactomodels AIM-9X Sidewinder Set
AMS Resin ACMI Pod, No. AMS32094
Master Brass M61 Vulcan Gun, No. AM-32-029
Archer Resin Decal Rivets
Afterburner Aggressor Eagles Decals, No. 48-007 (Includes 1/32 decals)
Speed Hunter Graphics, Big Scale Eagles Decals, No. 32007
AirScaleModern Cockpit Instruments, Data Plate and Warning Decals, No. AS32 DAN, HAC

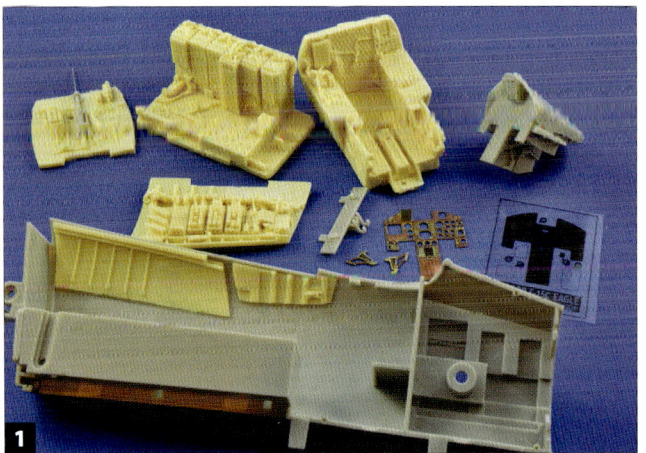

1 The kit cockpit is fairly crude, so I used the best parts from both Avionix (No. AV32023) and Aires (No. 2063) resin cockpits. Overall, the yellow Avionix parts had more detail, but the Aires instrument panel and other small details (gray and metal) were superior, so I used those.

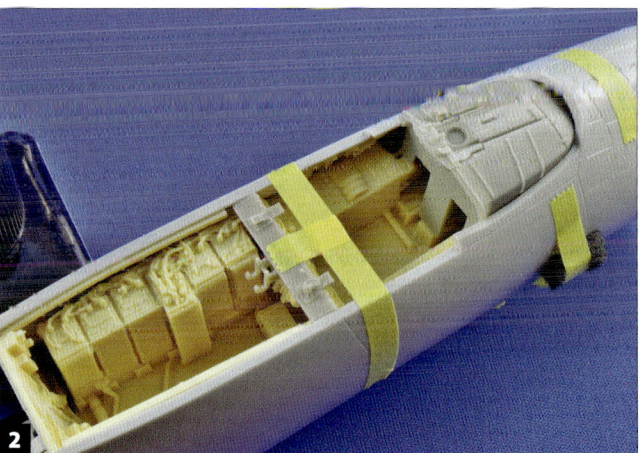

2 With lots of sanding, trimming, and dry-fitting with the kit fuselage halves, the two resin cockpit kits come together fairly well.

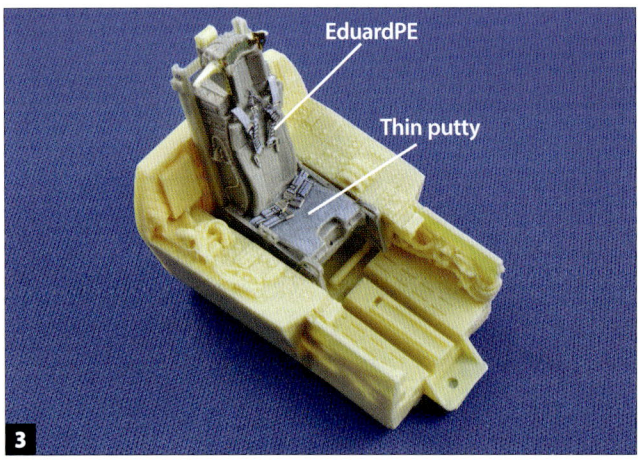

3 I used the Aires ejection seat embellished with a few Avionix parts and Eduard photo-etched (PE) seat belts (No. 32538), which are nicely detailed and already painted. To replicate the sheepskin seat covering, I used thinned putty dabbed on with a cotton swab to add texture.

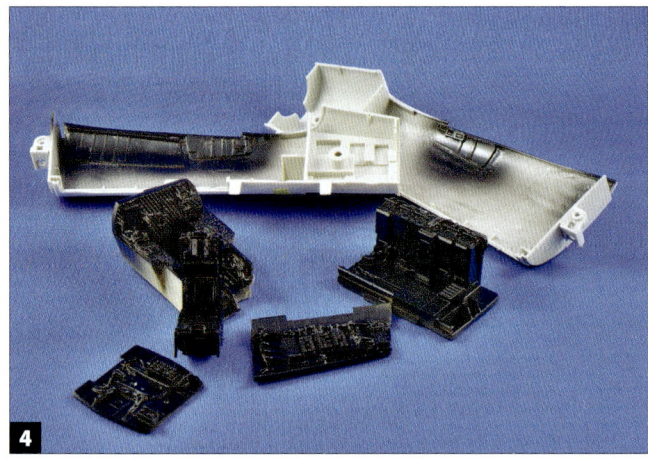

4 After assembly, all cockpit pieces were base-coated with gloss black lacquer that adds shading in tight areas and allows easy cleanup of subsequent detail painting.

5 I masked the areas to remain black with tape and Microscale Micro Mask solution.

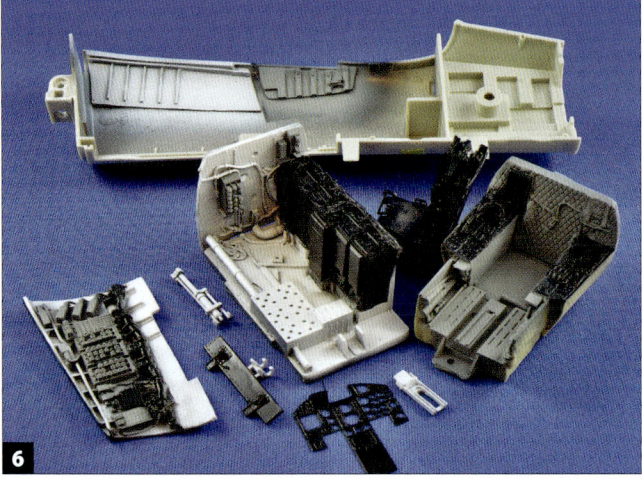

6 Them, I airbrushed the cockpit with FS36321 dark gull gray (No. 1740). Behind the seat in bay 5, my 1980 vintage jet was white.

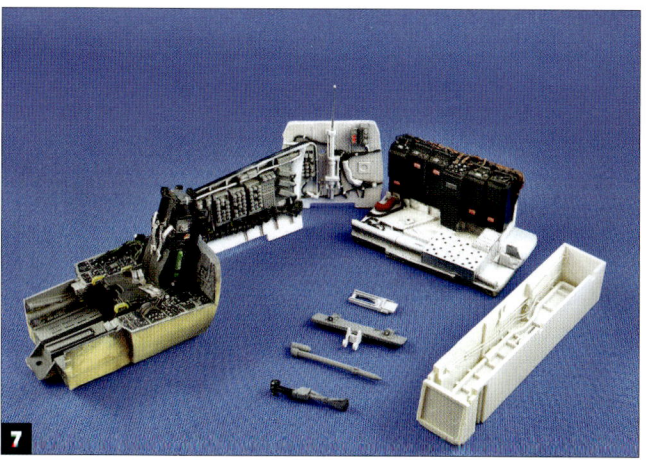

7 Fine details were picked out with a paintbrush, then wiring and placard decals were added and everything was sprayed with a clear flat to knock down the shine.

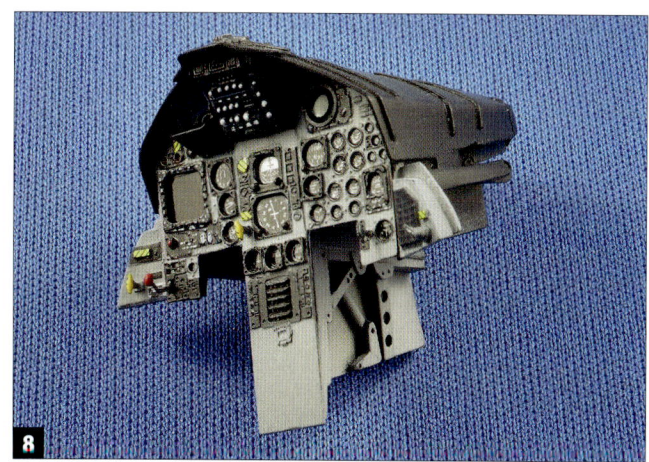

8 After painting the Aires instrument panel, I detailed it with tiny handles and placard decals from AirScale (No. AS32DAN and AS32IIAC).

9 For the HUD display, I attached iridescent film to the plastic glass parts using Pledge Floor Gloss (PFG) as an adhesive.

10 With the cockpit complete, it was ready to be glued into the front fuselage.

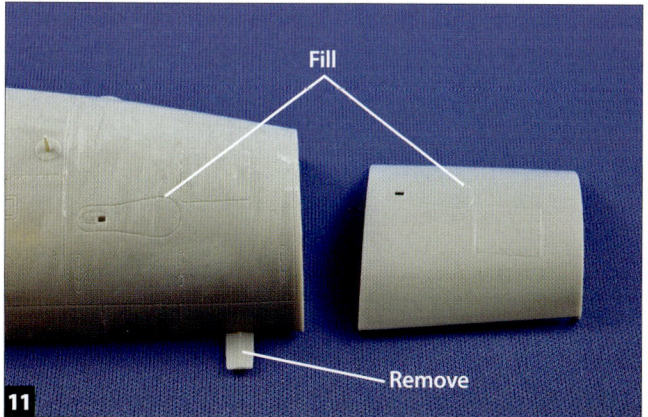

11 The front fuselage has a large oval panel line surrounding the pitot tube attachment, which is the outline of a cover that is placed over this tube when the aircraft is parked—fill it. Also remove the antenna forward and below the panel. Note: F-15Cs have a variety of antennas that vary from jet to jet and change over time, so check your references!

12 As I modified fuselage detail, I used black Tamiya Panel Line Accent Color to check my work. This wash allowed me to see minute surface detail I added, as well as ensure that flaws are totally removed, like the pitot tube surround that I filled with superglue and sanded smooth.

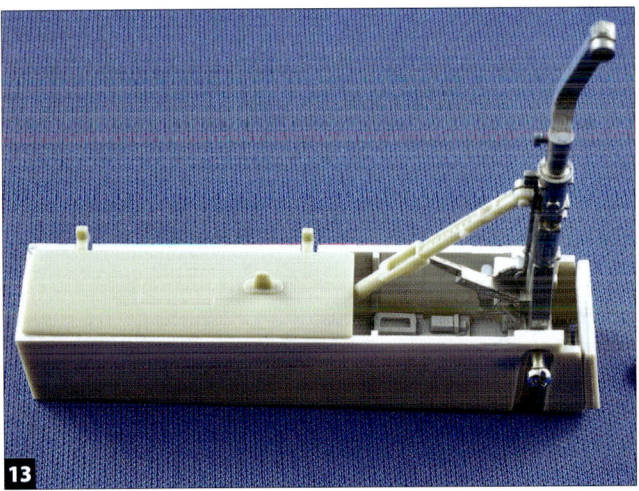

13 Before the front fuselage halves are joined, the nose gear bay must be inserted, as well as the front landing gear, which is attached using a screw from the side.

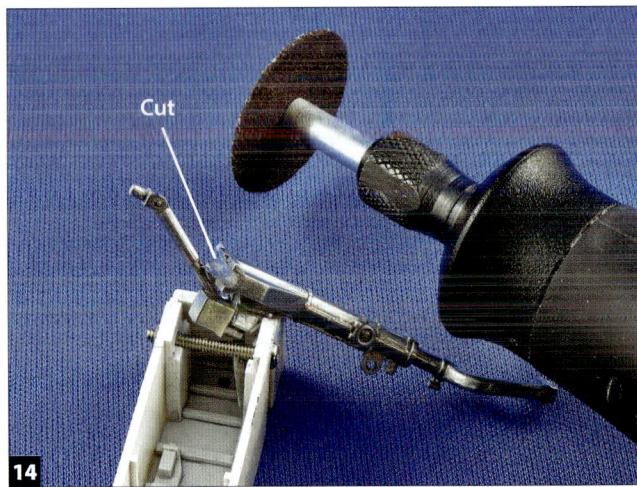

14 Since the front landing gear leg will always be in the way during construction and painting, I cut the mounting hole in the gear in half. That allowed the gear to be glued onto the screw at the end of the build.

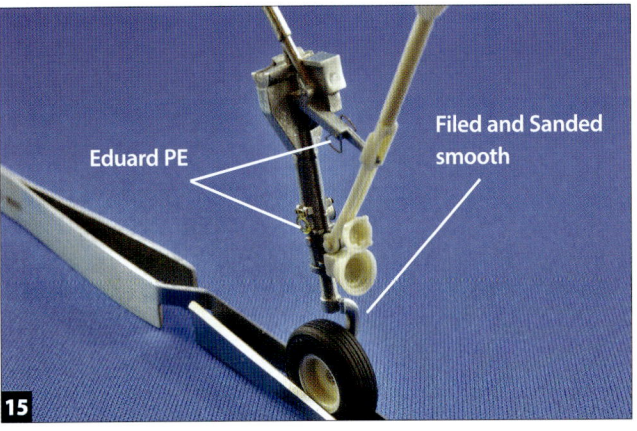

15 All of the metal landing gear is rough and needs to be cleaned up. The fork on the front gear is square like the F-15E, so it needs to be filed to a round shape instead to match the C. Fine details were added using Eduard PE.

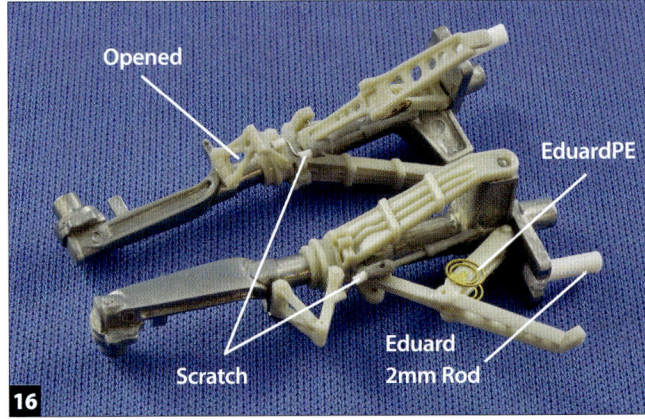

16 The main landing gear received Eduard PE (No. 32169) and scratchbuilt details. I glued a styrene rod in the spot where a screw would normally be inserted to attach the leg to the fuselage. This way, the main gear could be glued instead, eliminating an unsightly screw head at the end of the build.

17 After painting, placard decals were applied, as well as some hydraulic lines. For the wheels and tires, I used the GT Resin set (No. 32022), which are much more accurate than the kit wheels.

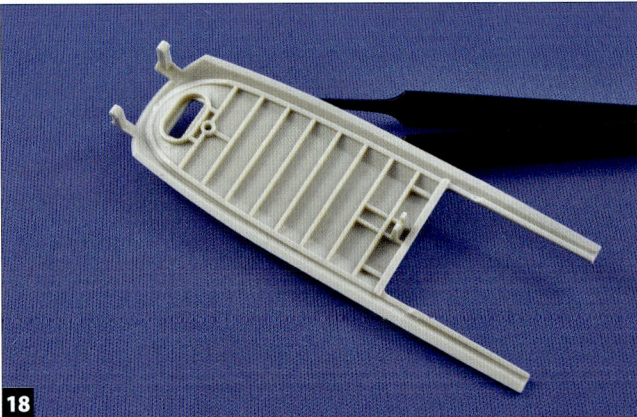

18 The bottom of the kit canopy frame is fairly plain, lacks detail, and has several ejector-pin marks. So I cut off the molded cross braces and sanded the area smooth to remove the pin marks.

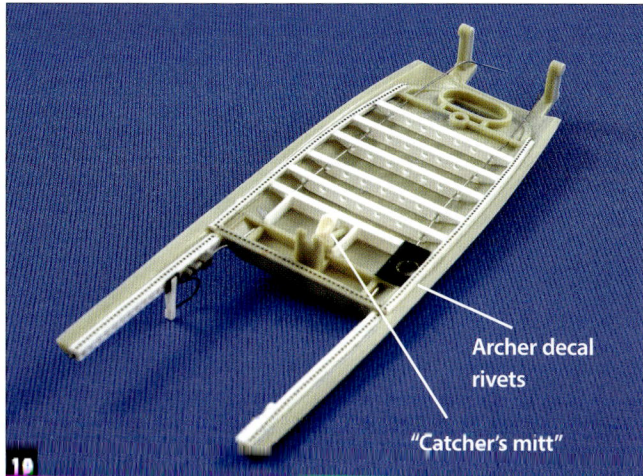

19 I replaced the braces with styrene I-beam detailed with drilled holes; Archer resin rivet decals dress the outer frame. I also created a "catcher's mitt" circular recess that attaches to a spear-like canopy ejection device behind the seat.

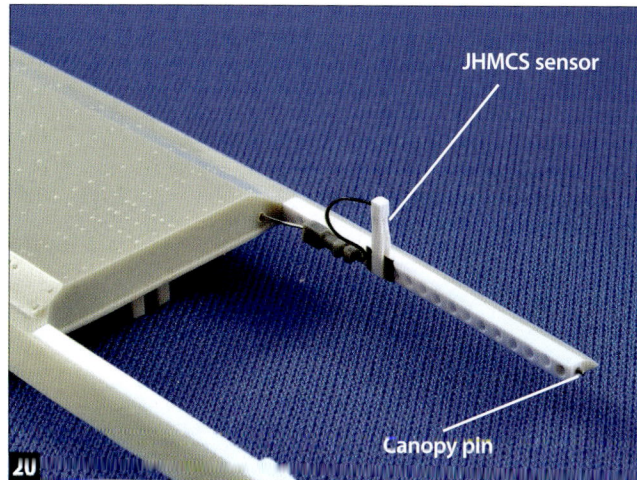

20 Topside, the edges of the canopy were trimmed and replaced with square styrene with drilled holes and canopy pins. On the left side, I added a Joint Helmet Mounted Cuing System (JHMCS) sensor—required for the deployment of AIM-9X Sidewinders made from 1.5mm styrene I-beam.

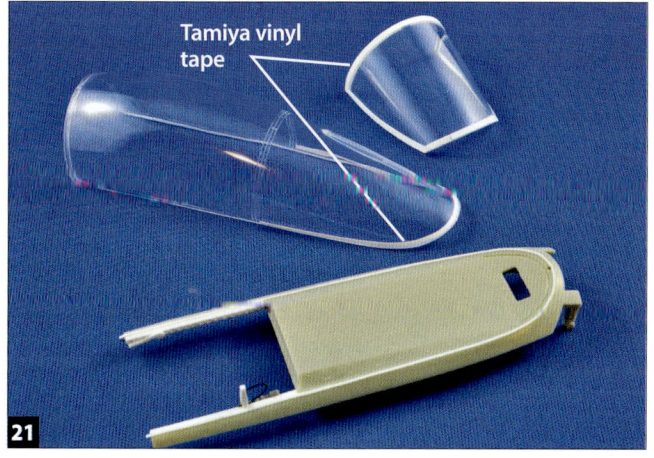

21 After removing the mold seam from the canopy, I used thin strips of Tamiya vinyl tape to replicate framing missing on the kit parts.

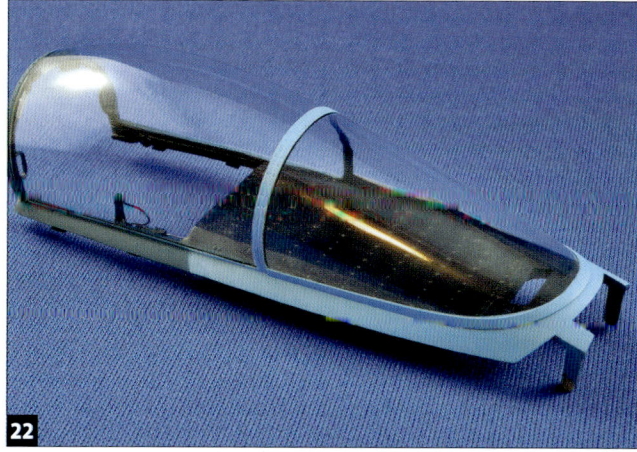

22 More detail was added to the front of the canopy, then all parts were painted, weathered, and glued together.

23 At the front of the windscreen are thin vents that keep the windscreen dry and free of ice. I created this 4-part assembly using styrene strips cut to size and sanded to shape, then detailed with rivets using a needle in a pin vise.

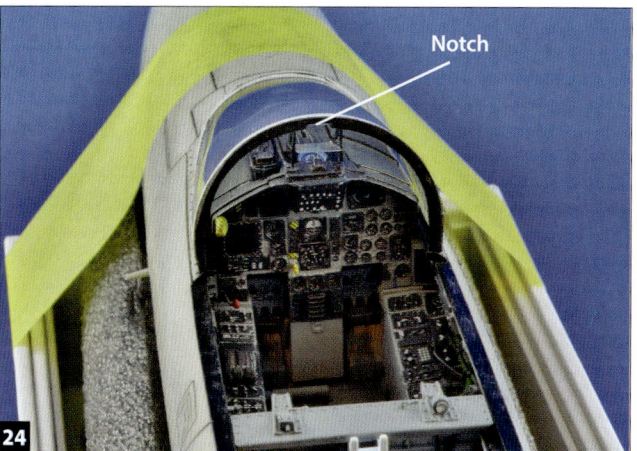

24 At the rear of the windscreen, I built up the frame with styrene, cutting a notch at the top that is part of the attachment between the canopy and the windscreen.

25 The hinges at the rear of the canopy are OK if the canopy is closed, but in the open position they are much too long, forcing the rear of the canopy to be raised in an awkward position (left). Trimming the ends of the hinges back put the canopy flush at the rear (right).

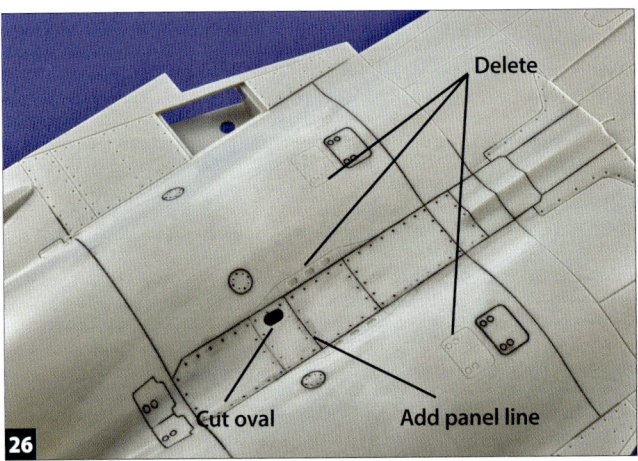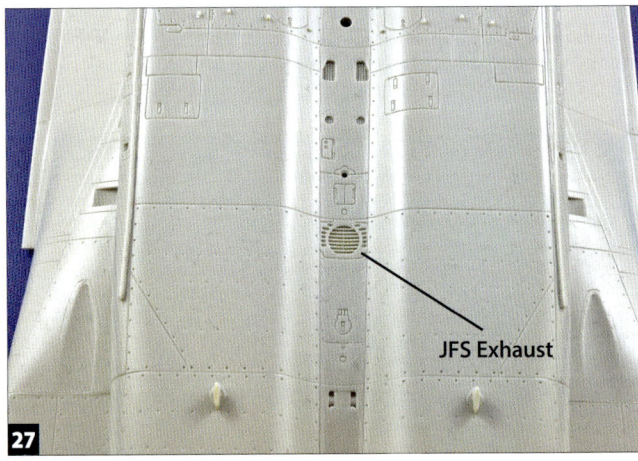

26 Some panels and vents on top of the fuselage are correct for an F-15E, but not a C, including the oval vents and the surrounding panel lines as well as a pair of access panels (top). I filled them with super glue, then added an oval vent and its panel lines and rivets.

27 Underneath the fuselage, I cut out the jet-fuel starter exhaust screening.

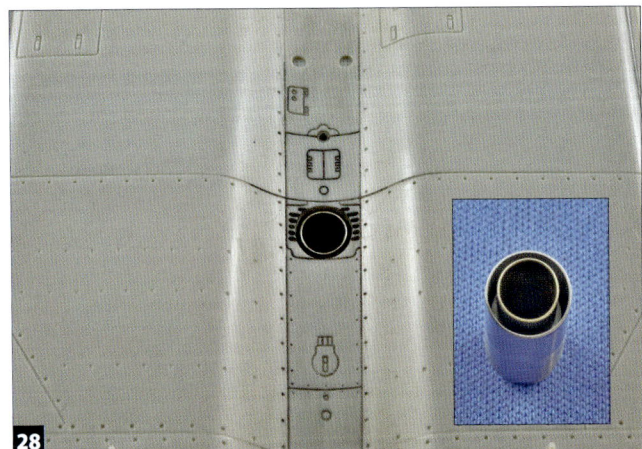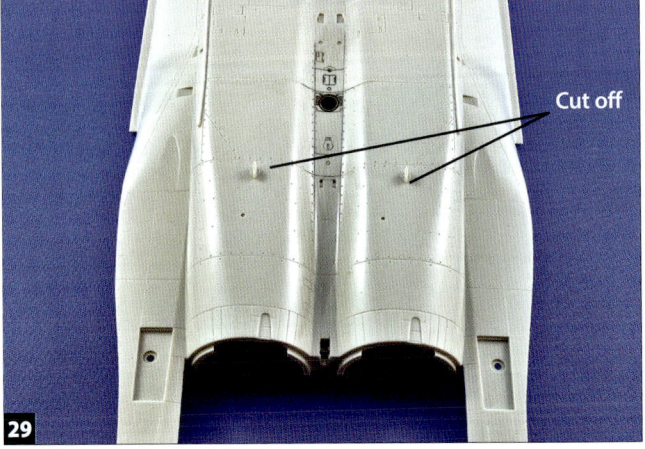

28 A metal JFS exhaust was created, using parts from a ballpoint pen barrel—brass tube would also work—glued to the inside of the fuselage at a rearward angle, flush with the bottom surface.

29 Aft of the JFS exhaust are two large fins—shrouds around fuel drains—that should be removed. I drilled new drain holes in their places.

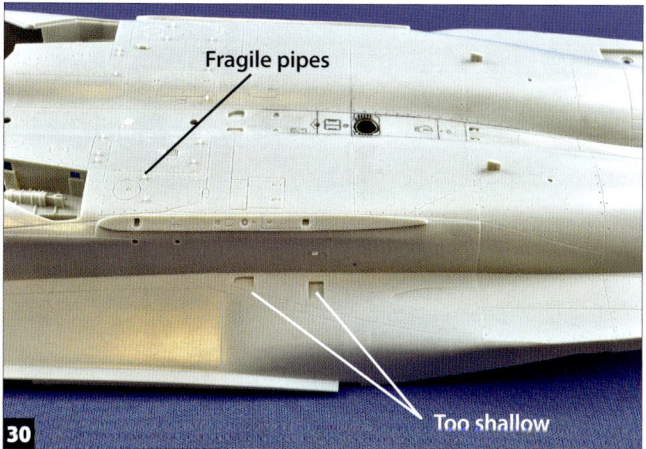

Also under the Eagle are three vents on each side that can be improved. Be careful of those tiny drain pipes that are easily broken—more on that later.

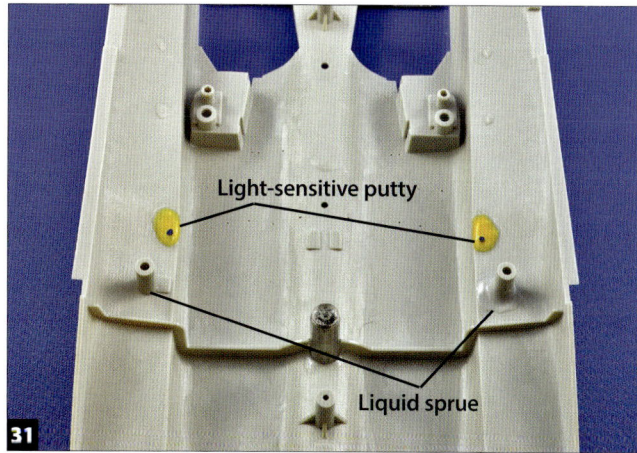

To back the forward vents, I used light-sensitive putty because it dries quickly. Then, I drilled out the vent at an angle. For the aft vents, I used liquid sprue as a backing instead, because the vent interfered with an important anchor point used to screw the fuselage halves together.

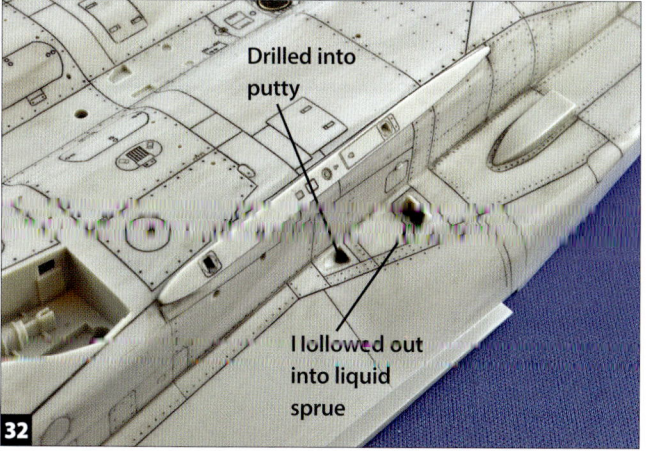

The vents are now much deeper and more realistic. I enhanced the surrounding detail with more panel lines and rivets.

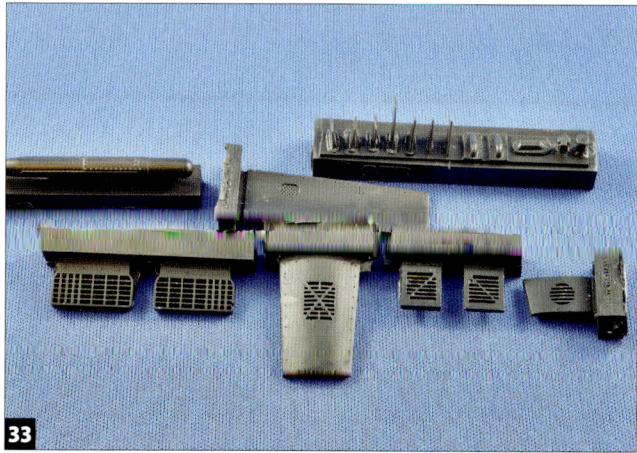

For many of the vents, I used GT Resin parts (No. GTR32015). The set also includes antennas and a large bullet-shaped fairing for the port vertical stabilizer (left), to replace the kit part, which is too small. This fairing is part of the Tactical Electronic Warfare System and is called a TEWS pod, while on the starboard side is a much thinner ballast to counter the weight of the pod.

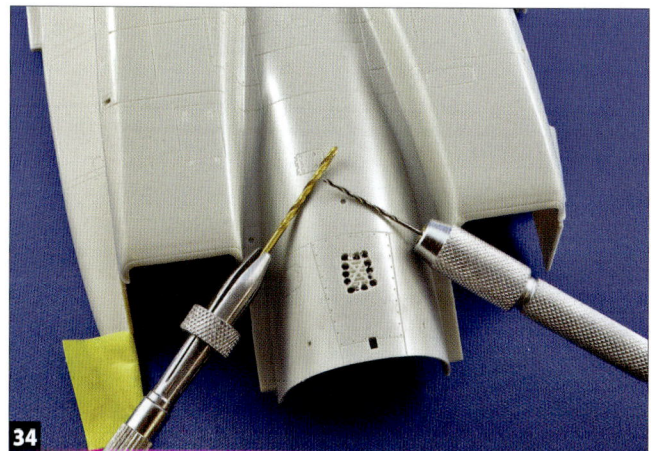

To install these vents, I drilled pilot holes in a rectangular pattern, then carefully cut out the molded vent with a No. 11 blade.

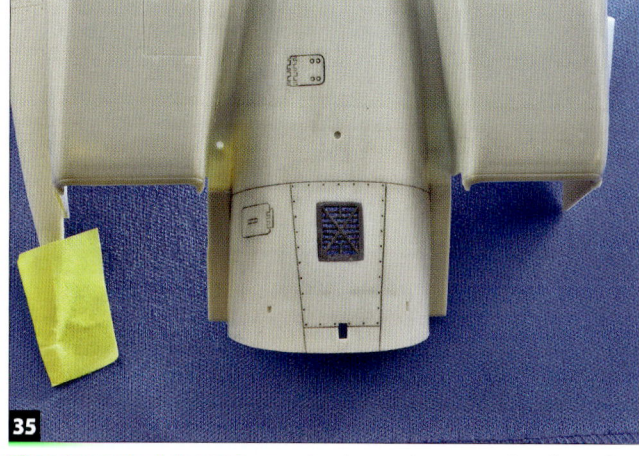

Then, I attached the resin vent in place using superglue flowed in from behind so it won't show.

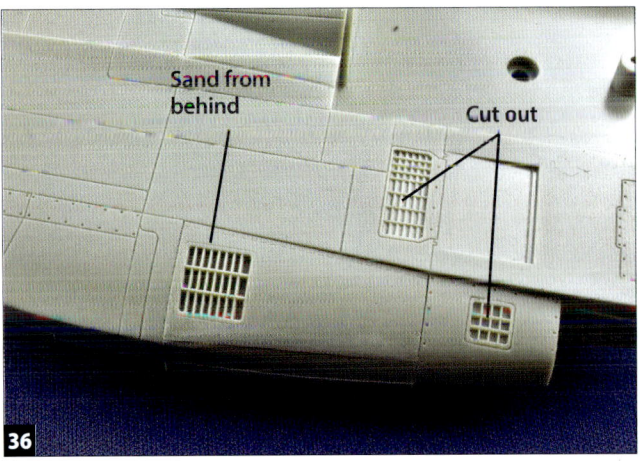

On top of the fuselage along the sides of the intakes are two vents that can be replaced with GT Resin parts. I sanded the starboard-side gun door from behind until I could see through it, then cleaned up the grill. The front vent was scratchbuilt.

After adding the vents, I added significant new panel-line and rivet detail over the entire upper fuselage based in references.

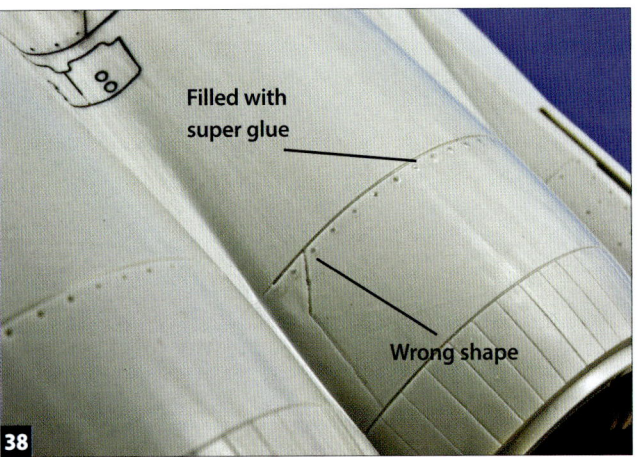

Working from references, I corrected panel lines and rivets on the rear fuselage around the engines. Much of this detail was filled with superglue and sanded.

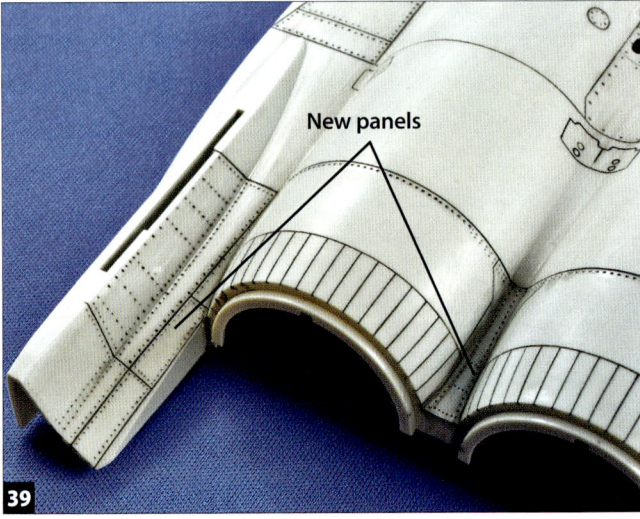

I applied Archer resin decal rivets for raised details, added several missing panels with a scriber, and added recessed rivets with a needle in a pin vise.

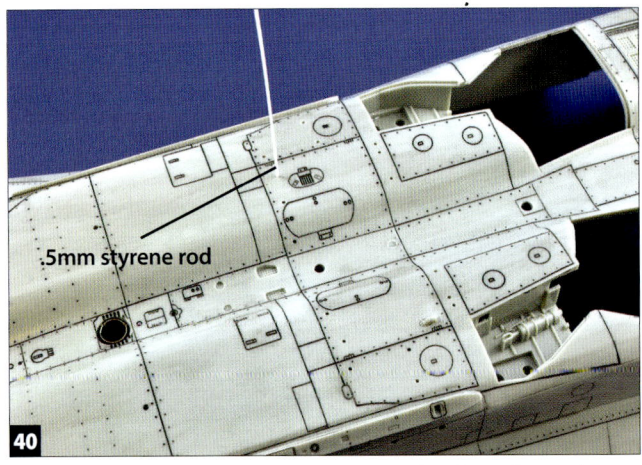

I filled and re-scribed many panel lines under the airframe, but, with extensive handling, I broke off many of the small drain pipes. I cut the remaining ones off, drilled holes in their place, and glued .5mm styrene rod into the holes.

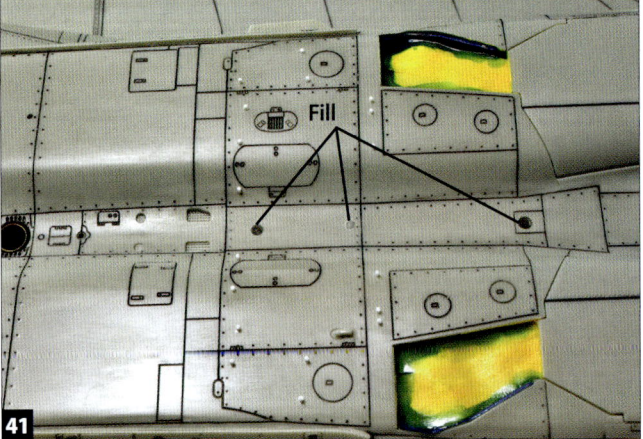

The pipes were then trimmed to the correct length. Other circular holes used for the centerline pylon, which I wasn't using, were filled with superglue and sanded smooth.

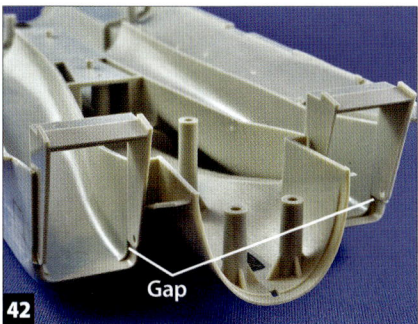

42

The engine intakes, which come in two pieces, have large, awkward gaps at the corners of the front.

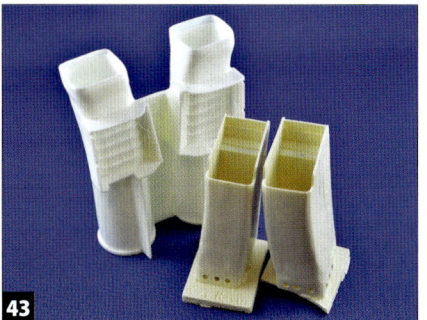

43

To avoid this problem, I used more GT Resin parts (No. GTR32003). These comprise three pieces, with the rear conveniently molded in white, the same color as the rear of the intake and the main landing gear wells attached to them.

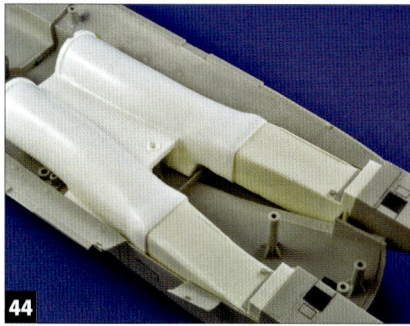

44

With a bit of clean up and dry fitting, they are a direct replacement for the kit parts with no seams to fill.

45

The front of the intakes fit flush and the gap is minimal and easily filled with putty and sanded smooth before painting.

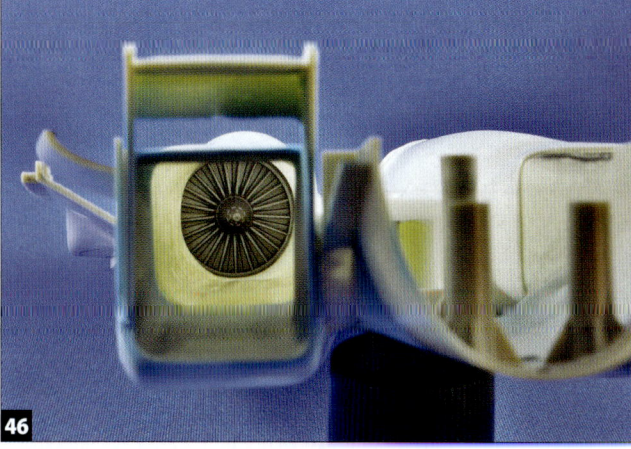

46

I left the rear of the intake unpainted in white as found in references but soiled it up a bit using pastels. The engine fan faces were painted with Alclad II steel, then glued to the rear of the intake.

47

To replace the rear sections of the kit engines, I used a set of seamless afterburner ducts from GT Resin that included upgraded flame holders. The tubes were painted with flat off-white; a variety of Alclad metal shades and pastels finished the flame holders.

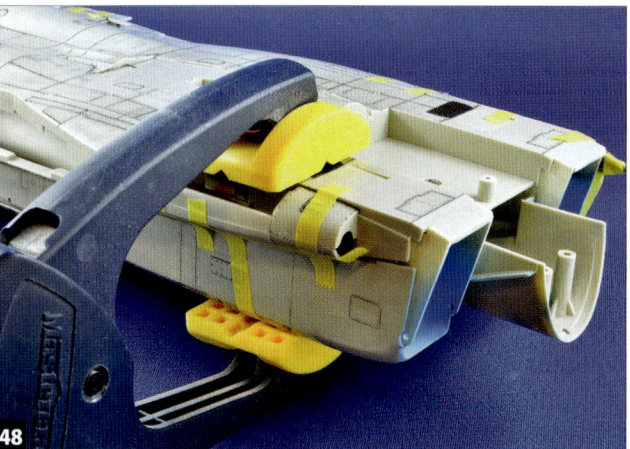

48

The top and bottom fuselage halves were then glued together, using Tamiya Extra Thin Cement and, in some cases, superglue to form a strong bond. Make sure that you dry-fit, sand, and trim these parts many times to ensure that the fit is not forced, or you will have issues with wing fit and alignment.

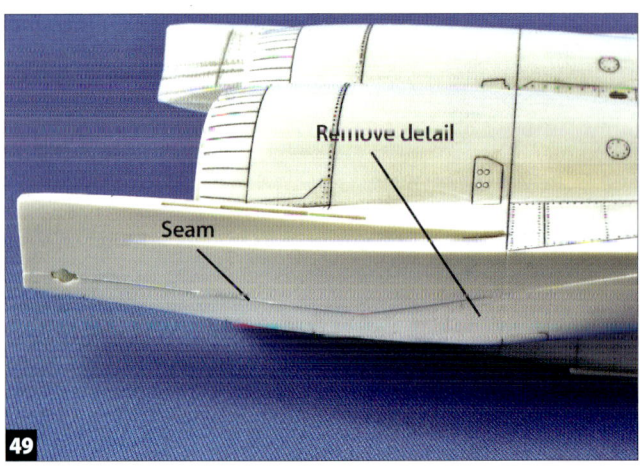

49 Many of the seam lines on the sides at the rear are offset and unsightly, and some of the panel line and rivet detail needs to be removed.

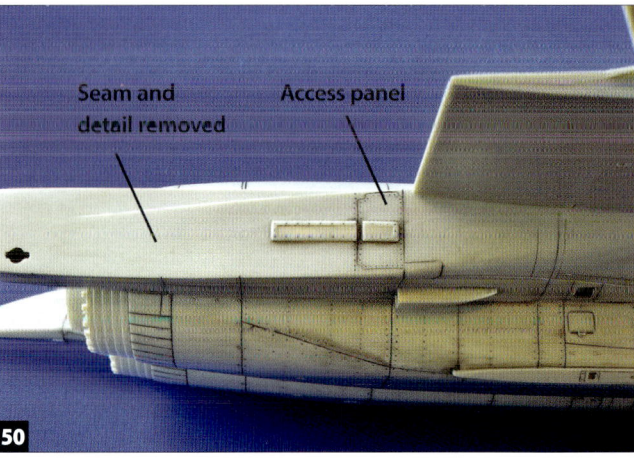

50 Careful filling and sanding eliminated the seams and other detail that should not be there. Note that the starboard formation light has been cut, with about a third of it attached to a new avionics access panel scribed behind it. The F-15C doesn't have the door and split formation light on the port side.

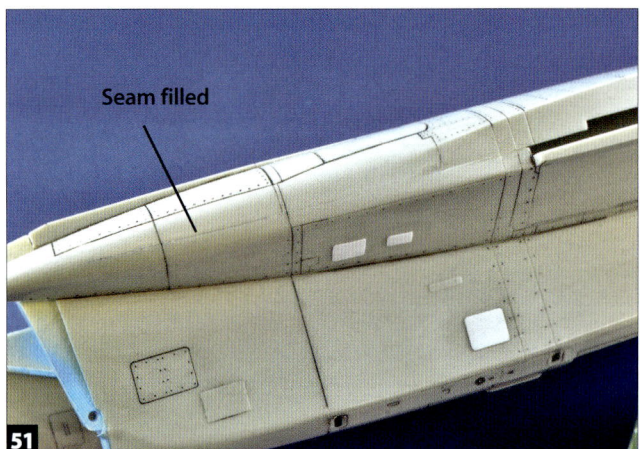

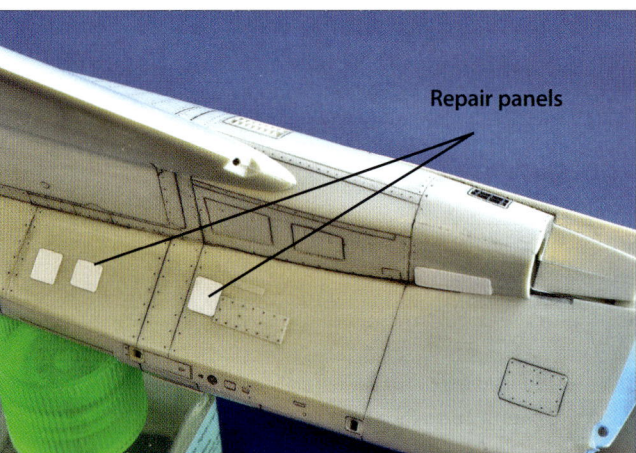

51 An interesting feature of all F-15s are small panels on the fuselage that are random in size and location. They are there to repair stress cracks and they are most common on the engine intakes and front of the wings. The kit has a few molded on, but I created a few more from styrene sheet specific to my subject.

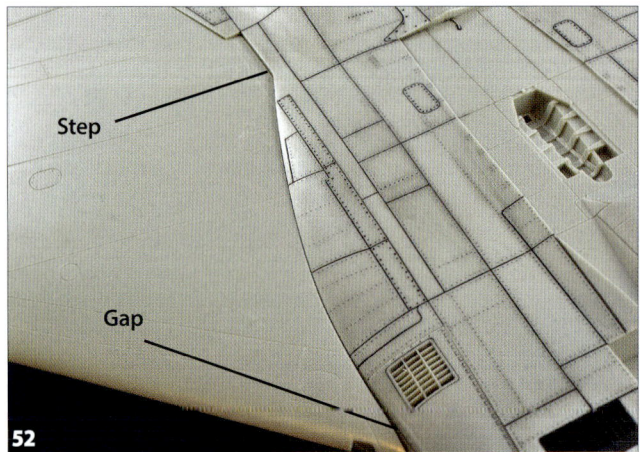

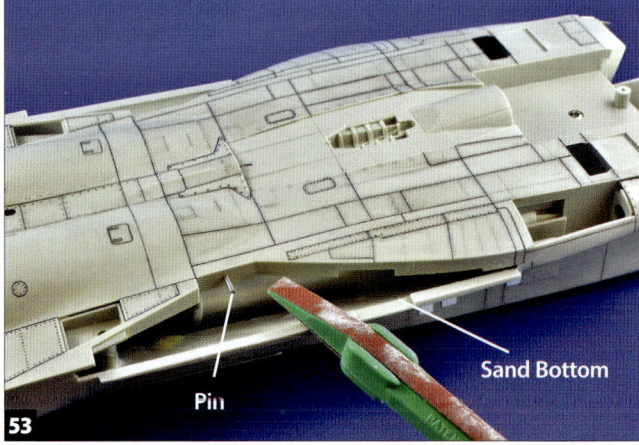

52 Without modification, the fit between the wings and fuselage can leave a step at the rear and a large gap at the front.

53 To mitigate this problem, I sanded the wing mating surfaces on the lower fuselage half and placed pins in holes on the upper half. Those pins fit into matching holes in the wings.

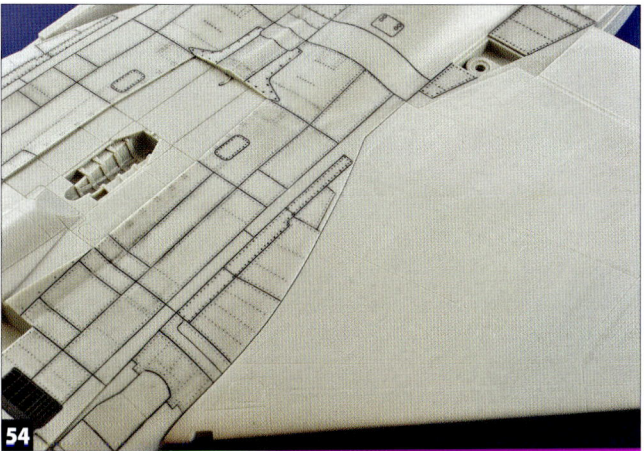

54. The pins force the upper wing surface up, reducing the step; the sanding reduced the gap at the front. Before attaching the wings, the trailing edges of the flaps and ailerons were thinned with sanding.

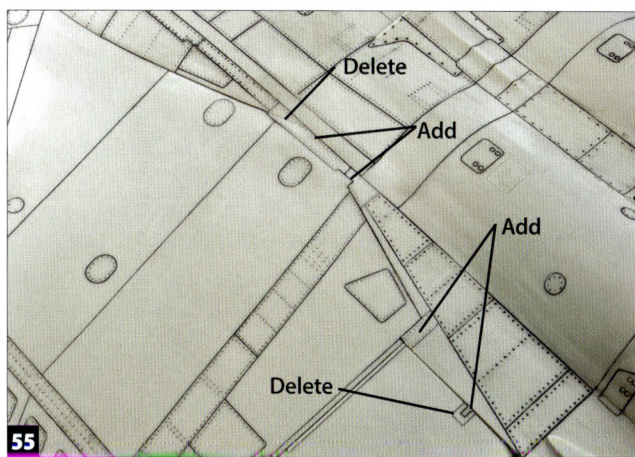

55. The wing was attached and the gap filled with super glue. Some panel lines were then re-scribed, while others were eliminated or modified along with rivet detail as shown.

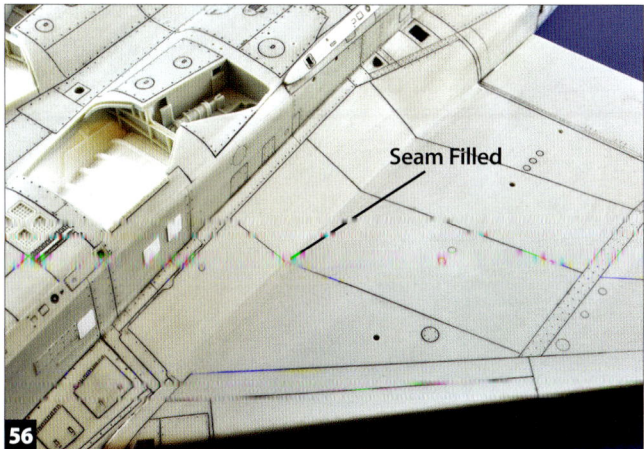

56. Underneath the wings, there should not be longitudinal panel lines along the joint. I filled the gap with super glue, then re-scribed panel lines that cross them.

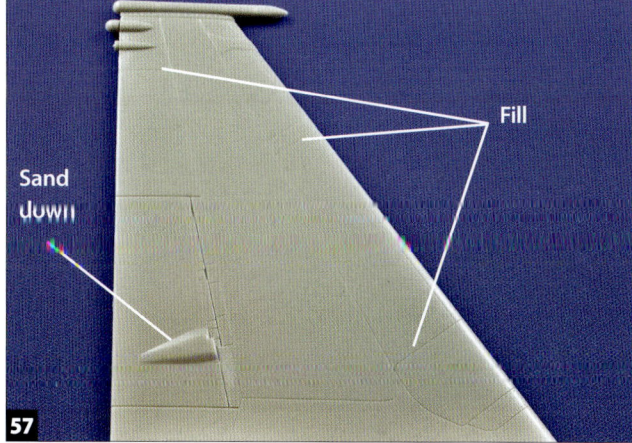

57. The vertical stabilizers have pronounced bulges on the rudders that are too big, so I sanded them down until they were barely visible. Some panel lines should be eliminated as well.

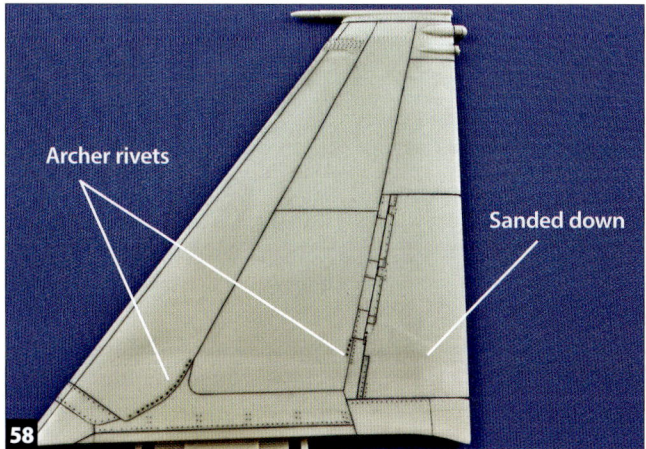

58. Some panel lines on the inside faces needed to be altered. I added a few Archer rivet decals, paying attention to the spacing as they are not always even. Fine rivet detail was also added with a needle in a pin vise.

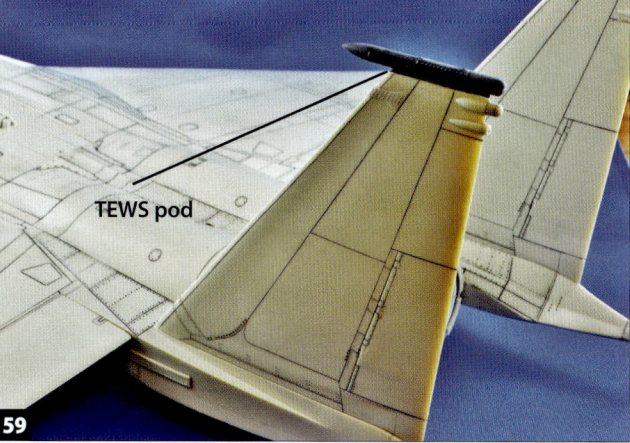

59. On the port vertical stabilizer, I attached the resin TEWS pod from GT Resin. The trailing edges of the vertical stabilizers and stabilators were also sanded to a thin edge, because the kit parts are too thick for scale.

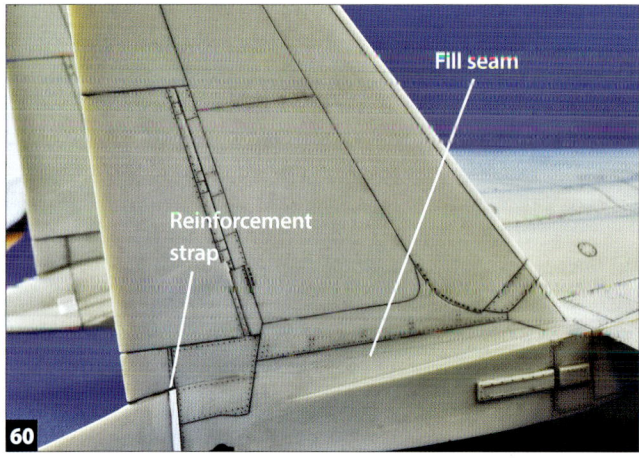

60 The gaps at the base of the vertical tails are too low, so I filled the gaps and scribed new panel lines above and at the rear. Note also the vertical reinforcement strap outboard and the reinforcement plate on the opposite side; both are made from styrene.

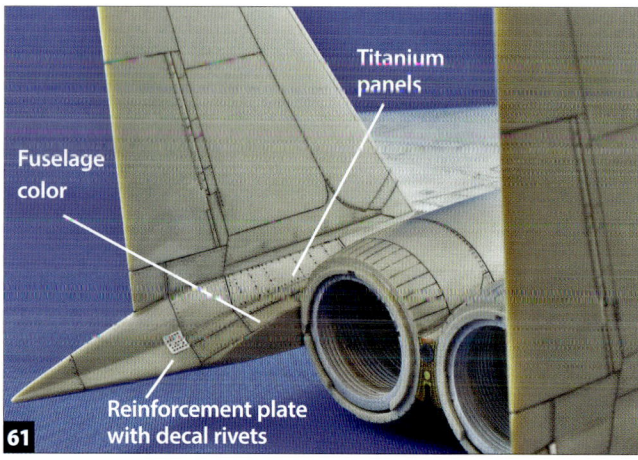

61 More panel lines and rivets were added next to the engines where the panels are made of titanium and unpainted due to heat. One small panel on the top and bottom, however, should be painted fuselage color instead.

62 The rear stabilators have thin plastic pins that are a loose fit with the fuselage. I cut them off and replaced them with metal pins—actually the base of a drill bit—inserted into holes drilled in the root. This modification provides a more solid base and the pin replicates the pivot arm of the real aircraft.

63 The rear of the intake ramps show large steps and circular panels that should not be visible when they are in the upright parked position. I added thin strips of styrene to the front of each intake, eliminating both problems at the same time.

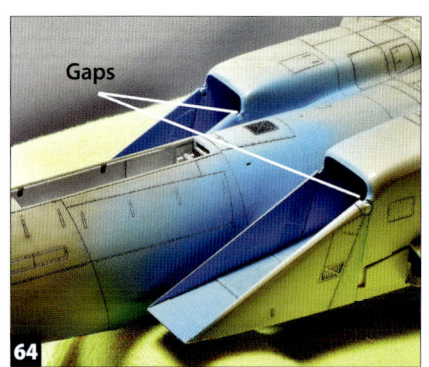

64 Large gaps mar the hinge areas at the lower edge of the intake ramps (left). I filled them with superglue, then scribed all four hinges inside and out (right). The lower fuselage was painted before the intake ramps were attached to prevent air turbulence from the airbrush that can produce a gritty finish.

65 I replaced the kit's fragile angle of attack (AOA) probes with Master brass parts designed for the 1/32 scale F-4s. Small holes drilled into the fuselage anchored them.

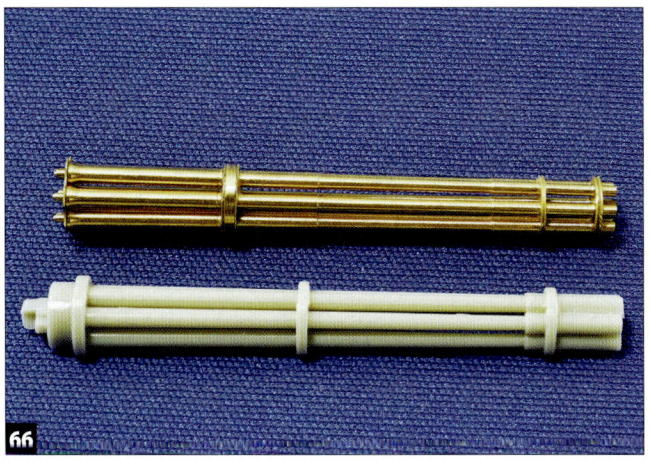
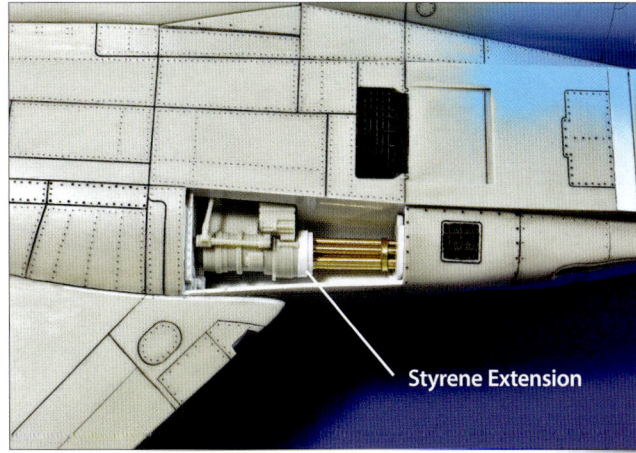

The kit's M61 Vulcan gun is crudely detailed on the bottom, so I replaced it with a brass weapon from Master. I created a styrene extension to match the brass parts with the plastic kit parts; it was all painted with Alclad gunmetal before installation in the bay.

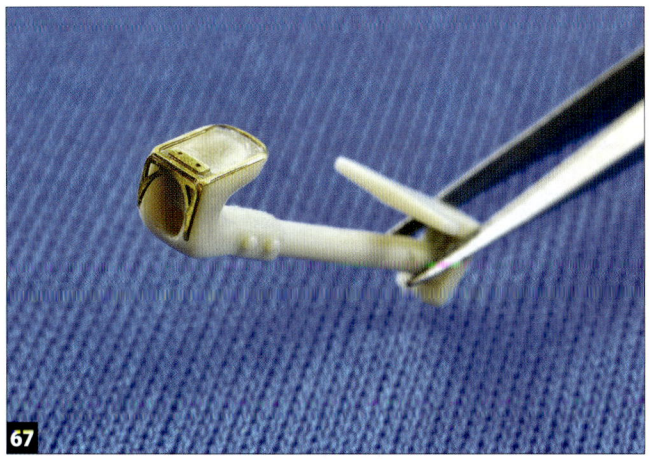
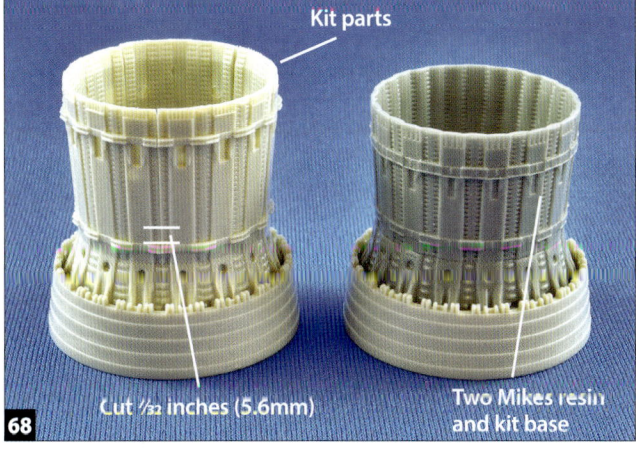

After hollowing out the tail hook on two sides with a drill, I detailed it with Eduard PE. Liberal amounts of superglue applied to the edges of the PE parts and sanded unified the brass and plastic.

The engine nozzles on this kit are about 7/32-inches too long, so they should be trimmed at the base before assembly. Or you can do as I did and use shortened resin nozzles from Two Mikes.

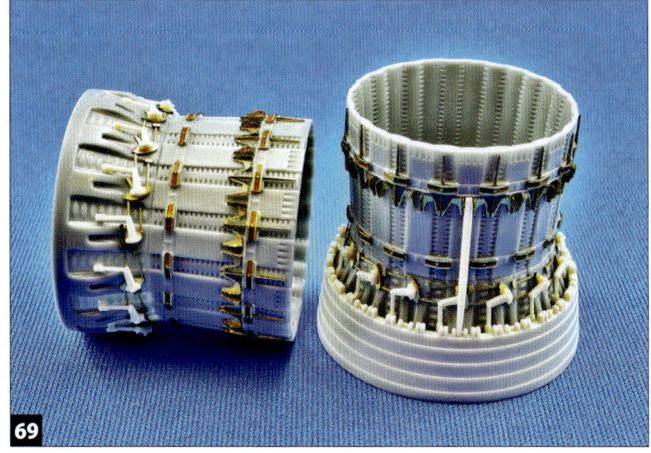
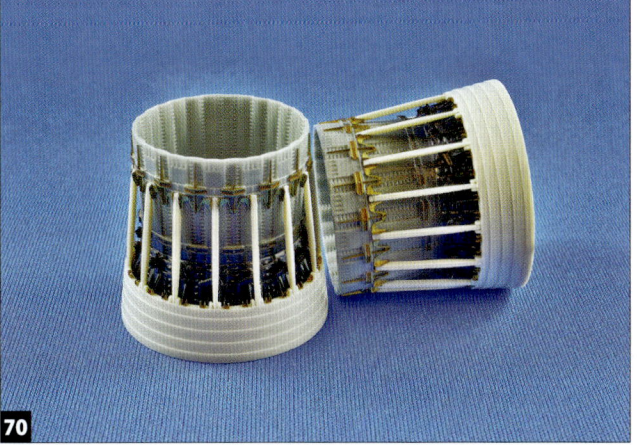

I detailed the nozzles with Eduard PE and the kit's L-shaped linkages and actuators trimmed to fit the shorter resin parts. With nine brass and two kit parts for each of the 30 nozzle petals, there are 330 tiny parts on both nozzles along with six major components.

Before gluing the nozzles to the base and adding the control arms, the base of each nozzle was painted with gloss black lacquer while it was still easily reached as a primer for Alclad metallics.

71 Then I painted the assembled nozzles gloss black and taped thin strips of styrene to the inside of each petal, leaving gaps between them.

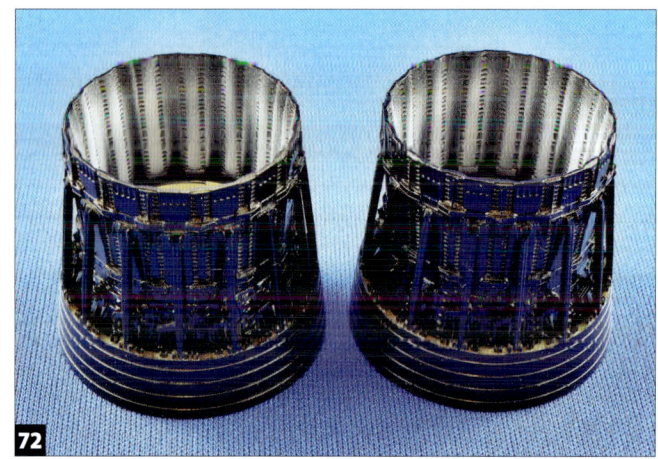

72 I sprayed flat white from the forward end of each nozzle (the direction of exhaust flow). When the styrene strips were removed, it left the characteristic streaked look of light and dark soot within.

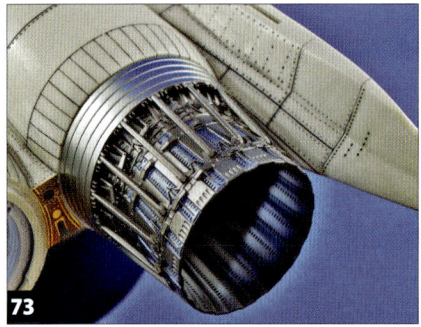

73 The outside of each nozzle was painted with Alclad steel lacquer followed by clear flat. For the bluish section between each petal, I brushed on Tamiya burnt blue pastel dissolved in water, a mix that's easy to apply, and to remove inevitable mistakes.

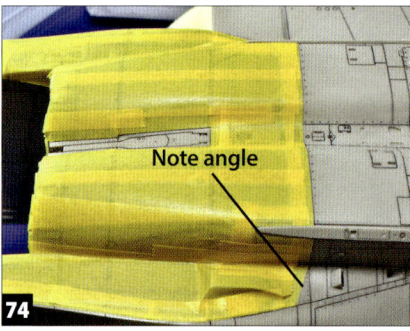

74 I masked the rear titanium panel areas to avoid paint build up over the fine details I added earlier. I could have painted this area first, but I wanted to avoid masking over fragile metallic paint, which can sometimes lift.

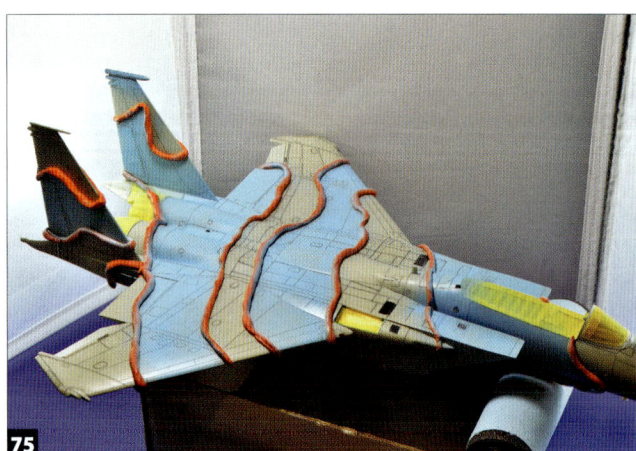

75 The model was then painted in the flanker scheme, using FS35450 for the light blue, FS35109 for the dark blue, and FS36176 for the radome. I avoided spraying the first color over the entire model to negate paint build up.

76 I edged the areas with poster putty to give the demarcation lines a softer edge as seen on this aggressor. All of the colors were lightened for scale effect and slight weathering from UV exposure.

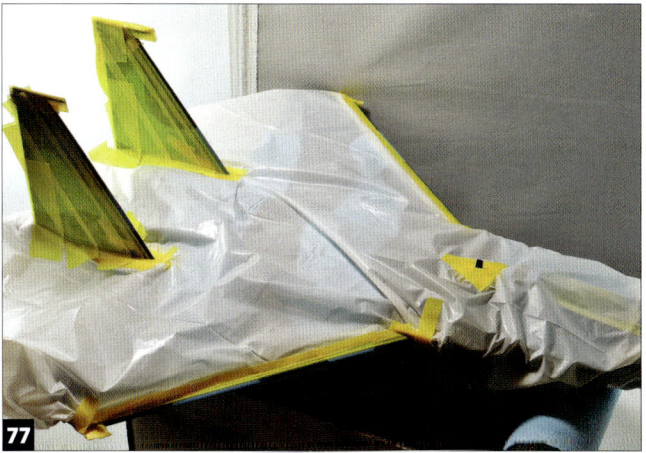

77 The leading edges of the wings, stabilizers, and stabilators were masked with tape and the rest of the model covered with a kitchen garbage bag to avoid overspray. I airbrushed the leading edges with FS36251 light gray.

78 I masked and painted other details, such as the white interior of the gun bay and the black surround for the gun opening on the wing.

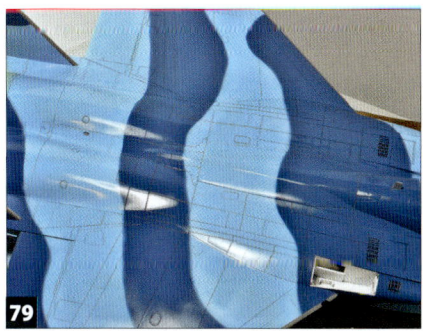

79 Due to minimal paint build-up, all of the fine detail that I worked so hard to create still shows through. To prepare for decals, I sprayed two good coats of Tamiya clear gloss (X-22), which dries harder and faster than Pledge Floor Gloss.

80 The titanium areas were then masked off and sprayed with gloss black lacquer to prep the surfaces for Alclad.

81 I painted those panels with a variety of Alclad metallics, including smoke staining around the JFS and other vents.

82 Many decals were then added, including a few on the titanium panels and engine nozzles, using Microscale Micro Sol to settle them without any silvering.

83 Decals should be applied to horizontal surfaces if possible, so I used a soft chair to handle this big bird while applying decals to the sides. Once all of the decals were applied and sealed with another coat of Tamiya clear gloss, I sprayed Tamiya clear flat coat to knock down the shine.

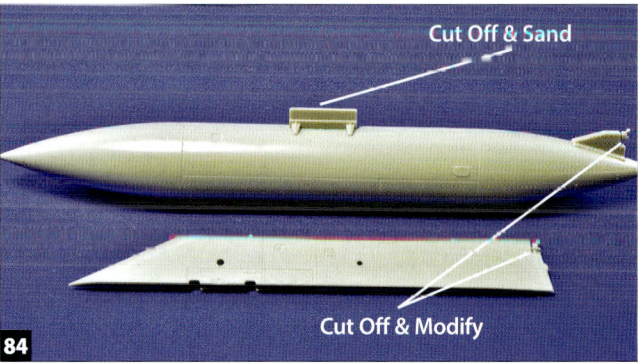

84 The sway bars that attached to the kit fuel tank are BRU-47A bomb release units specific to the F-15E. For the C, they should be the older style MAU-12 units with traditional sway bars and stabilizing pins, so I cut the F-15E versions off. At the rear of the fuel tank and wing pylon is a metal ball fitting used to help jettison the pylon or the tank if required. I cut these off for painting.

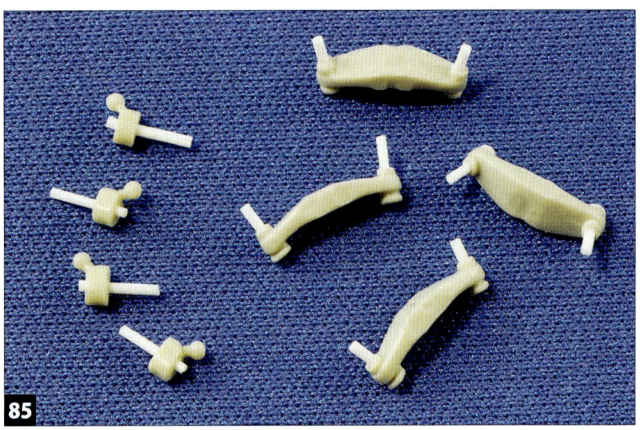

85 I had old-style sway bars left over from a Trumpeter A-10 and created new pins with styrene rod inserted into drilled holes. Styrene rod also produced attachment points for the rear ball fittings (left).

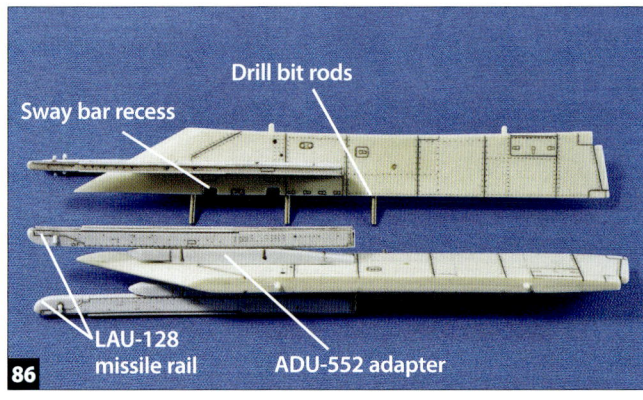

86 Notches cut into the pylons made way for the sway bars and I attached three small drill bits—brass rod would work, too—to attach the fuel tanks to the pylons. I replaced the kit's LAU-114 missile rails, which are no longer used, with LAU-128 rails with ADU-552 adapters from Wolfpack.

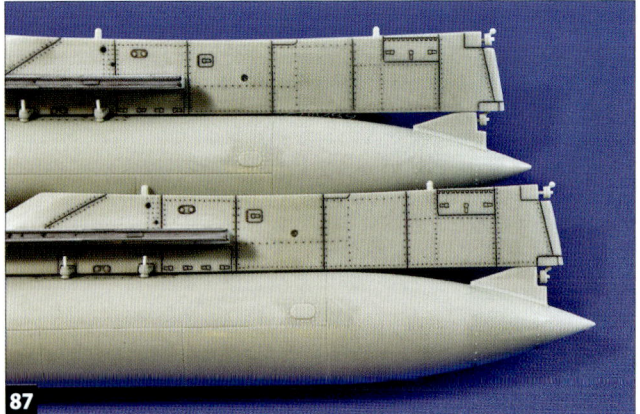

87 Before painting the pylons and tanks, I scribed missing panel lines and rivets and dry-fit everything to refine the assemblies.

88 After the pylons were painted FS36176 dark blue and the tanks FS36251 aggressor gray, I assembled, painted, and decaled a resin AIM-9X Sidewinder from Zactomodels. The missile was attached to the port pylon with fine pins that allow for easy attachment and removal.

89. ACMI pod

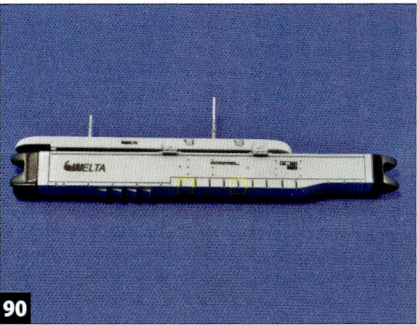

90.

To equip the starboard side pylon, I used an Air Combat Maneuvering and Instrumentation (ACMI) pod from AMS Resin.

Unique to USAF aggressors is the ELTA 8222 Electronic Counter Measures (ECM) pods from Israel. I fitted my Eagle with Wolfpack's resin pod—it includes terrific decals—and attached it to the port intake using the LAU-106 missile rails and more pins.

91. Ball fitting

92. Fine sandpaper

Note the clean ball fittings at the rear of each pylon and fuel tank.

As a final touch, I detailed and painted a boarding ladder to match the Flanker blue camouflage. Fine sandpaper replicated the antiskid material on the steps.

After almost two years and hundreds of hours of work, my F-15C Eagle aggressor was finally finished! Although it required a great deal of work and patience, the added details and corrections make this model stand out from the crowd. At approximately 2 feet long, it takes up a lot of shelf space as well!

MAKE THE MOST OF YOUR MODELS

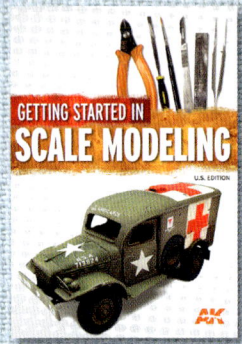

Getting Started in Scale Modeling
is a comprehensive how-to book from the experts at Damaged and AK Interactive, a Spain-based producer of model paints, finishing supplies, and scale modeling books.
#12818 - $18.99

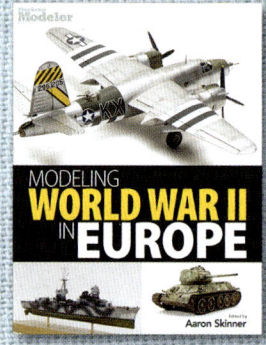

Modeling World War II in Europe
features a variety of modeling subjects from the invasion of Poland in 1939 until the end of the war. You'll find armor, aircraft, ships, figures, and dioramas.
#12811 - $24.99

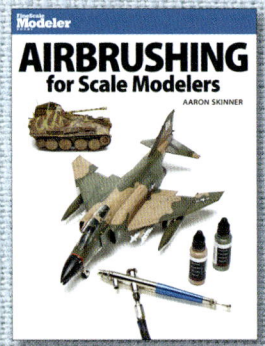

Airbrushing for Scale Modelers
Aaron Skinner provides a comprehensive guide to airbrushing. Inside this indispensable tool, scale modelers will find advice for modeling armor, aircraft, automobiles, figures, ships, and more.
#12485 - $22.99

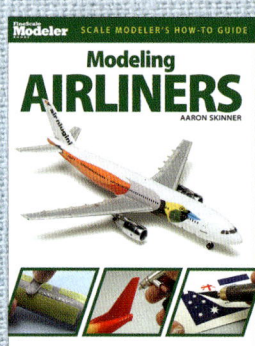

Modeling Airliners
This is the definitive guide for commercial aviation enthusiasts. From simple, out-of-the-box construction to conversions, painting, and decaling. Learn about masking, detailing, and more.
#12470 - $19.95

Kalmbach Media

Shop now at KalmbachHobbyStore.com